Loeb Classical Monographs
In Memory of James C. Loeb

The Roman World
of Dio Chrysostom

C. P. Jones

Harvard University Press
Cambridge, Massachusetts
and London, England
1978

Copyright © 1978 by the President and Fellows of Harvard College
All rights reserved
Printed in the United States of America

Library of Congress Cataloging in Publication Data

Jones, Christopher Prestige.
    The Roman world of Dio Chrysostom.

    (Loeb classical monographs)
    Bibliography: p.
    Includes index.
    1.   Dio Cocceianus, Chrysostomus, of Prusa—
Contemporary Greece.   2.   Greece—History.
I.   Title.   II.   Series.
PA3965.D22J6   938'.09   78-5869
ISBN 0-674-77915-0

Preface

In his own day, and throughout antiquity and the Middle Ages, Dio of Prusa enjoyed a high reputation for eloquence: the name Chrysostomus, "Golden-Mouthed," was early bestowed on him and is still used. At present he is comparatively neglected: eloquence is suspect, and Dio was never loved for himself, even in his lifetime. Perhaps more than most Greek authors of the Roman period he has suffered the ultimate indignity of a creative writer, and become a mere "source," though one useful to historians of Greek philosophy and of imperial history.

Yet sources have personality, to neglect which is to diminish the value of the information derived from them. Moreover, Dio is worth examining not only to correct an optical illusion. It is not by chance that two contemporaries so great and so diverse as Jacob Burckhardt and Theodor Mommsen esteemed him highly; the first published a lecture which is still the best general appreciation of him, the second paid him tribute in a conspicuous paragraph of his *Römische Geschichte*. Both Burckhardt and Mommsen saw Dio as a man intensely expressive of his age and, what is not always the same, a keen observer of it; and both had the breadth of vision to regard his age as interesting for itself, and not merely as a dreary stage in the decline of classical culture.

Mommsen's son-in-law Wilamowitz guided his pupil Hans von Arnim to the study of Dio, and by his edition of 1893–1896 and by his study of 1898, *Leben und Werke des Dio von Prusa*, Arnim did more for his author than anybody in modern times. Yet while his edition is still unsurpassed, the book is long out of date. On points of chronology and history it encountered prompt and damaging criticism from Hermann Dessau; and Arnim's view of Dio's development, from sophist to Cynic to philosopher, already questioned by Dessau, has not worn well with time. The very length of Arnim's work, however, imposed authority and daunted dissent; and since 1898 none of the few books on Dio has reconsidered his relation to the times in which he lived.

The present book is an attempt to fulfill that need. The emphasis is not on Dio's thought, though I have disagreed with Arnim on one essential matter of doctrine, Dio's supposed Cynicism. My subject is rather Dio and his relation to his age, especially to the theater of most of his public activity, the Greek city. I consider his background, his education and early career, and those civic speeches which I believe to belong to his first period; I survey his exile under Domitian and his return under Nerva and Trajan, the civic speeches of his last years, and the works centered on the emperor Trajan. Finally I view his attitude toward the leading city, Rome. Detailed questions of chronology are relegated, so far as possible, to the Appendix. This study complements and on some points modifies my previous *Plutarch and Rome* (1971).

My debts are many and various. Among institutions, I am grateful to the Canada Council, which awarded me the Leave Fellowship in 1971–1972 on which the basic work for this book was begun; to the Institute for Advanced Study, Princeton, where I spent that year amid ideal surroundings, both personal and professional; to Harvard University and its Widener Library, where much of the subsequent work has been done in vacation; to the Department of the Classics there and its Chairman, Zeph Stewart, for accepting the book in the series of the Loeb Classical Monographs; and to my own university, Toronto, for support and encouragement given in countless ways. (I particularly mention the patience and promptness of my typist, Donna Burns, and the skill of the Cartography Office.)

Four friends read an earlier draft of this book, and by their comments persuaded me to rewrite it entirely: Glen Bowersock, Richard Duncan-Jones, Christian Habicht, and Fergus Millar. I cannot thank them enough for their help, and for giving me the kind of sympathetic criticism that looks at the picture and not only at the paint. Glen Bowersock read a second draft, and has aided the book in many other ways. At a later stage I was also greatly helped by the comments of Friedrich Solmsen, who read my manuscript for the Press. To the teachers thanked in my *Plutarch* I would add one from whose writings I have learned more than I can say, Louis Robert.

Toronto   C. P. Jones
February 1978

Contents

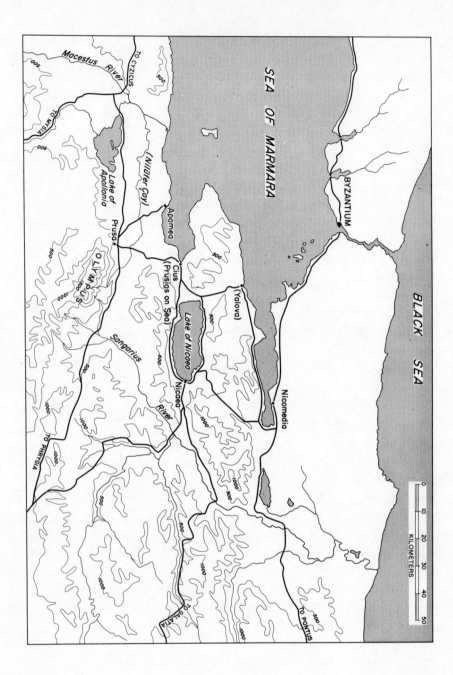

1
Prusa

Dio was born about the middle of the first century A.D. at Prusa, now Bursa in northwestern Turkey. Bithynia, the region in which Prusa lay, took its name from a Thracian tribe which had crossed over from Europe and settled this corner of Asia Minor several centuries before. From Alexander's conquest of the Persian empire, and until Bithynia was incorporated in the Roman one, it was ruled by kings who were of native stock but influenced by Greek institutions and culture. In the early second century B.C. one of these, Prusias I, founded Prusa in a part of his kingdom that he had only recently detached from the neighboring region of Mysia.[1]

It was said that the Carthaginian Hannibal, then an exile at Prusias' court, had influenced his choice of site, and the tale was justified by the reality. The new city occupied a terrace on the northwestern flank of Mount Olympus, the highest mountain of Bithynia and its most marked geographical feature.[2] The slopes behind Prusa gave it an endless supply of timber, which in Dio's time it exported to other cities. Before it lay a broad and fertile valley watered by streams from the mountain. There were also thermal springs, which were exploited under the name of the "Royal Spa" throughout later antiquity.[3] These fostered a local school of medicine, and the first Prusan to attain wider fame was a doctor called Asclepiades who attended the great of Rome in the early first century B.C.: another Prusan doctor of the same name was a contemporary of Dio and, like him, received benefits from the emperor Trajan.[4]

Prusa also had handicaps. It lacked a navigable river and access to the sea through its own territory and had to depend on the port of its neighbor Apamea, which was about a day's journey away and not always well-disposed. The city's springs had a noted and more generally accessible rival in those of the modern Yalova, and were finally eclipsed by them.[5] Despite its fertile soil, like all ancient cities it remained prey to a dearth of the most essential commodity, grain. Thus, for all its endowments, Prusa was not in the first rank of Bithynian cities, "none too large nor of very ancient foundation," as Dio reminded his compatriots.[6]

Similarly, Prusa's situation gave it a good but not preeminent place in the road system of the region.[7] It could not rival the two chief cities, Nicomedia and Nicaea, both of which lay at the start of major routes into the interior. Prusa's advantage lay in its position on the lines of communication between these two cities and those of the northwestern Aegean, since the great natural obstacle of Olympus deflects these routes around its shoulder. In addition, traffic moving from the great port of Cyzicus on the Propontis into the interior passed through the territory of Prusa. At the same time, the city was connected by easy roads with other cities of the vicinity, notably Apamea and Prusias on Sea, also called Cius, another foundation of Prusias I.

The history of Prusa before Dio's time is obscure. A fragmentary decree of the council and people survives from soon after the foundation and honors a royal governor.[8] When the last king of Bithynia died in 74 B.C., leaving his kingdom to Rome, it was immediately seized by the ruler of the neighboring Pontus, Mithradates VI. In the ensuing war Prusa and its neighbors were recaptured by Rome, no doubt with the usual consequences.[9] After the final defeat of Mithradates, Pompey combined Pontus and Bithynia into a single administrative region or "province." The new province was thus born from the accidents of war, with little regard for geographical or ethnic demarcations, or even for the convenience of the governor.[10] Nevertheless, this awkward conglomeration survived until the reforms of Diocletian. So also the law drawn up by Pompey to regulate the governance of the constituent cities, the lex Pompeia, remained valid until well after Dio.[11]

Little is known of the province, and nothing of Prusa, between the settlement of Pompey and the end of the Roman civil wars. The wealth of Bithynia soon made it the cynosure of Roman businessmen, and the corporation farming the Bithynian tribute became large and influential.[12]

Papirius Carbo, the first governor after Pompey's departure, was later convicted of extortion;[13] the long roll of prosecuted magistrates of the province was to include at least two proconsuls in Dio's last years. Shortly after Carbo, Bithynia was ruled by C. Memmius, whom the attacks of his subordinate, the poet Catullus, have made notorious; but besides plundering his subjects in the accepted way, Memmius also seems to have taken measures against brigandage, which was endemic in this mountainous and heavily wooded region.[14] The order imposed by Roman arms, the attractions of Bithynia for speculators, and its situation on the great roads linking Europe and Asia, all contributed to its rapid and profound Romanization.[15]

The accession of Augustus marked an important stage in the history of Bithynia and its cities. In 29 the emperor allowed Nicaea, now the largest city of the region, to build a temple of Rome and the deified Julius: Nicomedia, Nicaea's rival and the old royal capital, received in compensation a temple of Rome and Augustus himself, and thus became the center for Bithynia's worship of the emperors.[16] The hostility between the two cities was to involve Dio in difficult diplomacy and to persist to late antiquity.

Augustus' measure is the earliest evidence for a body in which again Dio was to be involved, the Bithynian council (*koinon*); it is unclear whether Pontus already had its own, as it did later. The council included delegates from all the cities, and the chairman or "Bithyniarch" was simultaneously the chief priest of the regional cult of the emperors. It also represented the interests of Bithynia by sending embassies to Rome; these had usually only formal business, but sometimes the graver task of prosecuting an indicted governor.[17]

Under the general settlement of 27, Augustus allowed Pontus and Bithynia to be governed by annual proconsuls chosen by lot from among the senators of praetorian rank, and assisted by a legate and a quaestor.[18] Though it was thus regarded technically as a province not requiring the emperors' close attention, in fact they kept a strict watch on it, both because of its strategic importance and because of the administrative problems it continued to pose. Their chief agent and source of information was the overseer (*procurator*) of imperial estates in the province, whose powers and responsibilities put him effectively on a level with the proconsul.[19] On occasion the emperors became impatient with proconsular rule, and instead put the province under legates of their own appointment, who were expected to maintain close contacts with them. The earliest known of these is the younger Pliny, sent by Trajan in Dio's last years. After further vacillations, the province was permanently governed by legates from the reign of Marcus Aurelius.[20]

A few years after transferring Bithynia to proconsular rule, Augustus visited it himself and made certain changes in its internal organization.[21] The constitution of Prusa now probably attained the form in which it was familiar to Dio. It was essentially an oligarchy of wealth, with the name, and sometimes the substance, of democracy. The two governing bodies, the council (*boule*) and the assembly (*ecclesia*), retained the classical names, but not the forms.[22] The assembly probably included not the whole free population, but only those with property above a certain valuation; it could not initiate legislation and could be suspended in emergencies by the governor.[23] Real power now resided with the council, of which the membership was carefully regulated by the law of Pompey. It was a permanent body, recruited chiefly from those who had held a senior magistracy, and its roll was regularly revised by censors (*timetai*) modeled after the Roman ones.[24] Within the council executive power was vested in an annual board called at Prusa simply "the magistrates" (*archontes*), and headed by a chairman (*protos archon*).[25] Probably to this board alone belonged the power to bring proposals before the council, whence they passed to the assembly for ratification. Another body whose powers were fostered by Rome was the council of Elders (*gerousia*); this in theory tended sacred moneys and formed a social club, but in practice if not in law it could have a marked influence on city politics.[26] Dio's forebears had certainly had a leading position in the council and the city, and no doubt among the Elders also.[27]

Under Augustus' successors, Bithynia continues to appear with unusual frequency among those provinces whose governors were accused of maladministration.[28] For the first time, moreover, there appears an incubus often associated with Roman misrule, that of internal faction.[29] But in general Bithynia shared in the general rise of prosperity which characterizes the early principate. The reign of Claudius, which probably saw the birth of Dio, is an important stage here as in other provinces of the empire. Under him the Bithynian council was first allowed to issue coinage, while Nicaea and Nicomedia resumed theirs after a long interval, and these signs suggest a growing affluence.[30] The earliest Bithynian known to have entered the Roman senate received his first advancement from Claudius, and the same emperor was perhaps the patron of Dio's grandfather.[31]

To this economic advance was joined a cultural one. There had been only a handful of distinguished Bithynians before the principate,[32] but now they became more frequent. Dio claims that his grandfather's culture earned him a fortune, though he does not indicate his profession.[33] A citizen of Nicaea who lived about the same time was a noted professor of rhetoric, and was succeeded by his son.[34] Dio's own contemporaries included a Stoic historian from the neighboring Prusias, and a philosopher from Prusa who found favor with Domitian;[35] in the next generation Nicomedia produced another Stoic historian in Arrian. The frequency of Stoics among the Bithynians of the period may reflect the prevailing ascendency of this persuasion, though there may have been some local teacher or school.[36]

Prusa in the middle of the first century was thus a typical, middle-sized city of the early empire. Under Roman rule, a city consisted both of the urban center and of its attached territory. The territory of Prusa must have comprised not only the wide valley in front of the city but also part of the mountain behind; it is not known where it touched the boundaries of its several neighbors. Similarly, there is no direct evidence for the size of the population, but including slaves it may have been about fifty thousand.[37] Like most of the Bithynian cities and of the empire generally, Prusa was stipendiary, that is, it paid an annual tribute to Rome based on an assessment of its population and property. Again like most cities of the empire, it lacked "freedom," though Dio's grandfather had tried to win this privilege for it:[38] the most important consequence of this lack was a potential rather than an actual one, that the city was unable to resist the authority of a proconsul or his legate who wished to intervene in its affairs.[39] Still less was Prusa "autonomous," and free to make its own laws; it could elect its own magistrates and regulate its ordinary affairs, but decisions of particular weight, such as the erection of a new public building, probably first had to be approved by the proconsul.[40] The proconsul again heard appeals in minor cases and tried all capital ones; here the Prusans did not even have the privilege of litigating in their own city, but had to go for the purpose to one of their neighbors, probably Apamea. This dishonor Dio managed to erase when he won "assizes" for Prusa.[41]

Almost all the physical traces of the ancient city have been obliterated by its medieval and modern prosperity. It must have contained the usual public places and buildings, a square, theater, council house, Elders' house, temples of the chief gods of the city and of the imperial cult. Some of the private buildings also probably were imposing, such as the town house of Dio's family, which was nearly burned down in a riot, the colonnades and shops that he built near the baths, or the private house left by a citizen to Claudius and allowed to go to ruin.[42] But a contemporary witness thought Prusa "very ugly"; the public baths were "old and dirty"; and Dio mentions "low, squalid ruins," among them a smithy in which the men "could practically not stand up, but worked crouching."[43] The cause of this squalor, in so well-endowed a city, is less likely to be general poverty than endemic mismanagement and negligence; as Dio was to find, attempts at reform were broken by immovable opposition.

Of the social structure of Prusa almost nothing is known. Apart from the slaves, the humbler trades may have included peasants and city-dwellers who lacked full citizen rights.[44] Above these was the class corresponding roughly to membership of the assembly, less poor but still "banausic." At the top stood the older, established families of the city, some of whom may have risen from the rank below; like Dio's, these families may have derived their wealth from land as well as trade.

On both sides Dio descended from such houses. His father, Pasicrates, was an "upright leader" of the city;[45] he must also have been a considerable businessman, since according to his son he died with four hundred thousand drachmas owing to him, almost none of it secured by bond, because he had "relied on his own influence" to recover it.[46] Pasicrates may have been at least in part a moneylender, as the wealthy sometimes were.[47] The size of the debt, if reckoned as a quarter of his estate, would produce a fortune of over six million Roman sesterces, a not unlikely figure for a very wealthy provincial.[48] Dio's mother came of an equally distinguished line. His maternal grandfather had spent all he had inherited from his own father and grandfather on public benefactions, and acquired a second fortune "from culture and the emperors."[49] Dio's mother must herself have been a generous benefactress, for the citizens built a shrine in her honor, and such a reward was the highest, because the most expensive, that a city could bestow.[50] Other branches of the family must have been equally eminent, since various relatives had received such distinctions as burial at the public expense and funeral games.[51] It is also likely that Dio was connected by hospitality or kinship with great families of other cities, especially Apamea, and this may in part explain his knowledgeable intervention in their affairs.[52]

Dio was not the only heir to his father's estate,[53] and even before the tribulations of his later years claims not to have been very wealthy,[54] though pleas of "modest means" were the etiquette.[55] His several estates, all in the territory of Prusa, included pastureland and vineyards as well as arable land, and he had many neighbors.[56] In addition, like his father, he may have lent money.[57] He also bought a parcel of public land near the city baths for the considerable sum of fifty thousand drachmas, or two hundred thousand sesterces;[58] in this frequented area he built colonnades, with shops that were rented out to retailers.[59]

The wealth of Dio's forebears put them in a class to which Rome was traditionally favorable. His mother and her father received Roman citizenship from the then emperor; his own father must already have been a Roman citizen when he was granted the franchise of Apamea, which was a Roman colony.[60] The fact that Dio was a Roman citizen on both sides amply attests his social standing; it is possible, if not recorded, that either he or his forebears raised the family to equestrian rank.[61]

His full names as a Roman are not known. The name "Dio," though very common, is perhaps derived from the local cult of Zeus.[62] In the usual way he must have used his Greek name as the third Roman one, while the first two were perhaps those of the emperor who granted his line the citizenship.[63] In addition, he used the surname "Cocceianus," by a fashion of the times placing it before his chief name so as to be styled "Cocceianus Dio": this surname was presumably acquired by kinship or some other tie with a Cocceius, perhaps on his mother's side.[64] The title "Chrysostom," "Golden-Mouthed," was devised later as a tribute to his eloquence, and perhaps also to distinguish him from the historian Cassius Dio, who appears to have been related to him.[65]

Dio was to be Prusa's most famous citizen. From his aristocratic background he derived a double tradition of culture and politics. But though he always retained the attitudes of his class, "the first people," "the leaders of the city," these attitudes were to be tempered by those drawn from a different source; it was as a philosopher, and not as a local politician of a type found in every Greek city, that he came to his later eminence. Prusa, therefore, was the nursery of his political thought, as it was the setting for most of his civic speeches: but the mature Dio was the product of wider concerns and more distant places.

2
Education and Youth

Dio's early years were presumably passed in Prusa, and here he must have received his basic education. Usually a boy was trained in the study of literature up to the age of about fifteen, and then for about three or four years in rhetoric.[1] Thereafter he might specialize under some noted teacher, perhaps in another city. This higher education could be in one of the liberal arts such as medicine, in philosophy, or in further study of rhetoric. In keeping with its avoidance of public expenditure, Prusa may not have had a public schoolmaster in Dio's boyhood;[2] but in any case, as the son of a wealthy family, he would probably have received his basic education from private tutors.[3]

An essay of Dio which cannot be dated (Or. 18) recommends selected authors to a wealthy man hoping to acquire eloquence. Among the poets Homer naturally takes first place; lyric, elegy, and the like are not recommended for a man of affairs;[4] Euripides and Menander are the preferred playwrights, a choice characteristic of the age; in prose Dio recommends the Attic orators, but praises Xenophon above all, especially the speeches of the *Anabasis*. Although this preference is appropriate for Dio's correspondent, it reveals his own tastes. All the authors chosen have in common clarity, energy, and directness: Xenophon had these and more, for he was renowned as a philosopher and as a man of sense and action.

Dio's admiration for Xenophon is visible in other of his works and reveals his own leanings. He too was to be a philosopher, but an interpreter of the wisdom of others rather than an original thinker. He was also to be an orator, but one who directed his art to practical questions, like the Attic orators and the speakers in the *Anabasis*, not to declamation or display. This double aspect of Dio results in part from the educational system of the time, which was the product of its literary culture. The spoken word was paramount: without oratory a Greek could not enter civic life, where he had to persuade his colleagues in the council or his inferiors in the assembly, to plead in courts of law, and to represent his city before governors and emperors. Even the applied arts required eloquence, for a doctor or architect might have to persuade his clients or refute his rivals.[5] Above all, rhetoric had invaded a field to which in theory it was a competitor and an alternative, philosophy. Not only did the philosophy of the age tend to be concerned more with moral guidance than abstract thought, but its exponents usually taught by lecturing to large audiences, and often performed so ornately that they became indistinguishable from teachers of the higher rhetoric.[6]

To this confusion of subjects corresponds an uncertainty of nomenclature that has often hampered discussions of Dio's development. The word "rhetor" was customarily applied either to those who taught rhetoric or to those who used their eloquence for practical ends, especially politicians and lawyers. A "philosopher" taught "philosophy" in the broadest sense, usually ethics but sometimes logic and metaphysics also. But a third term, "sophist," is applied both to speakers and thinkers.[7] In the age of Dio this word has several connotations. In a favorable sense it was used of those who had brought the art of rhetoric to a new brilliance. It is these who are the subject of the *Sophists* written by Philostratus of Athens in the second quarter of the third century. Their most characteristic skill was to speak *extempore* in imaginary situations borrowed from ancient history; thus, a coeval of Dio was "excellent at improvising a speech and taking both sides of an argument, but was particularly amazing on the more advanced subjects, above all those drawn from the Persian Wars."[8] But the same word, "sophist," is also used pejoratively, usually of philosophers; it implied that their teaching was mere words without thought,[9] that they failed to teach serious subjects,[10] that they took money for their services,[11] or simply that they were objectionable rivals.[12] The word thus came to signify nothing more than a "charlatan" or an impostor.[13]

This confusion of language is partly responsible for a debate about Dio's intellectual development which began already in antiquity. Philostratus included him in his catalogue of sophists, though not among those properly so named but in a preliminary survey of "philosophers who were thought to be sophists."[14] His account is so important for many questions of Dio's career that it is best given in full.[15]

"I do not know what Dio of Prusa should be called, so excellent is he in everything. For he was a horn of Amalthea [a cornucopia], as the expression is, consisting of all the best styles of the best authors, but particularly recalling the tones of Demosthenes and Plato, with which he mingles, like the bridge of a musical instrument, a note peculiar to himself and of a concentrated simplicity. Dio's speeches are also excellent for their variety of moods. With unruly cities he frequently used reproach without seeming insulting or tactless, like a man curbing unruly horses with the bit rather than the whip; well-behaved cities he praised without being thought to inflate their pride, but rather to warn them of the ruin which change would bring. In the general character of his philosophy there was nothing common or affectedly simple, but it was grave and weighty, though (so to speak) sweetly coated with mildness. He was also a competent historian, as his *Getic History* shows, for in fact he traveled as far as the Getae when he was driven out. His *Euboean Oration* and *Praise of a Parrot* should not be considered trifling but sophistic, for it is a sophist's task to treat with gravity even such subjects as these.

"As a philosopher he was coeval with Apollonius of Tyana and Euphrates of Tyre, and remained friendly with both even though they quarreled between themselves to a degree that does not become philosophers. His journey to the Getic tribes I do not think should be called exile, since he was not ordered into exile, nor yet a mere tour, since he avoided the public, concealing himself from eyes and ears, and doing different things in different lands in fear of the tyrannies in the city [of Rome], which had driven out all philosophy. He planted, dug, brought water for bathhouses and gardens, and did many things for a living; yet he did not neglect his studies, but sustained himself on two books, the *Phaedo* of Plato and the speech of Demosthenes *Against the [False] Embassy*. He frequently used to visit the camps in his usual tatters,[16] and seeing the soldiers starting to mutiny after the murder of Domitian he did not hesitate at the sight of the disturbance that had broken out, but jumped naked onto a high altar and began his speech thus: 'Then wily Odysseus stripped away his rags.' When he had said this and revealed that he was not the beggar or the person they thought but the wise Dio, he gave a violent denunciation of the tyrant and yet induced the soldiers to act more wisely and do the bidding of Rome. His persuasiveness was indeed able to charm even those not deeply versed in Greek culture. For example, at Rome the emperor Trajan took him in the golden chariot in which the emperors lead the processions back from the wars, and turning often to Dio would say, 'What you are saying I do not know, but I love you as myself.'

"The images of Dio are also very sophistic, for though he uses them frequently he does so clearly and appropriately to the subject."

Though several details of Philostratus' account are doubtful, here it is enough to note his general view of Dio. For him Dio is clearly a philosopher, a "wise" man (*sophos*), whose exile is part of the persecution of "all philosophy." But he also sees in Dio some features of the sophists who are his chief interest, the brilliant extemporizers and declaimers: these Dio resembled by his speeches on trifling subjects and his varied imagery.

About the year 400 Philostratus' account of Dio received severe criticism from one of the most interesting and cultured figures of late antiquity, Synesius of Cyrene.[17] This man wrote for the benefit of his unborn son an essay called *Dio, or on Living by his Example*, of which the first part sets out to refute Philostratus' account of Dio and replace it with a new one.[18] For Synesius, Dio was not a sophist and a philosopher in one, but underwent a conversion during his exile. Before that he had been a "hardened sophist," who "plumed himself like a peacock and, as it were, gloried in the sheen of his language";[19] in this period Dio was bitterly hostile to philosophy, "and as a result he composed his work *Against the Philosophers*, which is very pointed and spares no figure of speech," and his similar work *To Musonius*, "in which he does not skirmish with the subject but writes from conviction."[20] Later, however, Dio "departed under full sail from the calling of a sophist" and became a philosopher "by chance rather than design, as he himself has described."[21] Even now, however, he "does not seem to have laboured over technical questions . . . but to have derived from the Stoa all that is conducive to character, and thus became manlier than any of his contemporaries."[22] While in his first period Dio had attacked philosophers, he now "crowns them and makes them the model of a good and controlled life."[23]

In his dispute with Philostratus, Synesius' chief exhibits were works of Dio now lost, the sophistic trifles like the *Praise of a Parrot* and his anti-philosophical pieces. Nevertheless, enough evidence survives, in the works of Dio and in other authors near to him in time, to make Philostratus' account more plausible than Synesius'. This is not surprising, since Philostratus wrote as part of the same cultural tradition as Dio, while Synesius is separated from both by the great chasm of the late third and early fourth centuries. In particular, Philostratus was familiar with a cultural world in which rhetoric and philosophy were thoroughly intermingled; in the language of that world a man could readily be a "philosopher reputed to be a sophist." Synesius by contrast was a Neoplatonist, for whom a "sophistic" philosopher necessarily appeared a false one: since Dio was both sophist and philosopher, he must have been one before the other. Moreover, Synesius' account of him was not written without ulterior motives. As the title indicates, his main concern was with himself rather than Dio, and indeed the discussion of Dio is only the introduction to the work as a whole. The burden of this is that rhetorical and literary gifts are not incompatible with philosophy.[24] To prove his point Synesius had to show that the mature Dio was a true philosopher, not (as Philostratus had perfidiously suggested) one of the despised sophists.[25]

The student of Dio thus faces several obstacles in following his intellectual development. The first is the educational culture of the age, in which philosophy and rhetoric are difficult to distinguish. The second is the resultant confusion of terminology, especially the ambiguous label of "sophist." The third is the conflict, partly caused by this ambiguity, between the testimony of Philostratus and Synesius.

It is, therefore, best to adhere as closely as possible to the evidence of Dio himself and writers close to him in time. One of these casually reveals something which, if true, seriously weakens the view that Dio began as a pure sophist. He nowhere mentions a teacher: the orator Fronto, however, writing in the middle of the second century, includes him in a group of men "endowed with the greatest eloquence and yet no less celebrated for their wisdom than their oratory," all of them pupils of the famous Stoic, Musonius Rufus.[26] There seems no reason to doubt Fronto, since another of the same group, Athenodotus, was one of his own teachers.[27] That Dio at least admired Musonius is suggested by a passage of his *Rhodian oration*, in which he refers to a philosopher who recently visited Athens, "second to none of the Romans in birth, and with a reputation such as none has enjoyed for a very long time";[28] this can be none other than Musonius, who was a Roman knight of Etruscan descent and the most eminent philosopher of his day.[29]

Musonius Rufus first appears in history as a companion of Nero's cousin Rubellius Plautus, who had been compelled to retire to the province of Asia.[30] After Rubellius' death in 62, Musonius returned to Rome; in 65, however, he was banished for supposed involvement in the conspiracy of Piso.[31] He was confined to the barren Aegean island of Gyaros, a favorite punishment for political malcontents, and is said to have worked in one of the chain gangs employed to build Nero's canal through the Isthmus of Corinth.[32] Recalled by Galba, he was conspicuous in the turbulence of the first months of Flavian rule at Rome.[33] Musonius appears to have been acceptable to the new dynasty, at least for a while, since he was a friend of Titus and was exempted when Vespasian banished philosophers from Rome.[34] A not always reliable source makes Titus recall him from banishment, apparently while emperor; if that is right, Musonius eventually must have fallen from favor, but more probably the source has misdated the period of his exile.[35]

Like many of those who clashed with the emperors of the first century, Musonius was a Stoic. The fragments of his teaching show that he resembled other later Stoics in paying little attention to logical or theoretical inquiry, and much to practical ethics. He discourses on the manly appearance of a full beard, on the advantages of living off the land, on the need for women to receive a philosophical education (Stoic women of the period were formidable paragons); "sophists" who discourse lengthily on subjects that are only theoretical are dismissed contemptuously.[36] A similar preference for practice over speculation is shown by Musonius' most famous pupil, Epictetus, who frequently cites him.[37] One lesson, appropriate to a teacher who insisted on action and entered public life personally, seems to have been impressed on all his pupils, the value of persuasiveness. Epictetus, though he too despises "sophists," considers speech a faculty of paramount importance.[38] All the pupils of Musonius mentioned by Fronto were "endowed with the greatest eloquence and yet no less celebrated for their wisdom." Another one besides Dio and Epictetus was Euphrates of Tyre, commemorated by the younger Pliny in a sketch that might have suited any of Musonius' pupils: he had a long beard and eloquent tongue and held that to engage in public life was the better part of philosophy.[39]

If Dio did study with Musonius, it was probably in his early youth, approximately in the later reign of Nero. It is possible that he met him when Musonius was with Rubellius Plautus in Asia, the neighboring province to Bithynia, though it may have been in Rome, or even on

Gyaros, where many Greeks are said to have visited him.[40] The abhorrence with which Dio always speaks of Nero may be partly influenced by the emperor's treatment of Musonius, though similar views are expressed by many others.[41]

A glimpse of Dio soon after Nero's fall is provided by a work unfortunately of doubtful veracity, the *Life of Apollonius of Tyana*, written by the same Philostratus of Athens. According to Philostratus, Apollonius was visiting Alexandria when Vespasian arrived there at the beginning of his campaign for the throne. Dio and Euphrates of Tyre, who are supposedly agents and counselors of Vespasian, hold formal debate with Apollonius on the best constitution for Vespasian to establish at Rome, with Euphrates urging democracy, Dio proposing that the people be allowed to choose, and Apollonius arguing for monarchy. Although Vespasian follows Apollonius, he continues to confide in Dio as one who "gave delightful discourses, avoided quarrels, and had a beauty in his speech like the incense wafted from sanctuaries, together with an unsurpassed gift for improvisation." The emperor reconciles Dio with his old teacher Apollonius and also releases from military service a pupil of Dio's from Bithynian Apamea.[42]

Though Vespasian's visit to Alexandria is attested fact, very little else of this narrative is corroborated elsewhere. The constitutional debate is suspiciously similar to a famous one in Herodotus;[43] and generally the *Life of Apollonius* is so full of fantastic tales and unverified assertions that an incident for which it is the sole source cannot be credited.[44] Philostratus may have made it up to give Apollonius the credit of having taught Dio and, though an unpracticed speaker, of having proved the more persuasive. The stimulus was perhaps Dio's *Alexandrian* oration, which shows him in the city and as the friend of an unnamed emperor; it is possible that this speech has influenced another item in Philostratus' description of Apollonius in Alexandria, his denunciation of the citizens' passion for horse races.[45]

Even if Dio was not already a courtier of the Flavians in 69, he was to be one soon thereafter. He claims that before his exile by Domitian he had "known the houses and tables of the rich, and not private persons only, but both satraps and kings."[46] The word "kings" is frequently used of Roman emperors, and "satraps" of provincial governors.[47] Dio could have met the latter simply as one of the upper class of Prusa, but for a Greek an acquaintance with the emperor was less usual.[48] Though Dio might have seen the court only as an ambassador or infrequent guest, there are other signs of his closeness to the Flavians, and particularly to Vespasian's son and consort, Titus. Like his brother Domitian, Titus was a conspicuous philhellene, and it was usual for men with such tastes to have cultivated Greeks among their dependents.[49] Titus was a friend of Dio's teacher, Musonius; he also had a less philosophical attachment to a handsome boxer, Melancomas of Caria,[50] to whose memory two short works of Dio are dedicated.[51] Melancomas had died during a celebration of the Augustan Games (*Sebasta*) at Naples; since Dio usually cares little either about physical beauty or formal athletics, it is apparent that these are courtly essays written to gratify and console the emperor's son. He was also intimate with another member of the Flavian house, probably Flavius Sabinus, the son-in-law of Titus.[52] Yet another personage of the Flavian court, the future emperor Cocceius Nerva, Dio later claimed as an "old friend."[53]

Dio's connection with the Flavians may help to explain a difficult chapter of his early period, his "sophistry" and his attacks on philosophers. The most "sophistic" of his works—the *Praises of a Parrot* and *of a Gnat*, the *Description of Tempe*, and the *Memnon*—have perished,[54] but their titles are revealing. Laudations of trivial or refractory objects, as Philostratus observes, were favorite exercises of the sophists: Lucian's *Praise of a Fly* and another encomium of a parrot by Apuleius survive to show what could be achieved.[55] Similarly descriptions of natural or artificial wonders challenged a speaker to produce an equivalent in words; another laudation of Tempe survives from the pen of the sophist Aelian, and Philostratus' *Life of Apollonius* contains an elaborate description, perhaps modeled on Dio, of what is presumably the same Memnon, the famous colossus of Egyptian Thebes.[56] These essays do not suffice to prove what Synesius inferred from them, that the young Dio was a practicing sophist, for at least some professed philosophers also indulged in such descriptions.[57] Nevertheless, by making such concessions to rhetoric Dio cannot have pleased more determined Stoics like his teacher Musonius.

Dio's anti-philosophical works equally do not prove that he began as a sophist, though they are harder to reconcile with an attachment to philosophy. According to Synesius, Dio particularly attacked "Socrates and Zeno and their followers": if this is accurate, his target seems to have been that left wing of Stoicism which sympathized with the libertarian views of the Cynics.[58] The Cynics regarded Socrates as one of their paragons, and Zeno had been a pupil of the Cynic Crates before becoming the founder of Stoicism.[59] In Dio's day there was a measurable gap between such Stoics as Thrasea Paetus, whose views were not inconsistent with monarchy, and his son-in-law Helvidius Priscus, who stood closer to the Cynics;[60] in this division, Musonius and his pupils were nearer to Thrasea. Musonius preached that kings should be philosophers;[61] Euphrates exhorted Pliny to the political life; Epictetus, though he exalts Cynicism as a remote ideal, scorns the professed Cynics who do nothing but "haunt tables and gateways."[62] It may be that Dio's work *Against the Philosophers* was not against all philosophers, but only some, though if so it may also be that Synesius has abbreviated the title.

According to Synesius, Dio continued his campaign against philosophers in a work *To Musonius*. The title does not show that Dio attacked his teacher: conceivably he tried to justify his other work, as Aristides defends his previous attacks on Plato in his open letter *To Capito*. It may be relevant that when sending his *Dio* to his teacher Hypatia, Synesius too makes a bitter attack on unnamed contemporary philosophers.[63]

This sophistic phase may in part be no more than a sign of immaturity, as Plutarch's is usually held to be.[64] External causes may have contributed to it. Vespasian encouraged rhetoric and founded chairs in it at Rome.[65] Philosophy, by contrast, was in disfavor. Helvidius Priscus, the leading survivor of those senators who had opposed Nero under the influence of Stoicism, already had clashed with Vespasian in 70, and later was exiled and put to death.[66] Cynics who attacked the regime were flogged or executed, and eventually all professional philosophers were banished from Rome.[67] In this atmosphere it is not surprising that Dio indulged his sophistic abilities and checked his philosophic ones. Just as the two pieces on Melancomas appear to have been written for the court, so may *Against the Philosophers*. Synesius says of it that Dio urged the expulsion of philosophers "from land and sea as the pests of cities and conduct."[68] It seems evident that this plea was connected with Vespasian's ban, either to urge it or, more probably, to justify it after the event.[69]

Very few of Dio's extant works can be dated to the period before his own exile. Three of them deserve separate consideration, the speech on the riot at Prusa and the *Rhodian* and *Alexandrian* orations; but three others may be noticed here, the two pieces on Melancomas and the *Trojan* oration. The first of the works honoring Melancomas is a funeral oration (*Or.* 29), supposedly delivered by the president (*agonothetes*) of the competition in which the boxer had died; the cause of his death is not stated.[70] It is clearly implied that the scene is Naples, so that the competition must be the *Sebasta*, periodically held there in honor of Augustus; the date is probably 74 or 78.[71] Although Dio may have written his piece to be delivered on the occasion, its literary flavor suggests that it belongs to the tradition of invented funeral orations which goes back to the fourth century B.C.[72] Much of it is from the inherited stock of such orations, for example, the notion that an early death is desirable, and the exhortation to the survivors to imitate the deceased.[73] But some items are drawn directly from the conventional themes of athletic praise which recur in acclamations, epigrams, honorific decrees, and testimonials.[74] A recently discovered decree for another athlete who died at the Neapolitan *Sebasta* has several resemblances to Dio;[75] the praise of Melancomas' father as another notable athlete (3),[76] of his own courage and other moral qualities (9),[77] his invincibility (11),[78] the indifference to heat and fatigue which enabled him to fight all day (12),[79] all have echoes in the general language of athletic encomium.

In the second piece (*Or.* 28) an unnamed narrator describes a visit to Naples shortly after the same festival and how he learned of Melancomas' death from the trainer (*epistates*) of one of the other athletes.[80] This man and the narrator between them praise Melancomas in terms similar to the first piece; here again appear conventional ideas, such as his beauty unsullied by the usual boxers' scars (7), and his title of the "undefeated" (*aleiptos*, 9).[81] Thus, the second piece resembles the first in using traditional ideas to compose polished miniatures, which convey genuine feeling without exaggeration or bad taste.

The *Trojan* oration (*Or.* 11) is tour de force designed to refute Homer and show that Troy was never captured. The refutation (*anasceue*) was a regular exercise of the rhetorical schools, and this is the most sophistic of Dio's extant works.[82] Though this feature is the only indication of date, Synesius seems correct in placing the work among Dio's early ones.[83] The speech purports to be delivered in Troy itself (4), and though there is no independent evidence that any of Dio's occasional speeches were actually delivered, equally there is no reason to doubt it.[84] Ilion, as it was more usually called, remained an important and much-visited city in the Roman period. Its annual festival (*panegyris*) of Athena drew visitors from far and near, and might even be the occasion of Dio's speech, since such events were often used by speakers to attract attention.[85] Curiously, Dio speaks even here in the tones of philosophy, warning his hearers not to expect amusement (6) and against the blandishments of "sophists" (6, 14). This once again suggests that the young Dio was not so far from philosophy as Synesius believed.[86]

One passage of the speech is notable for its praises of Rome.[87] Recounting, or rather rewriting, the history of events after the fall of Troy, Dio describes how Aeneas was sent to colonize "Italy, the most prosperous land of Europe" (137) and, after becoming king of it, "founded the greatest of all cities" (138). Hector, who remained behind as king of Troy, assured the parting Aeneas that he deserved to have a kingdom as good as his own; perhaps he might conquer all of Europe, and his descendants Asia as well (141). According to Dio, the prophecy was now fulfilled since "both Greece and Asia are under others" (150). These praises of Italy's prosperity and Rome's greatness are conventional; and no doubt the occasion prompted them, since Ilion's supposed consanguineity with Rome had long brought it pride and profit.[88] Even if this passage proves nothing about Dio's real view of Rome, however, it is a useful reminder that such a speech as the *Rhodian*, with its faintly disapproving remarks about the ruling power, must equally be judged by the circumstances of its delivery.

Whether Dio would have continued on this middle path between philosophy and "sophistry" is impossible to tell. For the time being, he was secure and successful. In due course the elderly Vespasian died, and Dio's friend Titus ascended the throne, still in the prime of life. Within two years, however, Titus was dead, and the throne passed to his younger brother. The change of rulers was to affect the whole later course of Dio's life.

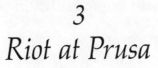

3
Riot at Prusa

Dio's civic speeches are the first of his works mentioned by Philostratus, and in modern times they have received the most attention. Most of them are addressed to Prusa, and of these all but one belong to the time after his exile. The exception (*Or. 46*) is probably from the reign of Vespasian and concerns a food shortage in the city.

Bread, preferably made from wheat, was the staple food of antiquity, and the provision of a cheap supply of grain was one of the chief tasks of government.[1] In normal times a city so fortunate as Prusa may have been able to allow the price to be determined by supply and demand, with no interference other than the usual supervision of the magistrate called the "market-overseer" (*agoranomos*).[2] In harder times, and perhaps usually, there would have been elected another official, the "grain-buyer" (*sitones*), who used public funds to ensure a supply of grain and to control the price.[3] At all times, however, another factor intervened that recurs constantly in Dio's civic speeches: public generosity. It was expected that the officials concerned with grain should contribute from their own pockets to guarantee cheapness and plenty.[4] In times of scarcity, when the regular machinery of the city became inadequate, generosity was essential. At this time there might be a call for a collective gift from the wealthy, a subscription (*epidosis*),[5] or one of them might be induced to be the "commissioner of the grain supply" (*epimeletes agoras, euthenias*).[6] This was not a recurrent office (*arche*), but a position created

19

in emergency and compulsory on the person elected, and thus a "public service" or "liturgy" (leitourgia).[7]

In making these provisions the cities were not actuated only by concern for the general welfare. Two other principal motives can be distinguished. One is the pervasive desire for "repute" (doxa) and "honor" (time), which will be seen later in Dio's plans to beautify Prusa. The link between this urge and civic generosity is shown by the fact that the word originally signifying "love of honor" (philotimia) early developed the meaning of "public munificence."[8] The other motive is a connected but negative one, natural in a small community, a fear of "dislike" (phthonos); again, it is symptomatic that the same word also connotes "envy," the dislike of those whose prosperity is conspicuous.[9] The people knew how to play on both feelings. Besides election to magistracies and liturgies, a leading citizen might receive "acclamations" (epiboeseis, epiphoneseis), whereby the assembled citizenry would chant his praises in unison, often for hours at a time, "Only Dio loves his city," "Good luck to our nourisher (tropheus) Dio."[10] At other times the shouts would be less gratifying, "Dio hoards grain," "Let Dio be made commissioner."[11] Violence might break out, and the mob stone the unpopular citizen, or try to burn his house down.[12] In such a crisis the victim felt the pressure not only of the people but of his own class, whose members were eager to quell trouble and to fasten the burden of expense on another. A grave disturbance might have the more serious consequence of drawing Roman attention and provoking retribution: loss of political privileges, exile, or even death.

It is in such a disturbance that the speech of which the published version survives was given. Since the members of his audience are the most affected by the shortage and are now debating measures to remedy it (10, 14), Dio must be addressing a regular meeting of the assembly, probably in the usual meeting place of this body, the theater.[13] The price of grain having risen above the normal (10), public wrath has turned on Dio. The only reason, by his account, is that he has recently bought a parcel of public land and built shops on it (9): evidently this display of wealth had attracted "envy" and created a justifiable impression that Dio had money to spare. He dismisses out of hand two other charges, that he is hoarding wheat and that, as a moneylender, he is profiting from the scarcity (8): the fact that he does not choose to take them seriously does not prove they were untrue. All these allegations may have been conveyed in shouts at public occasions or in the streets: finally the public fury had mounted so far that a mob carrying stones and firebrands had advanced on Dio's house and that of another man (2, 16). It was turned back from Dio's because it "feared the narrowness of the street" (12–13); in other words, his household had prepared to resist the siege by violence. Because the situation was becoming volatile, the magistrates had summoned the assembly to elect a "commissioner of the market" (10, 14). The scene can be imagined from a description that Dio gives elsewhere of an angry assembly. "Their fury was terrible to see. When they shouted against anyone, they threw him straight into a panic, so that this one ran about pleading, that one tore his clothes for fear. I myself was almost bowled over by their shouting, as if by a wave or a thunderclap. But other men, who either went up to the platform or stood up in the crowd, spoke to them either in few words or in long speeches. And some they listened to for quite a long time, others they grew angry with as soon as they opened their mouths, and stopped them before they had said a word."[14]

Dio's speech is delivered before an equally angry audience (1), which interrupts him with a disturbance (10). How far the published version represents a speech actually made cannot be exactly measured. Evidently it was not written before the occasion: but Dio may have hastily prepared, or improvised, an actual speech, which he later thought worthy of publication. That the speech is basically real is borne out by the fidelity with which it reflects the circumstances and the language of contemporary city life.

A circumstance which might seem implausible is that so well-endowed a city as Prusa should have suffered such a dearth as Dio suggests. Yet no region, however fertile, was immune from bad harvests.[15] Under Tiberius, Aspendus in the very middle of the Pamphylian plain was afflicted with such a famine that the inhabitants had to eat vetch; under Claudius the city of Acraephia in the fertile region of Boeotia suffered a shortage which only the generosity of its rich citizens alleviated; under Domitian the price of wheat rose by more than double at Pisidian Antioch, which had a large and highly favored territory.[16] Similarly, the belief that Dio was hoarding grain was based on a frequent practice. At Aspendus it was allegedly the philosopher Apollonius of Tyana who shamed the wealthy into opening their stores; at Antioch the governor ordered all surplus wheat to be made available to the public buyers, "since it is most cruel for anyone to profit from the hunger of his fellow citizens."[17] Two centuries later St. Basil of Caesarea bitterly denounces the rich who profit from the wrath of God, opening their granaries only when starvation has driven the price high enough.[18]

The means adopted by the Prusan mob have their parallel. At Aspendus, Apollonius barely saved the chief magistrate from being burned alive; in second-century Athens a Cynic philosopher saved the official in charge of the grain supply from being stoned; in the food riots of the late empire house-burning was frequent.[19] The "siege" of an unpopular man's house is illustrated by a letter of Augustus, who found that during such an attack a citizen of Cnidos had been killed by a dropped chamber pot.[20] Resistance to the call for liturgists, and even for regular magistrates, is attested even in the early empire, and in late antiquity becomes frequent: Dio provides another example in his later attempt to avoid the chief magistracy of Prusa.[21] A situation like the present one, a shortage of wheat leading to the election of a market commissioner, is found in another city of Bithynia, Prusias ad Hypium, where a benefactor is praised for undertaking the liturgy.[22]

Just as the situation of Dio's speech reflects actuality, so also his language is that of the civic life of the period. The words he uses for "approval," "munificence" (3), "influence" (4), for "requesting" imperial favor (4) or "contributing" to the purchase of grain (8), his use of the term "leaders" for the Roman authorities (14), all recur in official documents and in other authors of the period.[23] As often, the language of Plutarch is especially close to Dio's, since both belonged to the same social class and had similar political views.[24]

The speech has a double purpose, to calm the mob and at the same time to rescue Dio from election to the liturgy. After a general appeal to the public's forbearance (1–2), he tries to win its goodwill by recalling his ancestors' and his own services to the city (2–7). This passage well illustrates how single families were expected to maintain a tradition of generosity; no doubt this expectation increased the pressure on Dio, all the more since he seems recently to have inherited from his father (6). Among the members of his family, he begins with his father, recalling how the public always "blesses" him as "no mean citizen" (2): these "blessings" are clearly acclamations.[25] Dio's grandfather had "spent in munificence all the fortune he had inherited from his father and grandfather, until he had nothing left, and acquired a second one from culture and the emperors": yet he requested nothing for himself, but channeled all the emperor's goodwill toward Prusa (3–4). Here again Dio's claim is entirely plausible. So strong was the love of honor that citizens could impoverish themselves by their benefactions;[26] while the sums which could be earned by men of culture, doctors, for example, might run into millions.[27] It was good form for men so placed to "request" imperial favor for their native or adopted cities: thus, Dio later used his influence with Trajan for the good of Prusa, and the false prophet Alexander "requested" favors for his native city from Marcus Aurelius.[28] The populace was expected to show its gratitude in return, and Dio claims that with such ancestry he and his kin deserve respect from the citizens rather than hostility (4).

He now turns to the present crisis. His father's estate was less than it was thought, since much of it was in unsecured loans (5); even so, Dio had "already performed the heaviest liturgies for you, and more often than anyone else, though you know very well that there are many richer than I" (6). Here again is the authentic language of Greek city life; the reverse of the same coin is shown by a citizen of Caunus who "helped to meet the needs of the city, competing even with the more affluent."[29] But there must have been many, like Dio, who pleaded poverty in order to avoid their duty. Again St. Basil denounces the rich man whose one refrain is "I have nothing, I will not give, I am a poor man."[30]

Dio claims that he had also been a good citizen toward individuals, and again it is instructive to see what goodness in a rich man was expected to mean. He has many neighbors, rich and poor, yet none has ever accused him of taking away their land or turning them off it (7). Such oppression of poor neighbors by the rich was no doubt common, and St. Basil denounces those who join estate to estate and drive their poor neighbors from their homes.[31] Dio also asserts that, though "perhaps not the least of all in speaking," he has never taken an innocent man to court, accused him of possessing Caesar's property, or betrayed his interests when summoned as his advocate. The first and third of these must always have been common: the second is characteristic of the principate, since the imperial estate (*fiscus*) was constantly increasing, and a man whose property was alleged to be Caesar's might not dare, or be able, to make reply.[32] If Dio's speech was delivered under Vespasian, his claim had particular force, since the emperor was notoriously watchful for the public treasury and for his own estate.[33]

As for the present shortage, nobody is less to be blamed for it than Dio. He is not hoarding wheat; nor is it true that he has money to lend, and yet none to contribute for the purchase of public wheat (8). The latter charge had a double point: not only must a moneylender have spare cash, but he might also turn a scarcity to his own profit by charging higher interest and, if necessary, foreclosing on his debtors. Hence St. Basil, preaching in a time of famine, exhorts the rich to destroy their promissory notes and usurious bonds.[34] Dio claims that the row of shops he has recently built near the baths is the sole cause of his unpopularity (9): again the charge against him must have been that he preferred to spend for his own profit and not for the public good.

Clearly because he is only now confident of his hearers' patience, Dio reserves the least palatable section of his speech to the last. Even if the price of wheat is abnormally high, it is still only what obtains in other cities at the best of times (10). Dio may exaggerate, but the fertility of Prusa's territory must have kept the usual price comparatively low. Its neighbor Apamea, with little or no arable land, had regularly to buy its grain elsewhere, sometimes from Perinthus on the opposite shore of the Propontus; presumably the price was always above that of Prusa.[35] Dio further reproaches his hearers for their recent attack on "citizens, honorable ones too and inferior to none"; "such actions do not look like those of people in need, lacking the necessities of life, for want induces restraint" (11). The callous tone well shows the gap between the small group of "honorables" (*epitimoi*), in which Dio includes himself, and the commons, who are expected to be submissive to their superiors even in time of hunger. He reinforces the reproach with a threat: such outbreaks will only make the victims leave the city, "for it is much better to be an exile and live in another land than to be treated like this" (12). The same threat recurs in Dio's later speeches, whenever his plans for Prusa had been criticized or thwarted.[36] It was a real one, for the loss of a wealthy citizen meant one less benefactor for the people, and even in Dio's day this flight of the rich was beginning to disturb those who thought: in the late empire it was to become a grave problem for the emperors.[37] Lastly, Dio warns the people of the danger of Roman intervention: "nothing that happens in the cities goes unnoticed by the leaders, I mean the leaders superior to those here; just as the families of little children who are naughty at home report them to their teachers, so the misbehavior of the assemblies is reported to them" (14). In the same way a riotous gathering of the people at Ephesus provokes a warning from the chief magistrate: "We are in danger of being held to account for today's uproar."[38] Dio's warning refers to two different levels of authority: the Roman one, principally the emperor and the senate, and the provincial, the proconsul and his subordinates. One of the chief duties of a governor was to maintain the tranquillity of his province,[39] and he had many ways of showing his displeasure with an unruly populace. He could banish or execute its agitators, forbid it to meet in assembly, or even to congregate for private purposes;[40] if he thought the whole city culpable, he would refer the matter to the emperor, who might deprive it of some privilege such as an honorable title, or its freedom.[41] Like Dio, Plutarch saw the subject peoples as "children" before these stern and omnipotent masters.[42]

This brief speech illuminates much of the life, thought, and language of a Greek city of the first century. It does so, moreover, from an angle very different from that of the usual source, epigraphy. Inscriptions tend naturally to mention those aspects of city life which were thought good examples for posterity: generous benefactors, grateful populaces, civic harmony. It is no accident that, in this speech above all, Dio anticipates the language of Christian bishops, since they too were more concerned with the vices than the virtues of their hearers.

The speech also reveals Dio. It is aimed directly at the issues in a way that recalls his great exemplar, Demosthenes. In this it anticipates Dio's later civic speeches, one of whose most attractive features is the sharp clarity with which he defines and attacks the problem at hand.[43] Yet other qualities mark the speech as an early one: a certain youthful brashness, and the essential selfishness of his position. If the young Dio was not Synesius' "heartless sophist," he was as yet far from the civic concern of his last years; and if exile did not convert him to philosophy, still it taught him to put the principles of his Stoic training into practice.

4
Rhodes

By far the longest of Dio's extant speeches purports to have been delivered in the city of Rhodes (*Or.* 31). There is no good reason to doubt that Dio spoke there, for, like Troy, Rhodes was a much visited city. In particular, it was a customary stage on the journey to Egypt, and a passage in Dio's *Alexandrian*, which also seems to be an early speech, suggests that he had come there straight from Rhodes.[1] It may well be, however, that the extant speech is expanded from the one originally spoken, like Pliny's published *Panegyric*.[2]

Situated on the northern tip of the island from which it derived its name, and with excellent artificial harbors, Rhodes had been a great naval power in the third and second centuries. It had extended its dominion over some of the neighboring islands and a part of the mainland opposite, the so-called Peraea.[3] At first Rhodes profited from the approaching power of Rome. It gave signal help to it against Antiochus III of Syria, and was rewarded in the ensuing peace by the extension of its rule over much of Caria and Lycia. Rome soon grew jealous of this prosperous empire and proceeded to encourage or enforce its dismemberment, notably by ordering the Rhodians to give up the city of Caunus in Caria. Only then was it prepared to guarantee the rights of the now humbled state by a formal treaty. Rhodes never recovered its former greatness, though it was still strong enough to hold out in the Roman cause against Mithradates of Pontus. When civil war broke out in Rome, Rhodes like many of the allied cities found that mere loyalty to Rome was no protection: after lending slight support to Cornelius Dolabella, previously a supporter of Julius Caesar, it was besieged and plundered by the tyrannicide Cassius.

The early principate was a period of outward prosperity for Rhodes. After Actium, when the young Caesar declared a general cancellation of debts owed to Rome, Rhodes was, according to Dio, the only city which declined the privilege (66–67).[4] Writing under Augustus and Tiberius, the geographer Strabo gives a description of the city which suggests the last days of the Venetian republic. The harbors, docks, and walls were still to be seen, as in Dio's time; there was still a fleet, though its duties were now ceremonial; like Dio, Strabo greatly admired the stability of the constitution.[5] Rhodes had become ossified, a haven for such lovers of antiquity and the Greek past as the future emperor Tiberius.[6] Its streets and squares were encrusted with ancient bronzes (Cassius had been mainly interested in gold and silver), and in comparison with such Greek cities as Athens or Corinth it still struck the tourist as unspoiled.

Yet the facade concealed impoverishment and unrest: wealth was in the hands of a clique. Already at the time of Cassius' siege, the people had favored resistance, while the rich secretly betrayed the city.[7] It may again have been moneyed interests which caused Rhodes not to accept Octavian's cancellation of debts to Rome, for this seems to have been conditional on a similar settlement between individuals.[8] Despite the name of democracy, Strabo considered Rhodes an oligarchy in which the poor were pacified by an elaborate system of liturgies.[9] Under Claudius the Rhodians were accused of having crucified Roman citizens, presumably not westerners but members of the city's upper class; the city now lost its liberty, and the old treaty, if it had not already done so, no doubt fell into abeyance.[10]

The accession of Nero temporarily halted the city's decline. As crown prince, he persuaded Claudius to restore its liberty.[11] Since Dio makes much of its prosperity (40, 55, 62, 100, 102, 106), it may also have gained a privilege which did not necessarily accompany freedom, immunity from tribute: this may have been granted by Nero as emperor, who gave the same two privileges to Achaea.[12] He was not only actuated by philhellenism, but more particularly by Rhodes's devotion to the sun-god Helios, whose statue was the famous, though fallen, colossus.[13] This god, by his kingly splendor and as the heavenly charioteer, had a special power over Nero; the emperor's head is given Helios' features on Rhodian coins,[14] and conversely Nero appears to have intended to give his own features to the new colossus he built for Helios at Rome.[15]

After Nero's fall, and probably after the original delivery of Dio's speech, Vespasian again deprived Rhodes of its freedom and, if it had also had immunity, of that also.[16] Its freedom at least was soon restored, probably by Titus.[17] From then on no other changes in its status are known, though there was further unrest under Domitian.[18] In the reign of Pius the rhetor Aristides wrote an open letter to Rhodes which resembles Dio's speech at several points; Rhodes was still free, but again rich and poor were opposed.[19]

Dio's speech is given before the people (*demos*) of Rhodes, probably though not certainly meeting in regular assembly (110, cf. 1, 4). He pretends that most of his hearers do not know his intended subject and that many will dislike his "correcting" a practice of the city uninvited (1). Presumably the magistrates or leading citizens had requested him, as a visitor of note, to address the people on a subject of his choice; so also Apollonius of Tyana was invited to address the Athenian assembly, and Aristides the Rhodian.[20]

Probably not long before, Dio's teacher Musonius had reproved the Athenians for their disgraceful passion for gladiators,[21] and Dio too selects a question of public conduct. The city naturally had many visitors and felt obliged to honor a large number of them, especially if they were Romans (43, cf. 26, 33, 75, 93, 105, 155). Since it still had many bronze statues commemorating ancient benefactors, it had fallen into the practice of reusing them in order to save the expense of new ones. The chief executive magistrate, the "general" (9, 52, 71, 87, 99, 132, 134, 141), would be instructed to select a statue, erase the name of the previous honorand, and replace it with that of the new one (9, 141). This practice Dio denounces at exhaustive length.

The topic is not so frivolous as it might appear. The machinery of Greek city life was sustained by interaction between rich and poor: the rich were led by love of honor (*philotimia*) and fear of envy to be generous to their humbler fellow-citizens, while these in turn rewarded them with an elaborately graded range of distinctions. Of these a statue was among the highest, so that in this period the word for "honor" (*time*) was synonymous with it.[22] Because statues were costly, it was polite for the honorand or his family to assume the expense,[23] or to accept a lesser honor. Hence Plutarch advises the intending politician to decline portraits and statues and be content with simpler ones like an inscription;[24] so also Dio assures the Rhodians that their visitors will be satisfied with presents or a generous reception, or if they are "of the better kind" with an invitation to the public table (*prytaneion*) or to a front seat at the theater (*prohedria*, 108).[25] A front seat at Rhodes is worth more than a statue elsewhere; merely to receive the people's acclamations is an honor, so decorously are they expressed (110).

Besides their costliness, statues had another feature that other honors lacked. Though there was a fundamental distinction, carefully observed by Dio, between cult-statues (*agalmata*) and ordinary ones (*andriantes, eikones*, 16),[26] yet even these had an aura of sanctity: the Rhodians are committing a kind of sacrilege (10–15, 95–100). The mutilation or demolition of a statue symbolized the disgrace of a ruler or a private citizen, as did the erasure of his name from public monuments;[27] Dio infers that the Rhodians were inflicting a shame on their benefactors which more than canceled the original honor (29).

Among the excuses for the practice, one which Dio is greatly concerned to rebut is that it existed in other Greek cities, notably Athens (39, 116–125). Literature and monuments attest it in many cities, in Athens above all; Cicero, for example, was anxious not to be honored there with falsely inscribed statues.[28] That it was practiced on Rhodes is eloquently shown by a decree of another city, Lindos, passed about fifty years before Dio's visit. This ordains that anonymous statues on the acropolis may be reinscribed, or even removed, on payment to the city. So also in Rhodes the practice had begun with damaged and anonymous statues and had spread to others (141); and just as the Rhodians pleaded the expense of making new ones (41), so the Lindians urge the shortage of sacred funds.[29]

Dio's arguments are drawn from the intrinsic unworthiness of the practice and from the situation of Rhodes. The recurrent theme of the speech is that by maltreating its old statues the city betrays its past; accordingly, he appeals to every argument that marks Rhodes's ancient glory and its resistance to change. Like Strabo, he applauds its stable constitution (146), under which the people assembles every day; others do so only "reluctantly and at intervals, with nobody attending except a few of those considered well-born" (4). The people makes its acclamations sitting down, "whereas others do not think they do enough honor unless they yell to bursting" (110); Aristides similarly praises the decorum of the Rhodian assembly and its habit of voting not with a show of hands but a mere nod.[30] According to Dio, the whole appearance of the Rhodians, their measured step, their hair style and dress, is such as to awe the visitor (162–163); later he recalls the same features in order to reproach the Alexandrians by the contrast.[31] Rhodes's past glory is reflected not only in its many statues, but also in the ancient walls and docks it so lovingly tends (125, 146) and its vestigial fleet (103).[32] Dio even speaks as if its ancient empire were intact, and it remained ruler of Caria and part of Lycia (47, 101): but this seems an exaggeration, though Rhodes still received tribute from nearby islands and the Peraea, including the hated Caunus (48, 50, 125).[33]

Dio makes several of his points by contrasting Rhodes with other Greek cities. This device was recommended by the intense pride and competitiveness of ancient cities, which is particularly observable under the principate: Dio appeals to the same sentiments when he urges Tarsus to outdo its neighbors in courtesy, or exhorts Prusa to emulate the civic pride of other cities of its region.[34] At Rhodes the argument to which he especially appeals, as Aristides does later,[35] is that the city is the last true heir of Hellenism (18, 55, 117, 157–161, 163); this again was a device that could be adapted to circumstances, so that Dio also urges the Tarsians to prove themselves Greeks and not Phoenicians and congratulates the Nicaeans on the purity of their Greek descent.[36] Several cities serve as a foil to Rhodes. The Ephesians have large sums deposited on trust in their temple of Artemis; though they regularly declare them at the "registrations" (apographai), presumably those made for the Roman census,[37] they never touch them for their own purposes, even so far as to loan them; and yet Ephesus is in worse condition than many cities (54–55). This is another exaggeration. It is true that the Artemision had long been famous as a sacred bank, but also that Ephesus was one of the great cities of the empire.[38]

Another city to which Dio compares Rhodes, though not for prosperity but conduct, is Elis in the Peloponnese. Elis' claims rested on its control of the Olympic games. So coveted, Dio observes, was the wreath of wild olive awarded at the games that many athletes have died competing for it;[39] the emperor Nero was in bliss when admitted to the contest (110). If the Eleans crowned every Roman visitor, the wreath would no longer seem desirable: yet they are so far from fawning on Rome that when great Romans recommend athletes to them, they do not open their letters until the results are decided (111). If the Eleans so value what is theirs, "when generally they are no better than any of the Peloponnesians," Rhodes must not be so servile as to honor every Roman with a statue (112). Dio is not exaggerating when he says that many athletes had died at Olympia, for such deaths, like that of Melancomas at Naples, were a frequent occurrence;[40] but he conceals the fact, which would have greatly weakened his argument, that the Eleans had bent every rule in order to give Nero the victory he so desired.[41]

Elsewhere Dio uses the example of four cities at once—Athens, Sparta, Byzantium, and Mytilene—to refute the claim that Rhodes must honor every Roman. These four also have to cultivate the Romans, but if they decide to set up a bronze statue, they always have a new one made (105). Dio admits that Rhodes's situation is slightly different, but holds that the difference should be a source of pride: while Rhodes is both free and prosperous, the other four cities have only freedom,[42] except that Athens has a few possessions as well (106). It is true that Athens was the only one of the four to resemble Rhodes in having a semblance of empire;[43] but all these cities, especially Byzantium,[44] must have been fairly prosperous, and despite Dio Athens was notorious for reemploying old statues.

Athens, which epitomized the history and culture of classical Greece, is in fact the city Dio most frequently contrasts with Rhodes. On some points he can praise it: it does well to have a law requiring that the names of those condemned to death should first be erased from public monuments (84–85); and it showed a proper respect for its benefactors when it condemned Leptines for trying to abolish their perquisites (128).[45] But modern Athens is no example for Rhodes; the inhabitants are no better than Phrygians or Thracians; a visitor would scarcely know he was in the city of the Academy and the Lyceum rather than one of Syria or Cilicia (163). "They have called 'Olympian' someone who is not even a citizen by birth, but some creature from Phoenicia"; they have set up the statue of some careless poet, who also gave a display in Rhodes, besides Menander's; they honored Nicanor with a disgraceful epigram simply because he bought Salamis for them (116). The Phoenician is unknown, though the acclamation of "Olympian" is a real one mentioned by Dio elsewhere and on inscriptions; he perhaps has in mind that Pericles had also received it, so that the profanation was all the greater.[46] The poet can be identified as a certain Pompeius Capito of Pergamum, since the base of the statue has survived; the inscription shows that his "carelessness" appeared in displays of improvised verse.[47] Some of the bases of Nicanor survive also and show that this Syrian's act of generosity gained him the title of "New Themistocles"—another instance of the Athenians' indifference to their ancient legacy; later they too seem to have thought better of it, since on most of the bases the title is erased, together with that of "New Homer."[48]

A further symptom of Athens' decline is its addiction to gladiatorial displays. Even the Corinthians, the carriers of the pest, watch these shows in some gully outside the city, while the Athenians have remodeled the theater of Dionysus immediately beneath the Acropolis (121). When rebuked by an eminent Roman philosopher (evidently Musonius Rufus),[49] they were so indignant that he decided to leave the city and stay elsewhere: in Rhodes, where the law even forbids the public executioner to enter the city, such a thing could never happen (122). Dio's description does not fit the present stadium of Corinth, which was probably built much later;[50] but the remodeling of the theater at Athens may be attested by the extant parapet which separates the orchestra from the seats.[51] As a Roman colony, the governor's residence, and the focus of the provincial cult of the emperors, with which gladiatorial shows were especially associated, Corinth was naturally the chief scene of such displays in Greece.[52] After Dio, the Cynic Demonax is also supposed to have rebuked Athens for thus imitating Corinth; and Philostratus makes Apollonius denounce the city for defiling its ancient theater with blood, though the author may have invented the denunciation from Dio's speech.[53] What Dio says of Rhodes is confirmed by the remains, for among the hundreds of gladiatorial monuments from the Greek east not one has been found on the island.[54]

These criticisms of Athens need not be put down so much to personal reasons,[55] though Dio might have felt the insult offered to Musonius Rufus, as to the exigencies of the situation. Since his theme is the Hellenic tradition of Rhodes, it is strengthened by depicting the decline of the city normally thought the capital of Hellenism. This contrast was all the more attractive in that Athens and Rhodes were no doubt jealous of each other's culture and possessions.[56] For his purpose Dio could draw on the abundant arsenal of abuse to which contemporary Athens was subject, in particular its tolerance of foreigners and "barbarians."[57] When visiting Athens himself, however, or enumerating the honors it had shown him, he speaks of it with more respect.[58]

What Dio says of Rome in the speech must equally be viewed in context. Most of those who received reused statues at Rhodes were Romans, though new ones were made for "emperors and others of high station"

(107). Similarly, Rhodes's liberty depended on Rome's goodwill (106, 112–114); hence Aristides too warns the Rhodians that their dissension may cost them their freedom.[59] It is, therefore, natural that most of Dio's allusions to their history concern their relations with Rome. In one passage he enumerates the actions in which they have shown their "loyalty and goodwill" toward the Roman people (113):[60] they served it against Antiochus and Mithradates and handed over to it the rule of the sea which they had preserved through many dangers; they swore oaths of friendship with the Romans and joined them in a treaty still preserved in the temple of Zeus (on the Capitol);[61] they sailed with them to the Ocean[62] and finally suffered capture in their cause. This passage is full of traditional language, and Dio speaks much as a Rhodian ambassador would address the Romans.[63] As usual, he exaggerates, suppresses, or palliates. He pretends that Rhodes "handed over" its power to Rome, when in fact Rome methodically dismantled it; the treaty on the Capitol had long since been broken, and even the record may have perished before Dio spoke;[64] Rhodes was not captured in the Roman cause, but by Romans engaged in civil war. Dio says nothing of the more recent friction between Rome and Rhodes, such as the riot under Claudius in which Roman citizens had been put to death.

Dio does give a unique account of an incident in the reign of Nero. His argument is that Rhodes's abundance of statuary is a token of the Romans' goodwill; though they have plundered every other place, they have never touched anything at Rhodes.[65] Nero pillaged Olympia, Delphi, the Acropolis of Athens, "though that sanctuary belonged to him,"[66] and Pergamum, and yet considered Rhodes the holiest of holies (148). When his freedman Acratus arrived there after looting the world, and the citizens were indignant, he assured them that he was permitted only to look and not to touch (149). Other sources than Dio mention Nero's thefts from Olympia, Delphi, and Pergamum; it is not otherwise known that he pillaged Athens,[67] though Dio's language may imply that Nero's statue had been placed in the Parthenon.[68] Acratus had been sent to Asia about 61 to collect works of art for his master, and his visit to Pergamum caused violence there.[69] It is clear that Nero thought Rhodes "holy" because of his reverence for Helios and the god's favorite island. In turn, this mark of favor helps to explain the city's present predicament: Rhodes's abundance of statues not only made an invidious contrast with other cities, but was a conspicuous reminder of its relations with an emperor now fallen and disgraced.

Some have thought that Dio expresses hostility to Rome in the speech, or at least urges it to show greater respect for Hellenism: others see him warning the Rhodians against adoption of Roman ways.[70] It is true that, unlike Plutarch for instance, Dio divides the world into Greeks and barbarians (163), without putting the Romans in a separate class.[71] A note of resignation, though not resentment, is audible when he portrays the once sovereign Rhodians now subject to Rome (46, 125), or describes the decline of Greece (159, 161–163). He chides the Rhodians for respecting only strength when they fawn on the Romans (43); Rome's ascendancy was the work of good fortune as well as virtue (68). There is a hint of disapproval or mockery when he mentions the letters whereby the Romans recommend Olympic athletes (111), or their habit of traveling everywhere by litter (156). Although gladiatorial games had long since been popular among Greeks, Dio and his hearers knew that the disease had originally spread from Rome (121–122).

None of these ideas, however, marks Dio as an enemy of Rome; almost all of them are shared by Plutarch, of whose sympathy toward Rome there is little doubt.[72] Without expressing any warmth for the Romans, Dio represents them as reasonable and intelligent rulers, whose conduct is in some ways an example for the Greeks. They are not taken in by the fraudulent honors offered by the Rhodians, even if they are too polite to object (33, 44). They are not displeased when the Eleans refuse to be swayed by their letters, since they prefer to rule free men rather than slaves (111). It is true that they have carried off statues from everywhere, but it was to adorn their city, where the objects are better off than in some corner of Greece (151). In the matter of gladiators the Athenians showed less delicacy than the Corinthians (121), and it was a Roman who rebuked them (122). This last point recalls that, like Plutarch, Dio is no more critical of Roman failings than were reflective Romans. Several Latin authors rail against gladiators and ostentatious luxury, including the use of litters, far more loudly.[73] Romans as well as Greeks wished to see the traditions of Hellenism maintained and deplored those modern Greeks who stooped to unworthy and unnecessary flattery.[74] There is no doubt that Dio's Hellenism is sincere; but like other Greeks of his day, and many Romans, he accepted the compromise which gave the prize for culture to Greece, and for power to Rome.

The message of the *Rhodian* is not primarily political, but ethical. Like Musonius in Athens, Dio attempts to correct a moral failing in his audience; like the Athenians, though in a different way, the Rhodians err by neglecting their heritage. In other cities that he addresses, for instance Tarsus and Apamea, the general error is of another kind, an obsession with material wealth, and here too his speeches are above all concerned with ethics. It is only in cities with whose affairs he is personally involved, Prusa and to a degree other cities of Bithynia, that his advice is primarily political.

That is not to deny that Dio had other aims in delivering and publishing the *Rhodian*, and that one of these was political. When he urges Rhodes not to betray its past, the past that he dwells on is that of its cooperation with Rome. The kind of Hellenism he preaches is one that does not conflict with Roman supremacy, but is approved by the Romans.

Another of Dio's aims in publishing his speech was natural for a young author, a desire to display his skill. Indirectly he emulates the speech *Against Leptines* of his beloved Demosthenes, for the *Rhodian* not only alludes to that famous piece (128),[75] but also resembles it in its general argument. It is a tour de force, in which every imaginable consideration for and against the thesis is rehearsed with zest: in this it recalls the *Trojan*, with its exhaustive refutation of Homer, or the *Alexandrian*, where another city's vices receive an equally elaborate reproof. All three speeches, by their joining of earnestness and display, reveal Philostratus' "philosopher who seemed to be a sophist." In some of his later speeches, the *Olympian* and *Borysthenite* for example, the display is still present, though outweighed by the earnestness: in the later civic speeches, it has almost vanished. It was easy for Synesius to conclude that Dio had been converted to philosophy: but speeches like the *Rhodian* or the *Alexandrian* show that the truth is more complicated.

5
Alexandria

One of Dio's best and most celebrated speeches was delivered in the city of Alexandria;[1] it is addressed to the "people" (2, 4, 24–25, 29, 96), and so probably to the popular assembly.[2] The date is disputed, but one under Vespasian best fits the available evidence.[3] As at Rhodes, there seems no need to doubt that Dio did visit the city and give a speech roughly similar to the published version; Alexandria was one of the sights of the world, which every cultivated Greek would hope to see, and Dio would also have traveled in Egypt itself.[4]

In size and importance Alexandria is, next to Rome, the largest of the cities addressed by Dio. It was the second city of the empire (35), with a population of about three hundred thousand (cf. 2, 20, 41, 47, 87).[5] It owed its advantages directly to its location, being situated, in Dio's words, "on a kind of hinge connecting the whole earth and widely separated nations" (36). It faced the Mediterranean: behind, a system of canals linked it to the Nile, and ultimately to the Red Sea and Indian Ocean.[6] The "harbors" praised by Dio (36–37) lay on both sides of the city.[7] A visitor could see men from lands as distant as India (40). It was the greatest market in the world,[8] through which passed the products of almost every land (36). In addition, it drew an abundance of provisions from the proximity of salt and fresh water and the renowned fertility of Egypt (41). But Egypt was also the chief granary of Rome; the emperors jealously hoarded its grain for the use of the city on whose wellbeing their own rule depended, allowing Alexandria only enough to prevent public outbreaks (31, 59).[9]

Under the empire Alexandria was no longer the cultural center it had been under the Ptolemies, but its populace remained sophisticated and pleasure-loving.[10] Like other observers, Dio notes the Alexandrians' addiction to jokes and laughter (1, 99).[11] Every kind of "diversion" was to be found there[12]—mimes,[13] dancers (4),[14] tricksters (7),[15] and the two chief targets of Dio's speech, minstrels or "citharodes" (46, etc.) and charioteers (4, etc.). With its inbred love of diversion and dislike of authority,[16] Alexandria was a natural theater for a type of popular philosopher who appealed to these tastes, the Cynics. Dio refers contemptuously to the "crop" of these who stood at corners or in gateways amusing the "rabble," mainly sailors and children, with their jokes, gossip, and "vulgar repartee" (9).

No less than for its frivolity and turbulence, Alexandria was famous for its cults. Dio praises the multitude of its sanctuaries (41), but two were particularly notable. The presiding deity of the city was Serapis, whose great sanctuary, the Serapeum, had been built by the third Ptolemy.[17] It is to this god that Dio alludes when he mentions the "oracles and dreams" with which heaven favors the city (12), since Serapis regularly addressed his devotees in their sleep;[18] later Dio counts the god's "manifest presence" as Alexandria's greatest blessing (41). He contrasts disparagingly another famous oracle of Egypt, that of Apis at Memphis, in which the god gave his oracles through the random words (*kledones*) of children playing (13);[19] the rivalry between the two establishments was no doubt sharpened by the similarities and close connection of their gods.[20] The other sanctuary mentioned by Dio, less notable as a building but of even greater renown, is that of the Muses, the "Museum" (100). This was founded by the first Ptolemy, and was not only a temple but an academy of learning.[21] Dio must refer at least in part to members of the Museum when he deplores so-called philosophers who huddle in their lecture rooms rather than venture before the people (8),[22] or who amuse it with empty eloquence (10, 37, 39, 68); the "wise Theophilus," who lived in Alexandria without ever addressing the people, may be another member of the Museum (97–98).[23]

The history of Alexandria under Roman rule is one of continuous unrest. It had first been occupied by Roman troops in 56 B.C., when the king Ptolemy Auletes ("the Piper"), who had been expelled by the Alexandrians, was restored by A. Gabinius; Dio recalls how the citizens' factional strife caused the king to go into exile, and thus led to his restoration by Rome, "so that he lost the city by piping and you by dancing" (70). Later, Julius Caesar was trapped and besieged there; later still, it was the capital of Antony and Cleopatra. When Caesar's heir besieged and took it in 30, the citizens feared the worst; though he spared their lives and property, he put the last prince to death,[24] and from being a royal capital Alexandria became no more than the second city of a world empire. It was guarded with degrading vigilance; the prefect ruled at the emperor's pleasure and with almost royal authority; a legion was stationed in the city; the taxes were collected with rigor; despite repeated applications, Alexandria was denied one of the essentials of a Greek city, a council.[25] Augustus' suspicions were soon justified. One of the first prefects, C. Petronius, was stoned by the Alexandrian multitude, but with the troops he had at hand easily crushed the uprising.[26]

Under Tiberius his nephew Germanicus visited Alexandria and won favor by his affability and by distributing grain during a shortage. He was sharply rebuked by his uncle, for the emperors knew that a rival who held Egypt and its resources had the power to overthrow themselves.[27] The Alexandrians' dislike of the established order made them ever ready to abet pretenders, and they ardently supported several in the course of the principate. The first, and only successful, one of these was Vespasian, who was proclaimed there in 69.[28]

About twenty years after Germanicus' visit the Alexandrians' resentment found a new target. The city had a large population of Jews, and because of the privileges accorded them by Caesar and Augustus these were suspect as friends of Rome. In 38 violence broke out between Jews and gentiles which led to the dismissal and disgrace of the prefect Flaccus;[29] under Claudius two of the leading "Greeks" of Alexandria, who had led their party in the earlier trouble, were sentenced to death.[30] About this time a new type of literature began to circulate in the city and to travel up country, in which Greek "martyrs" rebuke the emperors for Judaizing, worst them in repartee, and are led off to glorious execution.[31] Under Nero, the rebellion in neighboring Judaea set off new violence in Alexandria. Some Jews were seen at a meeting of the assembly in the amphitheater and beaten; the Jewish population attacked the Greek with the usual weapons of urban violence, stones and firebrands; the prefect summoned his troops and crushed the riot, though on this occasion the Greeks were on the side of the Romans.[32]

When the Greeks of Alexandria supported the Romans in this outbreak, it was not simply because the Jewish rebellion had provided them both with a common enemy. Like Rhodes, Alexandria enjoyed Nero's favor, not only as a Greek city but also because it shared his passions for citharody and horse-racing. Soon after his accession the tribes of the city were reorganized and given elaborate names in his honor;[33] in 64 he canceled an intended visit at the last moment; until obliged to return to Rome, he may have planned to visit Alexandria after his artistic tour of Greece.[34] So impressed was the emperor by the Alexandrian claqueurs that he brought some of them to the capital and had them teach their rhythmical acclamations, novel methods of applause, and organization of factions.[35] It was later believed that he thought in his last days of escaping to Alexandria and earning his living as a citharode, a rumor born of the artistic sympathy between the emperor and the city.[36]

Shortly before the end of his reign Nero had sent his legate Flavius Vespasianus to deal with the Jewish rebellion. About a year after the emperor's death, Vespasian began his own bid for power; it was announced in July of 69, when the prefect of Egypt led his troops and the Alexandrians in swearing allegiance. While his supporters marched on Italy, Vespasian moved to seize Egypt and its grain. The several months which he spent in Alexandria gave the Flavian dynasty the necessary aura of imperial sanctity;[37] the Nile rose unusually high, the pretender was rapturously acclaimed in the hippodrome, and Serapis condescended to work miracles through his agency.[38] It has been seen that Philostratus makes Dio accompany the emperor from Judaea to Egypt: that is probably fiction, but if the *Alexandrian* is correctly dated to this reign the events of those months must have been in the minds of Dio and his hearers. The emperor's gifts to the city (92, cf. 26) were presumably made in gratitude for its early support; and when Dio suggests that the Alexandrians' good behavior may create in the emperor a "desire" to visit them (95),[39] he and they must both have thought of Vespasian's earlier stay.

That had ended less well than it began, as Vespasian turned from a pretender into an emperor. Expecting special favor, the citizens were instead burdened with new and heavier taxes; in return, they subjected the emperor to their powers of mockery and their peculiar rhythmic choruses.[40] Ever after, they dubbed him "the Fishmonger," after the most ephemeral and lowborn of their kings.[41] Titus, however, was as popular with them as Germanicus; and, like him, Titus was suspected of treasonable designs after visiting Egypt.[42] Later there was factional violence among the Jews themselves; and apparently unrelated causes led to an-

other serious uprising.[43] This may be what Dio refers to in describing a
recent riot which had ended, like that under Augustus, in open warfare
between the citizens and the occupying Romans.[44]

In tribute to the sophistication of his hearers, Dio has constructed his
speech with unusual care. The long preface (1–29) is not only designed
to win their favor, but also to announce the principal themes of the
speech, Alexandria's lack of "culture and reason" (3, 16, cf. 60), its ruin-
ous passion for entertainers, especially citharodes and charioteers (4),
and the irresponsibility of its professed philosophers (8–11, cf. 39, 68).
At the end of the preface, he artfully links his call for "reason" with a
plea for support of the reigning emperor: a good people is like a good
"king," who takes pleasure in the "order" of cities,[45] a bad one is like a
"tyrant" (25–29). Later in the speech the comparison is made more explicit: the Alexandrians must not be frivolous like Nero, but reasonable
like the present ruler. After the preface, Dio discusses the citizens' general duty to behave at public entertainments (20–40); he takes up his
two chief topics, citharody and horse-racing, together (41–46), and then
separately (46–74, 74–95). The epilogue (95–101) resumes several of
the themes of the preface, the relations between the city and the emperor (95–96), irresponsible philosophers (97–98), and the general frivolity (99–100). In a final anecdote, Dio recalls the earlier comparison of
cities with rulers by comparing himself to a piper who played before a
tyrant (101).[46]

Just as the speech is artful in its construction, so in detail it is decked
out with anecdotes (44, 63–66, 101), jokes (68, 77, 88), and a clever par-
ody of Homer, which seems to be made up by Dio.[47] Two of these orna-
ments deserve special attention, since they recur in later speeches. At
one point he gives a miniature encomium of Alexandria which contains
several ingredients traditional to such exercises,[48] praise of its size,[49]
situation,[50] river,[51] harbors,[52] and prosperity (35–36);[53] because Alexandria was unusual in that it lacked a real territory, and yet this was an
item in such laudations, Dio tactfully claims that the whole of Egypt is
a kind of appendage to the city.[54] After thus lulling his hearers, Dio jolts
them: he is praising not them but objects of nature (37–39). So again in
the first *Tarsian* (*Or.* 33) he warns his hearers not to pride themselves on
their natural advantages, or be misled by those adept at praising such
things;[55] in the *Apamean* (*Or.* 35), he discourses at length on the city's
material endowments, but in a way which shows him to be speaking in
irony.

Another device of the *Alexandrian* shared with other speeches is that of self-depreciation. Dio is a "nobody from nowhere, in a cloak, neither a good singer" (a sarcastic word for "declaimer")[56] "nor with a louder voice than others" (22); other rhetors and sophists may panegyrize the city, but his style is too "humble and prosaic" (39). So also Dio ironically contrasts himself with fine speakers in the first *Tarsian* (*Or.* 33), and avertises his squalid appearance in the second (*Or.* 34); both these devices occur in the preface of the *Apamean* (*Or.* 35).[57] Similar themes occur in other of his late speeches, such as the *Olympian* (*Or.* 12) and that *On His Exile* (*Or.* 13).[58] There is no need, however, to infer from these similarities that the *Alexandrian* is also late, since Dio may well have used such devices at widely different periods of his life. In particular, the close resemblances between the *Alexandrian* and the first *Tarsian* are no proof of proximity in date: Tarsus had much in common with Alexandria, and an artful speaker might use the same means to sway audiences in both cities.

The heart of the speech is Dio's double denunciation of citharody and chariot-racing. The cithara was a portable harp, which was usually played by a singer as an accompaniment, though it could also be played solo.[59] The art of citharody was an ancient one, but enjoyed a particular vogue in the age of Dio.[60] Antony appointed a favorite citharode to collect his taxes;[61] Antony's descendant, the emperor Nero, scandalized Rome less by his devotion to the art then by exhibiting his own skill on the stage.[62] Terpnus, a contemporary of Dio, was an international celebrity;[63] he could be the celebrated citharode who was announced to be in Cyzicus when Dio was lecturing there, and drew away his entire audience.[64]

With its love of entertainment, Alexandria must have produced many citharodes of its own as well as attracting them from elsewhere. They and other artists had their supporters organized into claques, whose rivalries could cause riots even in less volatile cities: Alexandria, famous for its claqueurs, was tinder awaiting ignition.[65] Dio describes the effects of citharodes on their Alexandrian audiences. During the performance the listeners would hum, jump up, and dance about (41, 50, 55–56, 69): they might acclaim the player as their "savior and god" (50),[66] and people might be crushed to death in the excitement (48–49). At other times, since the audience was quick to notice slips (46), the player would be mocked for his "growling" or "baying" (62), fights would break out (30, 69), and arguments continue for days at corners and in alleys (42). One such event seems to have led to a more serious consequence. He taunts the Alexandrians for "going to war" at the sound of a string, as if it were a trumpet (59–60); and it is within the part of the speech devoted to citharody that Dio describes a riot which had lately led to "war" with Roman troops (71–72). Since soldiers seem to have been regularly stationed in the theater during performances (51), fights between claques had evidently turned into an assault on their common oppressors. In the same way fights between factions in the Byzantine hippodrome could become demonstrations against the emperor, notably in the great Nika riot of 532:[67] while simple outbreaks of rioting in the theater, amphitheater, or stadium were not uncommon even in Dio's day.[68]

Dio's other chief topic is chariot-racing, another ancient art. In classical Greece it was mainly confined to special occasions, above all the Olympic games, and was an aristocratic preserve in which the owner of the chariot counted for far more than the driver.[69] The sport had early been naturalized at Rome, and there it became a regular item of public life through the circus games (*ludi circenses*) given by magistrates and, later, emperors.[70] These last attached the races to their own person and prestige, and used them with the corn-dole as their principal means of pacifying the people.[71] Since there now could be no rivalry among owners of chariots, attention was focused on the charioteers and their distinctive colors. As with citharodes, the animosity between partisans of charioteers readily led to violence; the rivalry between Blues and Greens at Constantinople caused many outbreaks besides the Nika riot. Emperors were not immune from the epidemic; as with citharody, Nero went the furthest, again by exhibiting his skill in public.[72]

The hippodrome at Alexandria, which Dio calls the "stadium" (74), had probably been built under the Ptolemies.[73] His description of the races, however, makes them sound more Roman than Greek, with the charioteer as the center of attention (4, 46, etc.), and the prize given in cash (75); oddly, he does not mention the colors. The reason for this Roman character is probably that the races were directly or indirectly given by the emperors: hence Dio talks of bread and horse-races being "thrown before" the Alexandrian mob (31), as they were at Rome.[74] Chariot-racing was a drug made necessary by "the feebleness and idleness of the many" (45); it need not overstimulate, if the subject were carefully watched, and it diverted his energies from undesirable outlets. At this time the drug was administered only to the largest cities of the empire, Rome, Alexandria, Antioch, Carthage, and Thessalonica: it was not until later that circuses on the Roman model became common in the East.[75]

As was to be expected, Alexandrian spectators were dangerously enthusiastic. "How could one describe," asks Dio, "the shouts, disturbance, passion, changes of posture and color, and all the different blasphemies you utter?" (74). Drunk on beer (an Egyptian specialty)[76] and wine, they would cheer on their favorite team and driver, quarrel with any neighbor who supported others, and fight "so that you would think neither sun nor moon safe from them" (83–85); in their enthusiasm they might throw items of clothing at the charioteer and go home naked (89).[77] Philostratus makes Apollonius of Tyana similarly rebuke the Alexandrians for their murderous conflicts over charioteers; that would be a welcome parallel to Dio's speech, if it were certain that Philostratus was not simply copying him.[78] Better evidence for the Alexandrian love of charioteering is provided by Philo, who often draws on the hippodrome for his illustrations.[79]

As with the *Rhodian*, Dio seems to have had several motives in delivering and publishing the *Alexandrian*. It is one of his cleverest speeches and shows his skill to best effect: there is little empty display of the kind evident in the *Trojan*, or even the *Rhodian*. At first it also appears to lack the underlying seriousness of the *Rhodian*. With so frivolous an audience, however, Dio could not make his points so directly as at Rhodes; and on inspection, many of the same ideas occur in the two speeches. Dio appeals to Alexandria to remember its Macedonian heritage (65) and to protect its reputation (31, 40–41, 96). He holds up the examples of other cities: Athens (3, 6, 92–93), Sparta (60, 69, 93), and Rhodes itself (52). Sometimes indeed he resembles one of the early Fathers in his fulminations. Just as he denounces the blasphemy of calling a charioteer "savior and god" (50), so Tertullian rebukes the Carthaginians for calling a charioteer "the greatest of all time";[80] Christian bishops also denounce the passion for entertainers and charioteers, ascribing it to the devil as Dio ascribes it to demons (77).[81]

As in the *Rhodian*, the moral message of the speech is inseparable from the political one. The Romans are mentioned more frequently than in any of Dio's other civic speeches. It is they who supply the city with food (31, 59) and watch over it as its "kind leaders" (71–72). The Alexandrians must imitate not Nero but the present emperor (60), to whom they are indebted for many fine buildings (95). All this suggests that Dio is concerned with improving Alexandria's behavior toward Rome. If he spoke under Vespasian, the question was particularly urgent. Nero had favored the city: Vespasian had been insulted by it. The insult was undoubtedly compounded by the numerous Cynics there; Vespasian had no patience for the tribe, and some of those he punished in Rome may have been Alexandrians.[82] That would add point to Dio's fierce attacks on the Cynics for doing "no good at all, but the greatest possible harm" (9). He may further hint at them in the "doggish (*kunikoi*) citharodes," who "overturn and destroy the city" (62); and Cynics must have been among "those foolhardy, shameless creatures who deliberately plotted general destruction and confusion" in the recent riot (72).

Alexandria, therefore, was now as low in Vespasian's favor as it had once been high in Nero's; the recent riot was caused by citharody, of which both Nero and the Alexandrians were devotees; it was probably fanned by the Cynics, perpetual irritants of Vespasian. When Dio identifies Nero with riot and folly, and the present ruler with reason and culture, he is trying to cure the city of a weakness that had once been profitable, but might now be fatal. It is possible that he speaks simply as one who sympathized with Rome and knew the mood of the court. More explicitly than in the *Rhodian*, however, he seems to insinuate that he bears a message direct from the emperor. He compares himself to Hermes sent against his will by Zeus (21), who was often identified with the reigning emperor;[83] in the same way, he suggests to the Alexandrians that their good behavior may gain the esteem of one higher than himself (29) and may induce the emperor to visit them (95–96). It was not unusual for the emperors to promote their Greek friends in their native cities, as Dio was later promoted by Trajan: but it seems unparalleled for a Greek to be sent with such a message to a city not his own.

The *Alexandrian* is, therefore, not altogether different from the *Rhodian* in its underlying seriousness of purpose; like that speech, it recalls Philostratus' "philosopher who seemed to be a sophist." Here, moreover, Dio refers to himself in a way that suggests an apprentice philosopher; he does not call himself by the name, but he wears the philosopher's cloak (22) and attacks not only "poets and rhetors" but also false philosophers (8–11, 38–39). Beneath the sophistic trappings, the outlines of the mature philosopher begin to be visible.

6
Exile and Return

The speeches of the young Dio reveal a speaker fully confident of his youthful powers. He dazzles the Trojans by refuting Homer; he composes elegant laudations of the athlete Melancomas; he rebukes the citizens of Prusa, Rhodes, and (if the speech is dated correctly) Alexandria. Intellectually he stands midway between rhetoric and philosophy. He is loyal to his teacher Musonius Rufus, but attacks Cynics and their Stoic sympathizers in his essay *Against the Philosophers*; he denounces sophists, yet makes "sophistic" speeches.

After the death of his friend Titus, possibly within a year or so, Dio was banished by the new emperor, Domitian, from Italy and Bithynia and spent many years wandering through Greek-speaking lands; allegedly his health was ruined and his estate plundered. When Domitian was assassinated, Dio's fortunes were restored with equal abruptness: he was recalled from exile, again became a favorite at court, and held a leading position in the affairs of Prusa.

Although the general outline of Dio's exile and return is clear, the details are controversial. As with his education and youth, his own testimony, however suspect, must come first. In the speech *On His Exile* he claims to have been banished as the friend of someone "very close to those who at the time enjoyed prosperity and power." Because of this same "intimacy and kinship," Dio's friend was put to death, and he himself attacked as his "friend and counselor." Thereupon, "such is the way of tyrants," he was unjustly banished (*Or.* 13.1). The "tyrant" is

45

evidently Domitian, as elsewhere in Dio's works:[1] the friend is likely to be Flavius Sabinus, son-in-law of Titus and a cousin of Domitian.[2] It is reported that Sabinus was executed because a herald at the consular elections had mistakenly proclaimed him not consul but emperor: this was evidently used as a basis for a charge of conspiracy. The date was perhaps early in the reign, when many of Titus' friends came to grief.[3]

In such cases it was usual for the humbler friends of the victim, especially his spiritual advisers, also to be punished, though less severely. Dio's sentence was comparatively light. He was condemned to exile, but to its milder form called "relegation."[4] He was forbidden to enter Italy and his native province, but able to meet his relatives and friends elsewhere and to travel freely.[5] His property at home, though it fell into neglect, was not confiscated.[6] He was free to speak in public; so far was he from being regarded as an outcast that in many cities he was urged to stay and take their affairs in hand.[7] His extensive journeys, even if made in the appearance of poverty, "with not even a single servant,"[8] not only were the wanderings of a mendicant preacher, but also satisfied the traditional Greek curiosity to see distant peoples and places.[9] Whether supported by his own income or by the generosity of others,[10] he was able ultimately to travel as far as southern Russia. By a curious fate, Dio's career followed that of Musonius, who was also banished for supposed complicity in treason and later restored: however, Musonius suffered the severer punishment of confinement to an island.[11] Dio's pupil Favorinus of Arelate was also banished for a while to Chios.[12]

Nothing in Dio's account of his banishment excites suspicion: it is otherwise with his description of the sequel. He claims to have decided to consult Apollo; he does not say where, but it was probably at the god's most celebrated shrine, Delphi. The oracle advised him to continue his wandering, since it was "honorable and appropriate," until he came to "the end of the earth." Encouraged by this advice, he put on humble clothing, disciplined himself, and began to wander everywhere. Many called him a vagabond or beggar, but some a philosopher; and so he acquired this honorable title spontaneously, unlike others who claimed it on their own behalf. Because people came to him for advice and asked him to talk in public, he was obliged to think about questions of good and evil (Or. 13.9–12).

To assess this account a feature of it must be noticed which is common to other of Dio's late speeches. In these he tends to assimilate his own experiences to those of famous men of old, such as Odysseus and Socrates.[13] Sometimes he goes beyond assimilation to self-identification and uses these predecessors as vehicles for his own opinions. Immediately after describing his exile, for example, he recounts how he gave advice using an "old speech" of Socrates; despite his pretense, this seems evidently made up by Dio.[14] The several works in which he purports to repeat speeches of the Cynic Diogenes convey in part his own views.[15] These devices are among the very few which distinguish Dio's late speeches from his earlier ones, and he may have developed them precisely because exile made it unwise to speak too freely. It is possible that Dio imitated his heroes in deed as well as word; but when he describes his actions in ways reminiscent of a Socrates or a Diogenes, it must be expected that he has adorned or even altered the truth.

Several of these suspect features appear when Dio explains how he went into exile. Above all, his account recalls his admired Xenophon, who consulted Apollo before setting out on the expedition of Cyrus; but there is also an echo of Apollo's oracle about Socrates mentioned in Plato's *Apology*.[16] Dio compares the oracle given to him with the prophecy of Tiresias that Odysseus should wander until he reached a strange and distant people;[17] since Dio was in fact "at the end of the earth" when he was recalled, it might also seem that this oracle was made up after the event. Another of Dio's heroes, Diogenes, was supposed to have become a philosopher only after going into exile and consulting Delphi;[18] and several other philosophers before Dio are said to have been "converted" to their true vocation, often by the Delphic oracle.[19]

It would be unwise to accept every detail of Dio's claim as literal fact: it seems certain only that he was banished as a friend of an eminent Roman, probably Flavius Sabinus, and wandered from city to city giving philosophic advice. Even if his account is taken literally, however, Dio does not say, as Synesius and others have assumed, that he suddenly deserted sophistry for philosophy.[20] If he did now begin to wear "humble clothing," he could have worn the philosopher's cloak before;[21] if he had not hitherto been called a philosopher, he need not have been hitherto an enemy of philosophy. Dio means rather to contrast himself, as he does elsewhere, with the sham philosophers who lightly claim the title without assuming the responsibilities:[22] for him, it is a prize earned by experience and self-examination. In speeches earlier than his exile, he does not call himself a philosopher, though he dresses and talks like one; only in later speeches does he lay claim to the title, though even now only by implication, or by comparing himself with philosophers of the past.[23]

Dio's exile lent itself to embellishment by his biographers. Philostratus, though denying that it was a true exile, nevertheless gives a vivid description of Dio's behavior in these years.[24] He traveled as far as the Getae on the Danube; he concealed himself from the public view because of Domitian's general persecution of philosophy; he "planted, dug, and channeled water for bathhouses and gardens" in order to earn a living; all the while he sustained himself by reading Plato's *Phaedo* and Demosthenes' speech *On the False Embassy;* he was in a Roman camp incognito when Domitian was assassinated and quelled an incipient mutiny by stripping off his rags like Odysseus before the suitors.

Judgments of this narrative have varied widely, some rejecting it entirely and others accepting all but the irretrievable details.[25] Yet Philostratus does not fare well when confronted by Dio. Dio states plainly that he was exiled: but this is a blemish that Philostratus does not like to admit in his heroes, and in the same way he dissembles the harsher exile of Favorinus.[26] He appears to think that Dio's journey to the Getae was the main object of his wanderings: yet Dio speaks as if he visited them after his sentence had been revoked.[27] He also seems to regard Dio as a victim of Domitian's general ban on philosophy, when in fact Dio was probably exiled several years before it; elsewhere Philostratus makes another of his martyrs, Apollonius of Tyana, a victim of the same persecution.[28] The assertion that Dio avoided publicity is flatly contradicted by Dio's own claim that he openly denounced the "tyrant."[29] Although he admits having been poor and ill during his exile,[30] he says nothing about manual labor. Although this might have appeared in a lost speech, it may instead result from a misunderstanding of extant ones. It is curious that, when describing a much later visit to a Roman camp, Dio says that he lacked the strength to dig a ditch; and the notion that he channeled water might derive from a general remark that the Indians divert their streams of milk and honey "as we irrigate gardens."[31] These and other details might also be imported from the lives of other famous men. The Stoic Cleanthes was supposed to have watered gardens, and Musonius Rufus to have helped dig a canal across the Isthmus.[32] Philostratus explicitly compares Dio in the Roman camp to Odysseus before the suitors; though Dio liked to model himself on Odysseus, it will be seen that this anecdote cannot be reconciled with his own account of his recall and must be apocryphal.

Philostratus makes exile drastically alter Dio's circumstances, but says nothing of an inner change: the view that it wrought his "conversion" is a refinement of Synesius'. For him Dio was turned from an outright sophist into a philosopher "by chance, as he himself has described"; he departed from the sophistic life "under full sail," and so adopted his true vocation.[33] When Synesius appeals to Dio's own testimony, he seems to allude to the passage in the speech *On Exile* already discussed: yet it has already been seen that Dio does not say there what Synesius infers. Dio's "conversion" may be considered an invention of Synesius, designed to serve two purposes at once: to explain what he rightly saw as a difference between Dio's earlier and later speeches, and to remake Dio in his own image, a cultured philosopher and not a sophist.[34]

Just as Synesius appears to have built a conversion on Philostratus' account of Dio, so modern writers have erected a further stage on Synesius'. Exile, so it has been proposed, turned Dio not just to philosophy, but into a Cynic.[35] This cannot be true of his last years. Not only does he sharply attack the Cynics in a late speech,[36] but his activities in this period are incompatible with Cynicism: he labored to restore his fortune, rebuild Prusa, advance his son's career, and obtain favors from consuls and emperors, whereas even moderate Cynics were expected to renounce the ties of home and city. A more plausible view might be that Dio leaned toward Cynicism in his exile, and returned to Stoicism thereafter.[37] The exiled Dio resembled the Cynics in his wandering, humble dress, and moral sermons. But these were not the exclusive property of the Cynics. They already characterize Dio in the *Alexandrian*, which seems to be an early speech; and in a late one, the second *Tarsian*, he urges his hearers not to confuse him with the ignorant and ostentatious Cynics just because his appearance resembles theirs.[38] Like Epictetus, Dio is a Stoic who admires the Cynic ideal, but deplores those impostors who falsely claim the title.[39]

Dio's admiration of Diogenes might also suggest that he temporarily converted to Cynicism: accordingly, the so-called "Diogenes speeches" have been dated to the period of his exile.[40] Again, however, admiration of Diogenes is not confined to Cynics, but shared by other schools, especially Stoicism.[41] For Dio, Diogenes is one of the figures, like Odysseus and Socrates, in whose guise he liked to dress. No doubt he had several motives: Diogenes resembled him in that he had become a philosopher in exile and had despised worldly power as Dio claimed to despise Domitian. But a lucky chance made the figure of Diogenes peculiarly apt. The Cynic was supposed to have conversed with Alexander of Macedon: and Alexander was the chief hero of the emperor Trajan.[42] It may be that

Dio did not even conceive the idea of modeling himself on Diogenes until the accession of Trajan, for nothing would forbid a date in that reign for the "Diogenes speeches."[43]

Exile left its stamp on the outer and the inner Dio. It weakened his health and reduced him to temporary poverty. It compelled him to think more deeply on moral questions and to put into practice the precepts he had learned from his teacher. But though exile hastened his development, it did not turn it in a new direction: as he had been taught by a Stoic, so he remained one in his own doctrines and in the eyes of antiquity.[44]

The number of Dio's works that can securely be dated to the time of his exile is very small. A speaker in the dialogue *On Beauty* bitterly maintains that all the Romans wish Nero were alive, and many believe it (*Or.* 21.10). Dio has often been thought to refer to an event of about 88, when an adventurer claiming to be Nero received vigorous support from Parthia.[45] This may be right: but Nero's memory long remained popular, and those who refused to credit his death could still have believed him alive even in the reign of Trajan.[46]

Another of Dio's works has been placed in Domitian's reign on the more remarkable ground that it predicts his fall. After mentioning the grim fate of Pelops and his descendants,[47] Dio remarks that "one may observe another house richer than that which was ruined by the tongue, and another one also in danger" (*Or.* 66.6). The house "ruined by the tongue" could well be the line of the Julii and Claudii, for Dio elsewhere ascribes Nero's ruin to his garrulity (*Or.* 21.9); if that is so, the last house should be the Flavian,[48] and the work should have been written shortly before Domitian's assassination, when his lack of heirs and persecution of opponents and rivals made it possible to foretell the end. This would be the only extant work in which Dio alluded at the time to the evils of Domitian's reign. Later he claimed to have denounced them openly, in speeches and writings that were widely known:[49] but either this claim is grossly exaggerated or almost all of these works have perished.

Dio's principal activity during this period was travel. Some details of his journeys are known, though again incidents that recall famous predecessors must be viewed with suspicion. Thus, he claims to have crossed with some fishermen from Chios to Greece and to have landed in emergency on the notorious Hollows of Euboea.[50] Here he was rescued by a huntsman, who sheltered him in his humble cottage. Dio's description of this incident is among his most admired works: though the outline may be true, he is evidently influenced by Odysseus' stay with the swineherd

Eumaeus.[51] Another supposed encounter in Greece provided him with further material. Near the end of his exile he was allegedly traveling from Arcadian Heraea toward Olympia when he met an old prophetess near a shrine of Heracles; the crone told him a story about a hero, bidding him tell it in turn to a great ruler whom he would some day meet.[52] This incident too is obviously influenced by literature, for the tale of Heracles is palpably modeled on Prodicus' famous myth recounted by Xenophon.[53] The woman's prophecy, like the earlier oracle of Apollo, seems to have been made up after the event; it fits too neatly with its setting, a speech delivered before an emperor who had a special devotion to Heracles.[54] Another anecdote of his travels, however, is entirely credible. When he was lecturing in Cyzicus, the most famous citharode of the day was reported to be in town, and Dio was deserted by his audience.[55] In all these adventures Dio claims to have been a free and unfettered traveler: there is no sign of the disguise alleged by Philostratus.

Apollo had bidden Dio to wander until he came to the ends of the earth. Even if the oracle is invented, it is fully consistent with something there is no reason to doubt, his account of his recall. He claims to have sailed into Olbia,[56] the Milesian colony at the mouth of the modern Bug, in the summer after his exile; he was then planning to go, "if possible, through the Scythians to the Getae, where I wished to see the state of affairs" (*Or.* 36.1). The Scythians are evidently the tribes of the northwestern Pontus: the Getae, as they are usually in Greek writers of the empire, are the people generally known as the Dacians in what is now central Rumania. Since Domitian had recently come to terms with them after a bitter war, it was a suitable time for an inquisitive traveler to visit the region. As Dio was intending to travel westward, it is natural to assume that he had been somewhere farther east when he heard of his recall, presumably in one of the Hellenized cities of the Crimea: such a place would count as the "end of the earth," as Ovid counted the much less remote Tomi.[57] News of Domitian's death in September 96 and of his own recall might have not reached Dio until the following spring: the summer he reached Olbia should then have been that of 97.

This reconstruction, however, is incompatible with that of Philostratus, who imagines that Dio was already on the Dacian warfront when he heard of Domitian's assassination.[58] If that were true, Dio would have had to sail to Olbia the following summer, and then have intended to return "if possible" thereafter. This itinerary seems so improbable that it has provoked a desperate measure: if the words "after my exile" are excised from the opening of Dio's *Olbian* oration, he can be brought to the city before the adventure described by Philostratus.[59] It seems easier to suppose that this too is a fiction of Philostratus or his sources; he or they may have been misled by Dio's description of his later visit to the Dacian legions.[60]

Dio's last years saw the peak of his worldly success and literary activity. This is the period of his major works, among them the four *On Kingship* which were greatly to influence later antiquity. Yet public success was to be balanced by domestic failure; to the same years belong most of his Prusan speeches, with their sorry tale of jealousy, mismanagement, and intrigue.

When Dio heard of Domitian's death, he was in the northern Pontus, perhaps in the Crimea. Simultaneously, or soon thereafter, he must have learned that his old friend Nerva had become emperor and had proclaimed a general recall of Domitian's exiles.[61] For some reason Dio was not eager to sail straight home, though communications between Bithynia and the northern Pontus were close. Instead, so he later claimed, he set out to see Nerva in Rome, but fell ill, and the emperor died before Dio could make use of his old acquaintance (*Or.* 45.2). The truth seems to be that he lingered on his tour to the boundaries of Dacia: he may already have been collecting material for the history of the Dacians that he was to publish under Trajan.[62]

When Nerva died the following January, Dio had still not reached Rome, and it is uncertain whether he continued his journey. He may have bent his efforts to making, or renewing, an acquaintance with Nerva's successor: but this could have been done elsewhere than at Rome, since Trajan spent the first two years of his rule on the Rhine and Danube. Eventually, armed with a letter from "the emperor" (presumably Trajan), Dio returned in triumph to Prusa.[63] Simultaneously he received congratulations and an invitation from Prusa's neighbor, Apamea, where he had family ties.[64] He deferred his visit, however, and was soon busy setting his affairs in order and participating in the complicated politics of Prusa.

Soon after his return Dio again started on his travels. Apparently in answer to an invitation from Trajan,[65] he led a delegation from Prusa to the emperor, and won several favors for his city, including the right to elect extra councillors and an increase of revenue; shortly after the embassy's return, the city was made the head of a newly created assize district, and a new delegation had to be dispatched to give thanks.[66] It is not stated that Dio's embassy met the emperor in Rome, though that seems likely:

since Trajan did not reach the capital until late 99 and left it again early in 101, Dio should have appeared before him in 100.[67]

The emperor's chief motive for favoring Dio and Prusa may have been zeal for his own fame, one of his most marked characteristics. Dio had been exiled by Domitian: promoted by Trajan, he could be an eloquent witness of the "new age" and its vaunted conciliation of the principate with liberty. If such were Trajan's calculations, he soon had every reason to think them well founded. It was probably on the occasion of this embassy that Dio spoke before him the first of his four pieces *On Kingship*, in which he implicitly contrasts the "kingship" of Trajan with the "tyranny" of Domitian and broadcasts the ideology of the new reign.[68]

Despite the success of his mission, Dio delayed his return to Prusa, so that his absence included part of two calendar years, presumably 100 and 101.[69] This delay may have been caused by an unforeseen development. The evidence is in Dio's *Olympian* oration (*Or.* 12), which was delivered during a celebration of the Olympic games and apparently after, though not necessarily immediately after, his return from exile.[70] Just before visiting Olympia, Dio had journeyed "straight to the Danube and the land of the Getae" and had there seen Romans and Dacians preparing for war.[71] At first it might seem that this visit to the Getae was the same as he was intending to pay after visiting Borysthenes in the summer of 97, which was an Olympic year: but that cannot be, since the Olympics fell in July, too soon for Dio to have visited the Danube on the way, and moreover there was no war impending in 97. This should, therefore, be a later visit. Now Trajan left Rome to fight his first Dacian war in March 101,[72] and Dio was in Rome the previous year and had delayed his return to Prusa. He may, therefore, have made his journey "straight to the Danube" precisely in the emperor's entourage, so that the impending war was the first against the Dacians. He would then have had time to linger on the front before visiting Greece in the summer and returning to Prusa in the same year. His friendship with the emperor perhaps explains the honors he now received from Greeks and Romans, and the fact that the Prusans had to pass a decree in order to obtain his recall.[73] Like Dio's earlier visit to the Danube, this one was presumably connected with his *Getica*; Trajan's motive for taking Dio with him may have been to secure a favorable account of the war in Dio's history.[74]

If Dio visited Greece and spoke the *Olympian* in 101, it may have been on the same visit that he delivered the speech *On His Exile* (*Or.* 13), which according to the title was delivered in Athens. The lectures that he claims to have given in Rome would then belong to his recent visit. When he returned to Prusa from his long absence, he named Athens and Rome among the cities which had lately done him honor.[75]

On his return to Prusa, Dio was decorated by his fellow citizens, and delivered the extant *Speech of Greeting*.[76] He was now at the summit of his success and popularity. From this time on, the tale of his life in Prusa is one of deepening failure. Already on this occasion his critics carped at the achievements of his embassy.[77] By intervening in the standing quarrel between Prusa and Apamea, he gained enemies in both.[78] In Prusa he undertook to build a grandiose portico, which was opposed at every stage. First he was accused of destroying old landmarks; next some of the subscribers were accused of embezzlement or default; and when the work was complete he was accused before the governor of being reluctant to have the books inspected.[79] No doubt Dio added to his unpopularity by overestimating his influence at court: thus, the suggestion made in an extant speech that he may gain Prusa's freedom was never fulfilled.[80]

The crisis in his civic career came about five years after his embassy. Perhaps from impatience and frustration, he entered into a political alliance with one of the proconsuls, who may be the Varenus Rufus known from several letters of the younger Pliny. Dio seems to have obtained by his influence the execution or exile of several of his opponents. The proconsul was duly indicted for maladministration, and probably also for the graver crime of governmental violence (*saevitia*), and Dio was alleged to have been his accomplice. He temporarily left Prusa, perhaps summoned to appear before the emperor in Rome. How long he was away is unknown, but Pliny, now appointed legate of the province, found him in Prusa about 110, still battling with his enemies.[81]

Yet these years of failure in Prusa saw Dio's greatest successes elsewhere. He spoke not only in Rome, but in other great cities of the empire. His speeches to the two chief cities of Bithynia, Nicomedia and Nicaea (*Or.* 38, 39), are both from this period; so also seem to be those delivered in Cilician Tarsus (*Or.* 33, 34) and Phrygian Apamea (*Or.* 35). Dio discussed his exile before the Athenians (*Or.* 13), and to the crowds assembled at Olympia praised Phidias' great statue of Zeus in a prose hymn which anticipates those of Aelius Aristides (*Or.* 12). What is perhaps his masterpiece, the *Euboean* (*Or.* 7), is from this period, as is the *Olbian* oration (*Or.* 36), with its lofty Zoroastrian myth.[82]

As before his exile, Dio traveled in the usual philosopher's garb of long hair and beard, humble cloak, and no doubt the staff that marked the itinerant sage.[83] He continues to attack the fluent, empty "sophists," though he now also mocks the pupils that flock behind them.[84] These attacks may reveal Dio's own discomfort; his relations with the emperor exposed him to the charge of insincerity,[85] and other philosophers viewed his eloquence with suspicion.[86] He too drew crowds of students to Prusa, among them two great sophists of the next generation, Favorinus and Polemo.[87] By 110, when Pliny refers to him, Dio would have been between sixty and seventy. He was probably still alive a few years later, when Trajan came to the east to fight the Parthians and now at last to win laurels worthy of Alexander's: unlike Alexander, however, Trajan did not pass through Bithynia.[88] Dio may even have lived to see Trajan's successor Hadrian, whose Hellenic tastes and antique appearance resembled his own.

Within a few decades of his death Dio was among the philosophic immortals. Favorinus saw him in a dream; Fronto praised his "supreme eloquence"; Lucian ranks him with Musonius among the philosophers persecuted by tyranny.[89] The authentic Dio was beginning to disappear beneath a varnish of anecdotes, by a process that he himself had begun. Many of these, which probably originated in the schools of rhetoric, were given permanence by Philostratus. In time, more accumulated. The name "Chrysostom," "Golden-Mouthed," gave currency to a story, once told about a Sicilian tyrant, that his breath was tainted; his own claims of Stoic hardiness caused it to be believed that he had dressed in a lionskin, like Heracles.[90] Synesius' picture of Dio, in its turn drawn from Philostratus, was imposed on the ever-thickening layer of accretions.[91] But these myths were the price to be paid for posthumous popularity; and without that, Dio's works would not have survived to give the myths the lie.

7

Ideal Communities

Two of Dio's works, the *Euboean* (*Or.* 7) and the *Olbian* (*Or.* 36), describe remote communities he claims to have visited, the first apparently during his exile and the second at the end of it. In a third work, now lost, he praised the Essenes of Palestine, though it is not known whether he also claimed to have visited them for himself.

The *Euboean* essentially argues that virtue is compatible with "poverty" (*penia*), the state of having to work (*ponein*) for a living; but since Dio considers the city intrinsically hostile to virtue, the piece is also an indirect laudation of country life. Its attack on extreme luxury suggests that it was intended for a Roman audience.[1] Only the first half of the work is about Euboea, and taken in isolation is nowadays Dio's most admired achievement.[2] Dio relates how, while crossing from Chios to Greece in a fishing boat, he was forced by a storm to land on the so-called "Hollows" of Euboea, the inhospitable southeastern coast of the island.[3] A huntsman shelters him in his hut, and Dio meets the other members of the family, among them his host's daughter and her cousin, who is also her ardent but modest suitor. Dio's stay sets in train the conversation that leads to the couple's simple wedding, which he attends with admiring pleasure (1–80).

This opening narrative is designed as a foil to the second half of the work, in which the simple style of the first yields to a more declamatory one. Dio first criticizes the behavior of the rich toward their guests, as it is portrayed by Homer (81–102). Next, after admitting that not all poor people can live in the country, he considers such honorable professions as are open to them in the city (103–124). After digressing to repel the charge of verbosity (125–132), he vehemently denounces those callings which pander to sexual appetites (133–152). The work ends abruptly and is often thought incomplete: but these sudden endings are Dio's way, and the second half complements the first in length and subject.

As he leads Dio to his hut, the huntsman describes a visit to the city which he was forced to pay when his little community was accused of cultivating public land for nothing. His father and uncle had once been the hired herdsmen of a wealthy landowner, whose property included flocks and herds, cultivated land, and "all the mountains here" (11). This man was executed for his wealth by the emperor (perhaps meant to be Nero),[4] and his estate was confiscated; since some of it became the property of the nearby city (27), the emperor must be imagined to have sold or given away at least a part. The livestock, including the herdsmen's own, was driven off (12), and they were left with only a few temporary huts and stalls which they had built in the mountains for the summer pasturage (13): this is one of the few references to transhumance in ancient literature, though the practice was no doubt common.[5] The two brothers turned the huts into permanent homes for themselves and their families, and so made a little settlement too small to be called a village (18, cf. 42).

Dio depicts this settlement as a small community of ideal virtue, practically independent of the civilized world. To sustain it the herdsmen had turned to hunting (16–17), in which they have now been joined by their respective sons. Of their quarry, mainly boar and deer, they use the skins (22, 43, 58, 62) and the meat, which they preserve by salting or curing (44). They also have goats and a single cow with her calf (47), presumably having hired the services of a bull; they lack horses, donkeys, and oxen (42). For other food they grow wheat, barley, millet, and beans (45), and they make their own wine (46). Their implements consist of a few farming tools and hunting knives and some earthenware, but they have no wineskin (46–47). For clothing the men wear the bare-shouldered tunic (*exomis*) characteristic of laborers, and over it a skin when necessary (32); the women wear a single tunic (58). This clothing, like the implements, pottery, and rope (71), presumably is obtained from the nearby village (73); the means of purchase must be barter, since the community does not use coinage (21, 48, 63). One of the daughters of Dio's host is married to a "rich" man in this village, and the two families lend or give to each other in need (69).

Dio's picture of the city is far less favorable. Though not named, it seems to be the important port of Carystos.[6] The city still has a strong wall with square towers; many of the houses are large (22), but many smaller ones even within the walls are uninhabited (50). There is a theater, in which the assembly meets (24). Of the two characteristic spaces of the Greek city, one, the exercise-ground (*palaestra*), is under tillage, so that the statues of Heracles and of other gods and heroes are hidden by crops in the summer: the other, the marketplace (*agora*), has become pasture, so that sheep graze around the council house and the magistrates' offices (39).[7] Two-thirds of the city's territory is deserted through neglect and underpopulation (34). As at Rhodes, economic decline seems to have been accompanied by a widening of social divisions. There is a small wealthy class whose members, presumably ranchers like the huntsmen's master, own huge stretches of mountain and valley (11, 34, 38–39). There are shipowners, also close to the upper class (55). Most of the population is poor and turbulent (24–26), ready to turn to banditry and theft (40); it is concentrated in the city, mainly no doubt to enjoy such amenities of civic life as distributions (49) and spectacles, but also because of the insecurity of the surrounding countryside, with its mountains hospitable to robbers (49). There are, however, villages on the territory (68, 73), and the sea supports some of the purple-fishers for which Euboea was noted (2),[8] even though they too supplement their earnings by robbing the shipwrecked (55, cf. 8, 32).

The huntsman pleads his case before the people assembled in the theater; it is implied that he appears before the assembly as an alleged public offender, just as Apuleius represents a supposed breach of the peace being tried in the theater of Hypata.[9] Before his case comes up other business is conducted; the people shouts its praise or blame; those blamed tear their clothes or run about imploring their fellow citizens; others calm the mob, either speaking before them (on the stage) or among them (in the audience) (21–26). The case against the huntsman is presented by a "rhetor" (38, 63), who is not necessarily a professional speaker, simply a man active in the courts of the city. He too appears to be a wealthy landowner (40), as does the man who eventually undertakes the defense (34): the only other intervention is made from the audience by the friend of a shipowner (53–59). In this as in most cities[10] only the rich and conspicuous would normally take an active part in politics: "private" persons (*idiotai*, 40) spoke only in unusual circumstances, or were confined to shouting in chorus.

At first the rhetor presents his case factually: the huntsman and his partners have occupied public land which they do not pay rent for and which they have not received as a gift of the people; they have performed no liturgy and paid no tax, as if they were free from both duties as public benefactors (27–28). The renting of public land is characteristic of the Roman period; about the same time Pliny tried to induce the Bithynian cities to invest their spare cash in land and thus increase their revenues from rents.[11] The gift of land, however, is less usual, since most benefactors were already wealthy, and preferred a more conspicuous reward, such as a statue. Immunity was also unusual, for though it had been freely given by cities to their benefactors in the Hellenistic age, the Romans did not look kindly on something that might lessen a city's ability to meet its obligations.[12]

Provoked by the huntsman's innocent replies, the rhetor grows abusive. These "animals" are being permitted to enjoy more than a thousand *plethra* of the best public land (about ten hectares or twenty-five acres), enough to yield three *choenices* of wheat (about three liters) for every citizen annually; the whole citizenry may as well embezzle the public moneys, as some do already, or divide up the public land (29). The rhetor further accuses the herdsman of living off wrecks, or even causing them by false signal-flares, as the mythical Nauplius wrecked the heroes returning from Troy (31–32).[13] There was always a risk of robbery when a ship was wrecked or beached on some wild coast like that of Euboea, Epirus, or the island of Seriphos;[14] and it was still a known crime in the Roman period to lure ships to their destruction.[15] The whole speech of the rhetor reveals a fear and contempt of rustics which was undoubtedly common among city-dwellers in time of decline and depopulation.

A "good" man intervenes, apparently spontaneously, silences the crowd, and addresses it "gently" in the huntsman's defense (33).[16] Since much of the city's land, public and private, is neglected, he proposes a scheme for the use of the public part. Citizens who agree to work it are to be leased parcels proportionate to their means; they may enjoy them free for ten years, and thereafter pay a small rent in kind. Noncitizens may join the scheme on less favorable terms, but will receive the franchise if they agree to undertake two hundred *plethra* (about two hectares or five acres) (36–37). This device of granting leases conditional on the improvement (*emphyteusis*) of land is an old one.[17] Close to Dio's time, one such scheme is found in eastern Macedonia in the middle second century; another appears at Thisbe in Boeotia, perhaps in the early third.[18] At Rome, Nerva resumed the lapsed practice of distributing public land to the urban poor;[19] under Trajan and Hadrian the cultivation of unused lands was encouraged by offering them on terms reminiscent of Dio's scheme.[20] It has, therefore, been supposed that the *Euboean*, with its exaltation of virtuous toil and rustic morality, was written to win public support for these emperors' schemes.[21] No doubt contemporary circumstances were in Dio's mind; but mainly he speaks as a pupil of Musonius, who also praised the agricultural life,[22] and as a member of the Greek upper classes: for these were no less interested than the emperors in making their cities less dependent on imported food, and their poor on public welfare.

Next the huntsman is called to speak personally. He recalls that his father had once received money when it was "being given to the citizens," and that he has inherited his status (49): he refers to the practice whereby the wealthy distributed money (*dianome*) to celebrate an occasion or by bequest.[23] The huntsman's children are thus also citizens and will help their fellows against robbers or enemies if need be: this recalls that cities were mainly responsible for the security of their own territory, and that a posse sometimes had to be raised to combat particularly dangerous or numerous bandits.[24] Far from profiting from shipwrecks, the huntsman claims often to have aided castaways and wishes that one were present to testify for him (51–53). Thereupon a member of the audience stands up and claims the floor. He and the man next to him are citizens (55), a detail which shows that, as at Tarsus,[25] noncitizens were permitted to attend the assembly. The speaker recalls that he and his neighbor had been rescued and sheltered by the huntsman after being wrecked on Cape Caphereus (54–58). This is a simple example of a very common feature of Greek civic life, the "testimonial" (*martyria*): thus, a wealthy citizen might receive one of these from his city in return for his benefactions, or another city to which he had done a service might send a collective testimonial to his native one.[26]

The people now "praises" the huntsman, presumably by acclamation (59), and the "good" man comes forward and proposes a motion. He does not consult the council first, an omission Dio elsewhere calls "demagogic":[27] it may be that this step could be omitted when a proposal was not controversial, but Dio may have left it out in order to avoid slowing the narrative. The man's speech is full of realistic detail. He proposes that the huntsman receive dinner in the public mess (60); this was one of the commonest of honors.[28] He is to receive new clothes in place of those he gave to his fellow citizens, "so that others too may have a stimulus to be upright and to help one another" (61); this is the so-called "hortative" formula very often found in honorific decrees.[29] Lastly, the speaker urges that the people vote the huntsmen and their descendants a perpetual lease on their land free of rent and offers to contribute a hundred drachmas to help equip them: again, it was customary for proposers of motions to offer to defray all or part of the cost, as Pliny does when urging Comum to hire a public schoolmaster.[30] The people votes on the motion, again by expressing "praise," and the decision is immediately put into execution (62–63).

If Dio's story is true, or at least based on the truth, it offers a unique glimpse into the urban and rural conditions of the period. It seems excessive to doubt that Dio visited Euboea at all.[31] His picture of social and economic conditions is corroborated for Greece generally by Plutarch, who asserts that large stretches of it were deserted and that scarcely three thousand men of means lived there:[32] but Dio could have learned this without a visit. The descriptions of the assembly, and of the huntsman's little community, seem plausible; but the first could well derive from the politics of Prusa, the second from the countryside of Bithynia. It cannot be denied, however, that many of the ingredients of this idyll have a literary flavor: some resemble the drama, especially the New Comedy,[33] others recall conventional descriptions of rustic or primitive virtue.[34]

Dio's *Olbian* oration (*Or.* 36) resembles the *Euboean* in that it describes a remote and uncorrupted community; here, however, the romantic exaggeration is palpable. According to the title, it was delivered in Prusa; and just as the attack on modern decadence in the *Euboean* seems largely aimed at a Roman audience, so Prusa is a suitable setting for this speech, which essentially glorifies civic and universal "order" (*kosmos*). The antique virtue of the Olbians, who are united by adversity, is a lesson to more favored cities torn apart by faction. At the same time, their supposed ignorance of literature after Homer justifies the unusually hieratic and lofty tone of the discourse which Dio claims to have delivered before them (29–60, cf. 27, 61). This discourse, devoted to Zeus, was supposedly delivered in his temple, just as the equally exalted speech of Phidias in the *Olympian* was.[35]

In this speech, like the *Euboean*, there can be no doubt that Dio's description of the city derives from his experience. The name he uses for it,

"Borysthenes" (1, 4, etc.), was sanctioned by literary tradition, as he uses "Soli" for "Pompeiopolis" and "Celaenae" for "Apamea":[36] but "Olbia" was now the customary one.[37] It was a foundation of Miletus and, according to Dio, maintained many of the traditions of the mother-city, among them pederasty (8): it is known that Miletus retained its contacts with Olbia even in the Roman period.[38] Dio accurately describes the city's location, properly on a branch of the river Hypanis, but with its older name borrowed from the more famous Borysthenes (1). These two rivers, now the Bug and the Dnieper, met in a large lagoon (2), on which there were salt flats: from these the Olbians obtained salt to sell to the Greeks and to the Scythians of the Tauric Chersonese, the modern Crimea (3).[39] The city had been reduced from its former dignity by frequent war and captures: the last of these had occurred about a hundred and fifty years before, when the Getae extended their conquests as far as Apollonia, now Sozopol in Bulgaria (4). Olbia is known to have been besieged in the late third or early second centuries and the early first:[40] the capture referred to by Dio is the one effected by the Dacian king Burebista, in the time of Julius Caesar.[41] After this disaster the Olbians rebuilt[42] their city with the connivance of the surrounding Scythians, who needed its trade (5): but even now it had not recovered its old prosperity (6). It is clear that the city was considered to have been refounded at this time,[43] and that its area was later a fraction of what it had been: but Dio has perhaps represented its recovery as less complete than it really was.[44]

In his description of his own visit to the city Dio combines exact observation with romantic fantasy. He describes a young Olbian horseman dressed in Scythian trousers and the black cloak peculiar to the region (7): while the cloak may be an antiquarian fiction, it is certain that Olbia and other cities of the Pontus depended on citizen cavalry to defend them from the Scythians.[45] Dio also observes the great reverence of the Olbians for Achilles, "to whom they have built temples both on the island called Achilles' and in the city"(9). This cult of Achilles is characteristic of the northwestern Pontus;[46] the island is Berezan, just outside the lagoon, where a dedication to Achilles contemporary with Dio has recently been found.[47] Dio vividly describes the effect of a recent Scythian raid: the gates are closed, the war-flag is raised, many of his hearers are dressed in armor (15–16). That these raids on Olbia had not ceased is shown by Antoninus Pius' measures to protect the city against them.[48] Because of the danger, Dio and his listeners retreat into the temple of Zeus (17): this cult is obviously connected with that of Achilles, and the very temple mentioned by Dio is attested by a document of Olbia.[49] The name of the old man who now urges him to speak, given as "Rhoson" in the manuscripts, has plausibly been emended to one frequent in the city, "Hieroson" (28).[50] However, the speech Dio claims to have given in the temple has no local color: though it might be tempting to associate his famous reference to Zoroaster (40) with Iranian elements in the population of Olbia, in fact this branch separated from the parent stock before Zoroaster.[51]

Although Dio's description of the city appears to be accurate, his picture of the inhabitants seems to exaggerate their distance from the modern world. Thus, he maintains that they admire only Homer among the poets and that almost all know the *Iliad* by heart, despite the corrupt condition of their Greek (9): it is true that they admired Homer,[52] but the language at least of their public documents is that of the average Greek city of the period. Dio pretends that philosophers are portentously rare in Olbia (24): yet a decree of about A.D. 200 honors a man for his innate philosophy, that is, as a man of such genius that he needed no instruction.[53] Dio claims that the few Greek visitors to Olbia are vulgar traders, "importing worthless rags and bad wine, and exporting nothing better" (25): actually the city still conducted extensive commerce, and had a large number of resident Greeks, many from Dio's own province.[54] He maintains that all the members of his audience wore their hair long in the Homeric fashion, except one: this man shaved, and was said to do so only to flatter the Romans and to advertise his friendship with them (17). Perhaps Roman styles were rarely seen at Olbia: but the implication that Roman culture was something unusual is again exaggerated. Already under Tiberius a prominent citizen dedicated a portico to the emperor and his predecessor, and the same man's son "advanced to the acquaintance of the Augusti."[55] The Roman protectorate of the city seems to have begun under Nero and, probably after an interruption, to have been resumed by Trajan.[56] All these touches further Dio's purpose of making the Olbians a community of ideal virtue and self-sufficiency: but, as in the *Euboean*, there is no reason to question his accuracy where this tendency is absent.

Yet another remote community appeared in one of his lost works. Immediately after mentioning the *Euboean*, Synesius states that "he also praises the Essenes, a whole city of happiness by the Dead Sea in the center of Palestine, apparently situated very near Sodom."[57] From this it is unclear whether Dio said much or little about the Essenes, and whether he claimed to have visited them. The geographical detail at least seems to be not his but Synesius', since Sodom is only likely to have been mentioned by one who lived in a largely Christian society. Moreover, if by "Essenes" Synesius means the now-famous community of Qumran, his location of it also suggests his own time; for while the true Sodom was at the south end of the Dead Sea, from the time of Constantine it was assumed for the convenience of Christian pilgrims to have been at the north, and so comparatively near Qumran.[58] But even if Dio spoke of the Essenes only briefly and by hearsay, it is easy to imagine how he would have depicted them. The elder Pliny, his contemporary, describes them as a "solitary race, miraculous beyond any in the whole world, without any women, all lust abjured, without coinage, with palm-trees as their companions," and constantly renewed by recruits fleeing to them from the corruption of the world.[59] Here was ready material for one who had praised the happy solitude of the huntsman's community and the rugged independence of the Olbians.

Dio's two surviving pictures of remote settlements appear to be drawn from his own experience, but tinted with utopian ideals. These reflect partly Stoic notions of self-sufficiency and dignifying toil, and partly concerns of Dio's own. In the *Euboean* his unfavorable picture of unprincipled politicians and the mob recalls his own tribulations in Prusa: in the *Olbian*, the theme of order reflects the lack of order he so often deplores in his own and other cities. These two communities are, therefore, a portrait of the contemporary Greek city, but with all the features reversed.

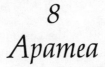

8
Apamea

A short speech of Dio (*Or.* 35) is addressed to a city which he does not name; but the indications he gives show that it is Phrygian Apamea (modern Dinar), often called Apamea Cibotus ("the Chest") to distinguish it from several namesakes. This inference is corroborated by the title given in the manuscripts, *In Celainae of Phrygia,* the old name of the city: however, this title may have been bestowed by an editor rather than by Dio.[1] There is no clear evidence of date, but the similarity to such speeches as the first *Tarsian* and the *Nicomedian* suggests a time in Dio's last years.[2] Like the first *Tarsian,* the *Apamean* is more concerned with the citizens' general behavior than with particular problems, and is referred to as a "talk" (*dialegesthai*) by its author: however, it appears to have been spoken before a formal meeting of the assembly (1).

Dio does not touch on any of the city's history, which was uneventful in comparison with that of Rhodes or Alexandria. For many years Apamea's chief claim to notice had been its great prosperity. It was an important junction of several major roads; it had a large and fertile territory; and it prospered under Rome as the head of an assize-district and as a flourishing center of commerce.[3]

In the characteristically long introduction Dio expatiates on a favorite contrast of his last period, that between his own lack of eloquence and humble appearance (1–6), and the ostentation and numberless admirers of the sophists (7–12). His main subject is the material advantages of

Apamea, which he first extols in the customary language of panegyric (13–17), and then compares to the fabled wealth of other places, especially India (17–25). In other speeches Dio speaks with contempt of panegyrics and natural wealth, and here palpably exaggerates the blessings both of Apamea and India: hence it is evident that his praise of the city is ironical, even though the picture that he gives of it is only slightly distorted.[4]

Dio begins his panegyric by congratulating the Apameans that their city is "inferior to none of the first ones" (13, cf. 17): this already may be a slight jab, for despite its importance Apamea was never able to gain a title like that of "first" or "metropolis." He then enumerates the city's endowments: its situation in the finest part of the continent of Asia, its advantageous position between plains and mountains, its abundant springs, its rich territory yielding every kind of produce, notably the essential items of wheat and barley, and its "greatest and most beneficial" of rivers, the Marsyas, Orgas,[5] and Maeander (13). It has been seen from the *Alexandrian* that all these items—situation, territory, rivers—were customary ingredients in praises of cities. Though Dio is mocking them, he scarcely exaggerates the city's advantages. The plain in which it stood was of notable fertility, partly because of the excellent water supply mentioned by Dio.[6] The three rivers he mentions all rise close to the city and flow even in high summer; the "springs," which he also mentions, must include the still existing thermal source.[7] Apamea's pride in its waters is shown by certain of its coins, on which the three rivers named by Dio, and also the "Therma," are grouped around the local Artemis.[8]

Dio turns to another of the city's endowments, its position in the road system of Anatolia:[9] "you lie in front[10] of Phrygia, Lydia, and Caria too, and many other very populous nations live round about, Cappadocians, Pamphylians, Pisidians; and to all of these your city provides a market and a meeting-place" (14). The great Southern Highway, which led from the Aegean coast up the Maeander valley, traversed Caria and Phrygia in order to reach Apamea; on the way it was met by another important route coming from Lydia; as it proceeded eastward from Apamea, it skirted Pisidia on its way to Cappadocia and the Euphrates. Another route from northern Phrygia came through the city and down to Pamphylia. Dio, therefore, exaggerates slightly when he implies that Cappadocia and Pamphylia were close to Apamea: but its situation made it the natural place for traders from these regions to meet.

Dio now takes up other proofs of the city's wealth, its "subjects" and "taxes" (*phoroi*), that is, the tribute paid to Rome (14). These two items were cognate, since the tribute a city paid was assessed on the population and property within its territory.[11] According to Dio, Apamea's subjects included not only "prosperous villages" but even "insignificant cities." It is known that Apamea's territory was large, since on the south it bordered that of Sagalassus, over fifty kilometers away.[12] The form and status of "villages" in the principate varied widely, but those to which Dio refers were agglomerations having no territory of their own but included in that of a city; the city formed the chief market for the villages' produce and made them share the burden of its tribute.[13] It was much less common for a city to be subject to another one, as Caunus was to Rhodes (*Or.* 31.125):[14] presumably such a city, though it had the usual council and assembly, was not treated as an independent unit of taxation but had to contribute to that of the superior one. With such territory and "subjects," Apamea's tribute was no doubt heavy, and Dio can ironically compare it to the loads drawn by the strongest draft animals.[15]

Dio reserves most of his praise for the city's chief pride, its position as the head of an assize-district. "In addition the assizes are held here every other year,[16] and a countless number of people gathers here, litigants, jurors, speakers, magistrates, servants, slaves, pimps, grooms, merchants, whores, craftsmen, so that retailers sell their wares at the highest prices, and nothing in the city goes idle, animals, horses, or women. Now that brings great prosperity, for where the largest number of persons congregates, that is necessarily where the most money is found, and the place naturally thrives. In the same way, they say, wherever the largest number of sheep is penned, that is where the ground is made most fertile for farmers by the dung, and many people beg shepherds to pen their sheep with them. And that is why the right to receive the assizes is considered to add very greatly to a city's health, and is an object of universal competition. The first cities all have a share in it every other year, but in future they say the interval will be longer, because people do not like constantly being dragged all around" (15–17).

By the system that appears to have obtained in all the so-called "senatorial" provinces, Asia was divided into a number of districts called "dioceses," which at the time of Dio's speech numbered about thirteen.[17] In the chief city of each such diocese, the governor or one of his legates held assizes (*agorai*); these were usually annual, though Dio seems to imply that the interval had recently been made longer. His description gives a vivid idea of the economic advantages of an assize-city; how valued these were is shown by an inscription from the eastern city of Gerasa, in which the citizens thank Hadrian for holding assizes there during the whole time of his visit.[18] As Dio says, other cities contended vigorously to obtain the same privilege. He won it for Prusa, and had to warn his fellow citizens to moderate their joy and not annoy the other cities now assigned to their district.[19] To have the assizes was not only an economic advantage but a mark of honor: the assize-cities ranked second only to the so-called "metropoleis" in importance,[20] and a city which declined in prosperity was liable to lose the privilege.[21] Yet another benefit accrued from the custom whereby Roman magistrates when hearing cases used provincials as assessors, or "jurors" as Dio calls them; since these would largely be drawn from the city in which the magistrate was holding court, a citizen of it who went to law against someone from elsewhere might enjoy an advantage.[22]

The only detail of Dio's description not corroborated elsewhere is his statement that the assizes were held every other year. It has been thought that he is supported by inscriptions which praise civic magistrates or liturgists for holding their positions "during the assizes": since magistracies at least were usually annual, it might appear to follow that the assizes were not.[23] This, however, is not the only possible interpretation of the phrase. The influx of visitors for the assizes greatly added to the burden of generosity already incumbent upon magistrates: thus, at Ephesus a *prytanis* is praised because he supplied oil "during the assize in all the gymnasia and baths in Ephesus."[24] Hence other inscriptions which call a man, for example, a "gymnasiarch during the assizes" may only imply that he was especially generous on the occasion, not that there were others in whose term the occasion did not fall. If that is right, Dio remains the only witness for a biennial rotation. It has been supposed that the phrase translated "every other year" really means "every year": but the Greek is unambiguous, and the context shows that there had been pressure to make the circulation of assizes less rapid.[25] It seems, therefore, that this pressure had succeeded in reducing their speed of circulation; it may be relevant that the younger Pliny, legate of Pontus and Bithynia not much later than this speech, only dispensed justice in Bithynia in the first year of his term, though it is true that this was not confined to a year as a proconsul's was.[26]

As the final item of praise Dio reminds the Apameans that they "share in the rites and expenses of Asia as much as the cities in which the rites themselves are" (17): in both places the word translated "rites" (*hiera*) may mean "sanctuaries," but the difference is not important. Here again the compliment is ambiguous. Dio refers to another institution of the province, the cult of the imperial house administered by the provincial league; probably his word "Asia" refers specifically to this league, as it does in inscriptions.[27] The league maintained sanctuaries only in the largest cities of the province, at this time Pergamum, Ephesus, and Smyrna, though the burden of maintaining them fell on all the cities alike.[28] Dio in effect is reminding the Apameans that they share the expense of the imperial sanctuaries, yet cannot enjoy the glory of being "temple-wardens" (*neokoroi*).[29]

Earlier in the speech Dio refers to another part of the apparatus of the imperial cult, the college of chief priests.[30] These were elected annually and were designated high priests (*archiereis*) of Asia: it seems clear that another term, "Asiarch," is an alternative title.[31] Like city-magistrates, they were expected to hold office and to spend generously, especially on gladiatorial shows. As a major city of the province, Apamea undoubtedly had many citizens wealthy and prominent enough to secure election to the position, and the names of some are known.[32] With his customary irony Dio describes these "lucky" people parading in their crown and purple of office, followed by a train of long-haired boys carrying frankincense (10). These priests wore unusually ornate and conspicuous crowns, adorned with miniature busts of the imperial family.[33] As in the second *Tarsian*, Dio shows no sympathy with the mania of the rich for "gold and purple"; and like Dio in the present speech, Epictetus rebukes a man who looked forward to wearing a crown as priest of the emperor. Neither Epictetus nor Dio speaks disloyally or subversively, for the cult of the emperor satisfied the vanity of the provincials as much as it did honor to the ruler.[34]

Dio's ironic intention is particularly clear in the last part of the speech. Most of this is devoted to a hyperbolical description of the wealth of India (17–22). The praise of its miraculous rivers implicitly belittles the merely natural ones of Apamea. The Brahmans, who despise such rivers and prefer the well of truth, seem to stand for those like Dio who value reality above appearances: it has been seen that these disguises are characteristic of Dio in his last period. He then portrays another nation of fabled wealth, "the most gilded of all men," who live by robbing gold-digging ants (23–24). Here again he seems to speak allegorically: the "gilded" people may be the Romans, whose love of gold Dio denounces elsewhere,[35] and the ants correspondingly the subjects of Rome, just as the Apameans were earlier compared to draft animals. Lastly Dio indirectly mocks the Apameans by praising the prosperity of the Byzantines: these have an excellent territory and yet can afford to neglect it, since without labor they draw wealth from the sea (25).[36]

The *Apamean* is a curious speech, full of graphic detail and yet consistently ironic and fantastic. It lacks the exuberance of the early Dio, but instead has a deftness absent from such speeches as the *Trojan* or the *Rhodian*. Nevertheless, what Dio's irony gains in elegance it loses in force; it is hard to imagine the prosperous merchants of Apamea cut by such glancing thrusts. There is already present something of that self-indulgent sarcasm of Dio's late speeches in Prusa; it is not surprising that in the end he was more successful as a teacher and an orator than as a politician or diplomat.

9
Tarsus

Two of Dio's speeches are addressed to the city of Tarsus in Cilicia (*Or.* 33, *Or.* 34).[1] They appear to belong to his last years.[2] Provided that the originals were actually spoken, Dio must have traveled to the eastern empire in his last period as well as to Greece and Italy.

Tarsus of Dio's day was highly prosperous (*Or.* 33.2), the largest city of Cilicia (*Or.* 34.7), full of splendid buildings (*Or.* 33.18).[3] It had no acropolis (*Or.* 33.39), but lay in the middle of a very fertile plain (*Or.* 33.17, 24, 28).[4] Its extensive territory stretched north to the foothills of the Taurus (*Or.* 33.2) and south to the sea (*Or.* 34.8), though in Dio's time some of this coastal area was claimed by another city, Mallos (*Or.* 34.45– 46). Among the many products of Tarsus' territory flax was particularly important, and the city contained a large number of linenworkers (*Or.* 34.21).[5] It also had a vital position in the road system of Cilicia, chiefly be-cause it received the great highway leading from the Anatolian plateau into Syria soon after it emerged from the pass called the "Cilician Gates."[6] It was also well connected by water, for the river Cydnus, the Tarsians' pride (*Or.* 33.2, 17, 24, 29), was navigable from the sea as far as the city: it was by this river that Cleopatra sailed up to visit Antony in Tarsus.[7] In addition, there was a regular harbor formed by a lagoon at the river's mouth.[8]

Tarsus was an ancient city, in which Greek became the language of culture only under Alexander and his successors.[9] However, like many cities of Asia Minor it early clothed its foundation and cults in Greek dress. Perseus, revered as its founder (*Or.* 33.1, 47) and protector (*Or.* 34.48), as in several other cities of Cilicia, appears frequently on its coinage.[10] Nonetheless, Tarsus also claimed to trace its descent from Heracles (*Or.* 33.1, 45, 47), and celebrated his festival by building a ceremonial pyre (*Or.* 33.47): both the god and the rite are Hellenized versions of older, Asiatic ones.[11] The city further took great pride in its claim to have been founded by Argive colonists (*Or.* 33.1, 41). This presumably refers not to Perseus but to a myth that Triptolemus led Argives in search of Io and left some of them there.[12] Other gods particularly venerated by the Tarsians were Apollo (*Or.* 33.1, 45), in his Argive form of the wolf-god (*Lykeios*),[13] and Athena, closely connected with the legend of Perseus;[14] Dio alludes in addition to myths, now unknown, which concerned a trident and oracles, and to one otherwise only attested in Byzantine sources which made a Titan one of the founders (*Or.* 33.1).[15]

As at Rhodes, Dio passes over the city's history in the period before its incorporation in the Roman empire. The part of Cilicia in which it lay, called "smooth" to distinguish it from the "rough," mountainous part to the west, had been brought under Roman control by the conquests of Pompey: when Dio spoke, the two Cilicias were united in a single province governed by a legate of praetorian rank. Like Rhodes, Tarsus had strongly supported the Caesarian cause in the civil war and been punished by Cassius for aiding Dolabella;[16] Dio discreetly refers to this as the city's "misfortune" (*Or.* 34.7, cf. 25). It was lavishly rewarded by Augustus, to whom it probably owed its status as the mother city or "metropolis" of the province and the principal assize-city.[17] The same emperor, in Dio's words, gave it "land, laws, honor, and control of the river and of your part of the sea" (*Or.* 34.8). The emperor must have increased the city's territory so as to give it complete control of the Cydnus: the reference to the sea suggests that he also gave it new or additional rights to levy duties (*portoria*) on ships passing along the coast.[18] Dio's "laws," and perhaps his "honor," seem to signify "autonomy," a city's right to use its own laws and not those laid down by Rome for the province. This privilege could not be enjoyed except by a city that was also "free"; and Tarsus' "freedom" had been given by Antony, was apparently renewed by Augustus, and still obtained in Dio's time (*Or.* 34.39).[19] Augustus' favor was not only the result of Tarsus' support of his father's cause, but also of the influence of his Tarsian friend, the Stoic philosopher Athenodorus.[20] Like other large cities of the east, Tarsus had a bad reputation for restlessness and immorality. Antony elevated to power a demagogue named Boethus: Augustus' friend Athenodorus drove out Boethus and his supporters and, with the emperor's approval, ran the city in the face of insult and factional opposition.[21] Dio talks of Athenodorus' ascendancy as a period in which Tarsus was famed for its good government (*Or.* 33.48): and Strabo, a contemporary if biased witness, depicts it as a city devoted to culture and philosophy.[22] A different impression is given by Philostratus in his *Life of Apollonius*. The young sage allegedly began his studies in Tarsus with a Phoenician teacher, but found it so devoted to wit, fine linen, and its river that he moved to the more salubrious city of Aegaeae. It is true that a native of Aegaeae, which was traditionally hostile to Tarsus, seems to be the source of Philostratus' information, but he also draws on letters in which Apollonius rebuked the city. Later, however, he makes the sage visit Tarsus in the reign of Vespasian and perform several benefactions for it.[23]

The same luxury and frivolity provided material for the first of Dio's *Tarsian* orations (*Or.* 33). As usual, while visiting the city he appears to have been asked to address the people (13): but as in the *Apamean* he refers to his speech as a talk (1), and unlike the second *Tarsian* it has no political content. As befits its audience, it is witty, allusive, and carefully structured. Dio begins with an idea, previously used in the *Alexandrian*, that his hearers must not expect praise from him but reproach (1–16). He develops another favorite idea, that material resources without moral ones are worthless, and a city that lacks the latter is sure to lose the former (17–30). Dio introduces the main subject, as often, only when the speech is well advanced, and denounces a practice which he describes by a word that may be rendered "snoring" or "snorting" (*rhenkein*).

Dio expects that his hearers will recognize the practice to which he refers, even if he cannot express it directly (32). To modern readers it is less readily intelligible, especially since it is unclear whether he is speaking literally or figuratively. It has been suggested that he reproaches the Tarsians, like Apollonius, for their neglect of philosophy:[24] but this seems too mild an offense for the vehemence of his diatribe. If he were reproaching the Tarsians for faulty pronunciation of Greek,[25] that would suit his references to "Phoenicians" (41–42) and to "nostrils" (50): but it would not explain why the practice is so reprehensible as to make the city like a brothel (36, 60) and its inhabitants like catamites (54) or hermaphrodites (64). It is possible that he is speaking literally, since there is abundant evidence to show that snorting was regarded as grossly indecent.[26] Dio may also be using one of his characteristic allegories and suggesting that the Tarsians are careless of their general reputation. Thus, he compares them to those who snore when "drunk or full or asleep in embarrassing circumstances" (33); and the connection between snoring and self-indulgence occurs elsewhere both in Dio and in his contemporary Epictetus.[27]

Certain details of the speech illustrate customs that are not only those of Tarsus. In his preface Dio dismisses other speakers in the same way as in the *Alexandrian*. They are masters of rhetoric, practiced in the art of eulogizing cities; Dio briefly parodies their stock subjects, the city's gods and mythical founders (1), its territory, mountains, and, above all, its river (2). These people, by whom he must mean sophists, are ready to talk on any subject (4) with extreme volubility (5). Their useless eloquence is like "the demonstrations of so-called 'doctors'" who make crowds gape by lecturing on abstruse medical subjects (6). Dio may be referring to real practitioners, since those who wished to be employed by a city had to persuade the assembled people of their competence.[28] Alternatively, he may mean a strange phenomenon that first appears in his time, the "iatrosophist" who gave displays of rhetoric on medical subjects.[29] In contrast to these, Dio is a "true doctor" come to cure the city's ills (6), not wearing fine clothes but "squalid, meanly dressed, and without attendants" (13–14). By a characteristic device of his late speeches, he compares himself to men of the past: he will speak as plainly to the Tarsians as Socrates to the Athenians (9), he comes to their riotous city dressed in rags like a slave, as Odysseus surprised the suitors (15).[30]

Twice in the speech Dio reminds Tarsus of its claim to be the mother-city or "metropolis" of the province, and he urges it to act with motherly dignity toward the lesser cities (17, 46). This word originally designated the founding city of a colony, as Miletus of Olbia: however, it came to mean the preeminent city of a region. Under the principate, titles such as "first" or "mother-city" were assigned by Rome. Originally the title of "metropolis" seems only to have been given to one city in each province: thus, in Bithynia, Nicomedia and in Asia, Ephesus were the first "metropoleis."[31] In time other cities that claimed preeminence in their regions were also able to obtain the title, sometimes taking it away from their rivals:[32] when Dio congratulates Tarsus on having had it "from the beginning" (*Or.* 34.7),[33] he means not only that its superiority was immediately recognized by Rome, but that no rival had been able to dispute it.

Another detail of the speech that reflects contemporary practices concerns Tarsus' origins. The citizens were proud of their Hellenic descent, and Dio mockingly calls them "Greeks and Argives, and even better" (1): one of their rivals, Aegaeae, claimed foundation by Perseus and kinship (*syngeneia*) with Argos, as is shown by a decree from the parent city.[34] This pride of Asian cities in their kinship with those of old Greece is a feature of the age, though it is noticeable long before; it was given concrete expression when Hadrian founded the Panhellenion, a council in Athens to which Asian cities could gain admission by proving Hellenic origins.[35] For a city like Tarsus the craving for Hellenic credentials was made all the keener by its proximity to the Orient. Even members of the upper class, like Athenodorus, were of Asiatic descent, and the city contained many Jews, of whom the most famous is St. Paul.[36] The teacher of Apollonius was a Phoenician.[37] It is, therefore, not only a play on words but a well-aimed thrust when Dio warns the Tarsians not to be thought to come from Arados rather than Argos, Phoenicia rather than Greece (41–42). Arados was an important city with its own claims to Greek descent, but for Dio's purposes it was enough that it was Phoenician: the same snobbery is evident when he elsewhere rebukes the Athenians for honoring "some Phoenician creature not even from Tyre or Sidon."[38]

By contrast, another detail that might seem oriental to a modern is adduced by Dio precisely to show the Hellenic sobriety of Tarsus' earlier days: "the women when they walk out are dressed in such a way that no one can see any part of them, either of their face or of the rest of their body, nor do they see anything that does not lie in their path" (48–49). This same practice is found in another city of southern Asia Minor, Pamphylian Perge, and there too it is not a sign of oriental influence but of conservative Hellenism.[39]

The first *Tarsian* is concerned solely with a question of behavior: the second is directly addressed to political questions, above all, the recurring problem of relations with Rome. One problem that arises in this speech is found frequently in Dio's works of this period, that of "faction" (*stasis*) and its opposite, "concord" (*homonoia*). The meaning of these terms, especially the second, will be examined later: for the time being it may be noted that in this speech "faction" appears in the same contexts as "hatred" (14) and "disturbance" (21), while "concord" between citizens (17) or cities (45) is the state of friendship or reconciliation that follows "faction."

The second *Tarsian* is delivered before a formal meeting of the assembly (1) and is not the first speech that Dio has made in the several days of his visit (38): the first *Tarsian* may be one of these other speeches. The second is perhaps the most carefully constructed in the whole collection. In the preface (1–7) Dio justifies his coming forward. It is usual only for citizens to address the assembly, and of them only the rich and munificent, not for strangers such as he: yet the wealthier are not necessarily the wiser (1). Dio graphically expresses the understood connection between wealth and political influence; he also anticipates a recurrent theme of the speech, the incompetence of Tarsus' present leaders. After this claim, he has to disarm suspicion. Some might judge from his appearance that he is a Cynic and despise him (2); and Tarsus is generally ill-disposed toward the local philosophers, because some of them have "harmed their city and conspired against their fellow-citizens." Such people, however, are not really philosophers, "even if they go around with less covering than a statue" (3). Because of his denial of Cynicism and of the reference to public nudity Dio seems to be thinking primarily of the Cynics. It would not be surprising if these had stirred up the poor of the city (21) or inflamed the mob against the governor (39).

Having won the people's attention, Dio announces the scheme of his speech: he will first show that the city needs advice, then that its present advisers are incompetent, and lastly he will offer his own suggestions (6–7). In accordance with this scheme, he sets out the city's problems under three heads, its quarrels with other cities (7–14), its dispute with the governor (15), and the divisions among its own classes (16–23): because most of this internal dissension has recently been healed, Dio treats it in this section, and does not return to it later. Next he criticizes the conduct of the upper class (28–37), and finally he gives his own remedies, considering the governor (38–42) and then the other cities (43–53).

Dio begins his review of Tarsus' problems by considering its relations with other cities of Cilicia. The favors shown by Augustus had made it grow rapidly (7–8); soon, however, prosperity had had less auspicious effects. Certain of the governors, whom Dio calls "generals" (*strategoi*),[40] acted "cruelly" and were successfully prosecuted by Tarsus: this made the city popular in Cilicia but disliked at Rome (9). Though Dio speaks as if Tarsus carried the burden of prosecution alone, it must have acted as the chief city of the provincial league, since only this could prosecute a governor.[41]

Dio next refers to an apparently later event: Aegaeae "absurdly competed" with Tarsus over the "registrations" (*apographai*), and even though Tarsus won its case it seemed to be oppressing the other cities (10). These feuds between cities are another feature of ancient life that becomes prominent under the principate.[42] Tarsus had several such rivals, but Aegaeae (modern Ayas) was perhaps the most formidable (*Or.* 33.51, 34.14, 47). This had a flourishing port and a famous sanctuary of Asclepius; like Tarsus, it claimed descent from Perseus and the Argives.[43] Dio's word "registrations" probably refers, as in the *Rhodian,* to the registration of property made by the tributary cities for the periodical census.[44] Since the two cities were not neighbors, their quarrel probably did not concern land: but since both had harbors, and Tarsus at least had "control" over the adjacent stretch of sea, the dispute between them may have been a maritime one.

Tarsus' most urgent dispute was not with Aegaeae but with Mallos (11). This city, whose site is not known for certain, was southeast of Tarsus on the river Pyramos.[45] The two cities were probably old enemies, for an inscription from over two hundred years earlier seems to show them already quarreling.[46] At present they were disputing a sandy patch of coastland "near the lagoon" which was the harbor of Tarsus.[47] The Mallians must have used physical force against their neighbors, for Dio claims that if the Tarsians had done the same they would have been thought to be starting rebellion and to require armed suppression (11).[48] Nevertheless, Dio urges that an adversary so much weaker than Tarsus should be treated with forbearance.

Tarsus feuded with more cities than Aegaeae and Mallos: Soloi, lying to its west, on the very edge of Smooth Cilicia, and usually known as Pompeiopolis,[49] Adana, Tarsus' neighbor to the east and an ancient rival,[50] and apparently other cities also (14, 47). All these were speaking ill of Tarsus and wanted to "follow others" (14). This phrase suggests that there was a cry for another city to be made the capital of the province and the center of the provincial league, perhaps Tarsus' later rival, Anazarbus:[51] in the same way Syrian Antioch later lost its primacy and its title of metropolis to its rival, Laodicea.[52] Dio urges the Tarsians to be conciliatory and to win their neighbors' goodwill. Since Mallos is far the weaker, it is better to end the feud amicably and not resort to the Romans for arbitration (43–46): exactly the same advice is given by

Plutarch to rival politicians.[53] With the other cities Tarsus should be equally gentle, and then they will "follow" willingly: "that is far more important than that Mallos[54] should sacrifice and litigate in your city; for it makes no difference at all if the citizens either of Adana or of Aegaeae come to sacrifice here" (47). The logic is not clear, and the text may be corrupt. If it is sound, however, Mallos must have been a member of Tarsus' assize-district and wished to be transferred to another one or made the head of its own: either could happen when Rome altered the system of assizes.[55] Dio's reference to "sacrifice" presumably concerns Tarsus' position as the center of the provincial league, to which the other cities sent delegates to join in the cult of the imperial house; other signs show that its guardianship of the cult was being challenged, perhaps by Anazarbus.

Like other Greeks who attempt to quell faction within or between cities, Dio argues that such disputes are worthless:[56] "whether Aegaeae quarrels with you or Apamea with Antioch or, further away, Ephesus with Smyrna, they are quarreling over a donkey's shadow, as the saying is, since mastery and power belong to others" (48). The issue between Antioch and Apamea (those on the Orontes) is otherwise unknown: later, Antioch's chief rival was Laodicea.[57] The quarrel of Ephesus and Smyrna is comparatively well attested, since it became entangled in the professional rivalries of the Second Sophistic: thus, Dio's two most eminent pupils, Favorinus and Polemo, were the leading sophists of Ephesus and Smyrna respectively and bitterly hostile to each other.[58] In the second century Pergamum was drawn into the dispute, and Aristides in an extant speech tries to restore "concord" between the three cities.[59] Like Aristides, Dio appeals for concord by recalling the fatal quarrels of Athens and Sparta (49–50); and like him he observes that Roman supremacy had made such things obsolete, "typical of fellow slaves squabbling over reputation and primacy" (51).[60] There is no slight to Rome when Dio calls the cities "slaves": rather, he mocks the pitiful degradation of the Greeks, just as he pities Caunus as the slave simultaneously of Rhodes and Rome (Or. 31.125). The "primacy" (proteia) presumably refers to Tarsus' danger of losing its position as the head of the league: these struggles to be "first" went on constantly between cities of Asia minor, as Dio's speech to Nicomedia shows.[61]

The second cause of Tarsus' troubles is its relation to the governors. As a proud, free, and ancient city, Tarsus was probably always suspicious of the Roman authorities;[62] and these for their part were the more readily tempted to abuse their powers by the distance of the province from Rome, which made accusation and detection more difficult.[63] As the chief city of Cilicia, Tarsus would have had a primary role in any action against the governor, and some time before Dio's speech had already prosecuted two "cruel" ones (9). Elsewhere Dio refers to "two governors in succession" accused by a prominent citizen, who may be the same, but are perhaps more recent.[64] Dio praises Tarsus for its courage and its concern for the other cities, but warns it of the attendant risks: it was invidious to prosecute senators before senators, and it created an impression of insubordination (9). It must often have happened that cities were deterred from prosecution by the senate's leniency toward its own members and its prejudice against provincials, especially Greeks: in Dio's time a Bithynian who presented the case against a corrupt governor was nearly convicted himself.[65]

Though Dio does not reveal the issue, Tarsus was quarreling with the governor once again. For some time he had merely sensed the Tarsians' ill-will; recently, when he was thought to have slighted them, they "said something, and he was moved both to write angrily and to take an unprecedented measure" (15). The "slight" may be connected with the disputes between Tarsus and its neighbors, or it may have been some affront to its prestige: cities were highly sensitive about their rights and titles and regarded as a mortal insult any failure to address them by their proper style.[66] The Tarsians perhaps retaliated by "saying something" in chorus at a public gathering; the "unprecedented measure" may be some expression of the governor's anger, such as the banishment or execution of troublemakers.

Dio advises Tarsus to be neither servile nor rash. "Those about Ionia" have recently voted not to prosecute any governor, but that is to throw away the subjects' only weapon (39). Dio seems to mean not the whole province of Asia, but the ancient league of thirteen Ionian cities which still met and retained a semblance of unity.[67] Presumably its members could not prosecute a governor independently of the provincial council, but by agreeing to withold their support for any such prosecution could effectively prevent it. The greater danger for Tarsus was the opposite. Dio urges his hearers not to expect every governor to be a Minos (38), the judge of souls who was the type of impartiality.[68] It is better to decide once and for all whether to prosecute than to tolerate the present "tension" (40) and the behavior of the chief magistrate, the *prytanis*.[69] Because a citizen had once made himself conspicuous in "critical times"[70] by prosecuting two governors in succession, most Tarsians think they must emulate him: but that is like applying a possibly lethal medicine without any expertise (42). Again Dio's language shows the risk that attached to prosecution of the Roman authorities: in the same way Plutarch observes that opposition to a wicked governor, though it may bring rapid glory, is less "safe and leisurely" than other means of ascent.[71]

The third source of Tarsus' troubles lies within the city. Several groups had recently been at variance: the council and assembly had been "apart," but were now "deliberating together," while the Elders were still "aloof" (16). In the Greek city, council and assembly tended to clash, since they drew their members from classes with inherently opposed interests: it seems to have been the end of such a clash that Dio celebrates in his speech given at Nicaea on "concord" (Or. 39).[72] The two groups in Tarsus had only recently been reconciled "by their anger" (17): they may have been driven to unity by the governor's recent rebuff, since the people depended on the chief magistrate to act as the city's spokesman, and he naturally belonged to the upper class. The involvement of the governor might also explain the "aloofness" of the Elders. Groups with this name are found in many Greek cities; their powers and responsibilities may have varied from place to place, but in general they were associations of a social and religious kind, which because of their organization and the seniority of their members could exercise great influence in civic affairs.[73] This must have been so at Tarsus, since Dio compares the Elders to the captain of a ship, with the assembly as the crew and the council as the pilot (16). The Elders at Tarsus may have derived their importance from the reforms introduced by Athenodorus,[74] himself an old man when he guided the city's affairs: the same body was also reinforced about the same time in Argos, Tarsus' supposed mother-city.[75] Rome had every reason to foster the position of the older and more conservative citizens, especially in a city so volatile as Tarsus. Yet another group at variance with others in the city was the association of Youths (neoi, 21); this widely attested body seems primarily to have been social in purpose, though it too could act as a political unit, for example, by sending its own letters to an emperor.[76]

Further unrest was caused by a large group called the Linenworkers. Most of these had been born in Tarsus, and some of them had been there for several generations. Though allowed to attend the assembly, they were too poor to pay the 500 drachmae necessary for enrollment as citizens; because they were disenfranchised, they had been causing "faction and disturbance." Dio now proposes, or supports a proposal, that they be enrolled as citizens immediately and free of charge (21–23).

This passage illuminates several features of the Greek city under Roman rule. Though Dio does not say so, it appears that the Linenworkers were organized into a professional guild, as they were at Anazarbus and elsewhere: these guilds were common in Asian cities, and ones of Porters and Graindealers are known at Tarsus.[77] They could apply political pressure, like the poor men's clubs (*collegia*) in republican Rome: thus, the Silversmiths at Ephesus organized a famous demonstration against itinerant preachers whose doctrines endangered their livelihood.[78] The same passage also illustrates a less well known feature of Greek city life, the restriction of full citizenship to those of at least moderate wealth. This may be another of Athenodorus' reforms, though there is no reason to believe it peculiar to Tarsus.[79] It must have excluded an ordinary artisan from citizenship, for a legionary in the same period earned roughly half this sum a year.[80] Dio may be moved by considerations of Stoic humanitarianism in speaking against this rule, but also by the desire to remove a source of political irritation; as in Prusa, he regarded the maintenance of order as one of the politician's first duties.

Although Dio ostensibly discusses the incompetence of Tarsus' upper class only to justify his own intervention, he regards it as a contributory cause of the city's troubles (28). The chief fault of the politicians is their empty ambition; most think only of their crowns, purple, and seats in the front row, and few are "truly concerned" for the city (29–30).[81] Just as a seat in the front row was a great honor for a visitor, so it was one of the most desired perquisites of a magistrate. The gold crown and purple robe were no less highly coveted; a contemporary of Dio considered the gold crown one of the chief inducements to becoming priest of the emperor.[82] Dio satirizes the tendency of the mob to listen only to the gymnasiarch, who was responsible for the maintenance of the public baths and gymnasia, or to the *demiourgos*, the eponymous magistrate who had to spend heavily on public amusements (31).[83] The true politician does not "gape after the noise of the many," but resists them if need be (33); so also Plutarch advises the rising politician to despise the baubles of popularity and keep the mob in check.[84] Others of the wealthy at Tarsus entirely avoid politics, or participate only rarely, considering public life too unsafe (34). Still others hold office for the required six months,[85] just long enough to win themselves glory by some "brave" act,[86] and thereafter neglect the city's affairs: as a result, it changes its policies like a ship puffed about by gusts of wind (35–37). This whole section not only shows Dio's satirical gifts, but is full of the brilliant similes for which Philostratus admired him.

In range and depth the second *Tarsian* goes far beyond all the speeches hitherto considered, and it exemplifies Dio's greatest strengths, his "clear grasp of the state of affairs" and his "practical energy."[87] There is no irony or allegory, and no use of trifling subjects to convey serious messages. That Dio was still capable of these devices in his last years is shown by such works as the *Apamean* and the first *Tarsian;* the second *Tarsian* is closer to his mature speeches delivered in Bithynia.

10
Concord

The subject of "concord" (*homonoia*) occurs frequently in Dio's political speeches. It was touched in the *Alexandrian* and the second *Tarsian*, and is the topic of four late speeches delivered in four cities of Bithynia—Nicomedia, Nicaea, Prusa, and Apamea (*Or.* 38–41).

The word translated as "concord" has several shades of meaning and would often be better rendered by "amity" or "understanding." In its commonest sense, especially when used by writers of the imperial period, it is the opposite of *stasis* ("faction" or "discord") and implies the resolution of recent or still existing disputes: this is the sense in which it was used in the second *Tarsian*.[1] It was perhaps originally coined in fifth-century Athens to express the ending of discord among citizens, as Dio uses it in Nicaea.[2] But it could also refer to the relations between two or more cities. Usually these were neighbors, like Prusa and Apamea, and the discord was caused by simple friction. Sometimes, however, proximity was of little or no account, and the issue was a disputed title such as "first" or "metropolis," as it was between Nicomedia and Nicaea.

On coins and inscriptions "concord" often lacks its negative connotation, and means merely "understanding" or "goodwill." Thus, one city that had agreed with another to an exchange of exports might celebrate the concord of the two, as citizens of Perinthus in Thrace celebrated their concord with Apamea on the opposite coast of the Propontis.[3] Two maritime cities might agree to give privileges to each other's ships: this is perhaps the significance of coins marking the concord of Side in Pamphylia and Alexandria.[4] Sometimes the word means nothing more than the goodwill created by a man with contacts in both cities,[5] or by a supposed bond of kinship (*syngeneia*).[6]

It must be noted, because it has sometimes hindered the understanding of Dio's speeches, that concord does not imply any formal treaty. The many coins signifying concord between cities are conventionally called "alliance-coins": and the convention has created the belief that they refer to treaties of alliance.[7] For several reasons this cannot be so. "Concord" and "alliance" (*symmachia*) are different concepts; the theory cannot accommodate coins which mark concord between different bodies in one city, such as the council and assembly of Nicaea; it is unlikely that any city of the empire could consider itself allied to any other except Rome;[8] still less is it likely that a subject city, especially one so restricted in its rights as Alexandria, could conduct an independent foreign policy; and no text of such a treaty has survived. Most of the same arguments apply against another theory, largely based on Dio, whereby concord is identical to the mutual exchange of citizen rights (*isopoliteia*) practiced in the classical and Hellenistic periods:[9] this institution appears no longer to have existed under the principate.[10]

The longest and most important of Dio's speeches on concord is that addressed to Nicomedia (*Or.* 38). This, modern Izmit, had been founded by Nicomedes I as the capital of his kingdom.[11] Its chief sources of industry and revenue were its natural and well protected harbor, and its position as the starting point of several major routes into the interior.[12] Its feud with Nicaea, modern Iznik, about fifty kilometers to the southwest, may well have been an ancient one, for as the older city, boasting an impeccable pedigree, Nicaea cannot willingly have taken second place to the new capital. In the Roman period this feud was expressed in the competition of the two cities over titles and privileges. For a while Nicomedia had been the "metropolis," Nicaea the "first city."[13] Domitian had allowed Nicomedia to add "first" to its other title, and now it was trying to have Nicaea deprived of it. But Nicaea continued to be confirmed in its right to be "first" until it made the error of supporting Pescennius Niger in his war against Septimius Severus. Nevertheless, far from coming to an end, the rivalry of the two cities continued into late antiquity.[14]

Feuds between neighboring communities readily arise in societies based on agriculture and petty trade, and it is partly because of the abundance of evidence that they are particularly well known in the Roman empire.[15] But these struggles for titles, which did not necessarily occur between neighbors, first appear under the emperors, and, as Dio observes (*Or.* 38.38), were considered peculiarly "Greek failings." Again, it is probably because of the distribution of evidence that they are particularly well known in western Asia Minor, in the provinces of Bithynia and Asia; similar struggles are sporadically glimpsed in Greece, Macedonia, and Syria.[16] Deliberately or not, the Roman system of administration encouraged them in several ways. Emperors played on the cities' vanities, granting or withdrawing titles as a mark of favor or displeasure; from the same motives, governors used or failed to use them when addressing a city; the apparatus of the provincial cult of the emperors, with its priests, temples, and processions,[17] fueled rivalries over precedence. But the quarrels sprang from deeper causes. Nicomedia, for example, probably desired the exclusive right to be called "first" because it had overtaken in prosperity its former superior, Nicaea. Desire for honor and glory was ubiquitous: cities struggled to be first in their province or to have a temple of the imperial cult, as individuals struggled to be the "first men" of their city or to wear the gold crown and purple robe of office. These yearnings for distinction were all the keener now that the dead weight of peace forbade more overt forms of aggression: it is not for nothing that those who opposed such rivalries, like Dio and Aelius Aristides, constantly compare them with the classic wars of Athens and Sparta.[18]

Dio's speech to Nicomedia, which can be dated securely to the period of his return, is delivered before the assembly (3). Like the second *Tarsian*, which it resembles in other ways, the *Nicomedian* is carefully constructed. In the preface Dio courts his audience's goodwill and announces his subject and its subdivisions (1–9). He then gives a general panegyric of concord (10–20); condemns the futility of struggling over titles (21–30); recommends that the city reform its behavior (31–40); and finally depicts the blessings of concord (41–51).

He begins by recalling that he has been made a citizen of Nicomedia (1). According to the law of Pompey, cities of Bithynia were forbidden to make citizens of those from other cities of the province, but by Dio's day this rule had often been broken.[19] Though such grants were sometimes a simple mark of honor, as when the recipient was a performing artist, they could be intended to bring tangible benefits: Nicomedia may have hoped to receive not only Dio's advice but the results of his influence with Trajan.

The most substantial part of the speech begins when Dio considers the causes of the present dispute. The sea is not an issue, since Nicaea has already come to terms (22). Dio does not say what the dispute here had been; it cannot have concerned access to the sea, for Nicaea was not dependent on Nicomedia's port as Prusa was on Apamea's.[20] Neither is land the issue between them, since again the Nicaeans have come to terms about revenues (22). The quarrel probably concerned the boundary between their adjacent territories, for any change in this might affect a city's income from rent or taxes. Dio speaks as if both these disputes had been settled at the same time, perhaps by a Roman official.[21] In addition, the two cities had many other bonds: trade, intermarriage, ties of kinship, public representatives of each other's interests, and private friendships. They observe the same gods and most of the same holidays and have no difference in customs to cause dispute (22). Such disputes over religious customs were notorious in Egypt,[22] and probably existed elsewhere.

The real cause of faction was the desire to be first, in a word, "primacy" (*proteia*, 24). Among the titles over which Greek cities fought, that of "first" was frequent. In the province of Asia there was a triple contest for the same title between Pergamum, Ephesus, and Smyrna, which the rhetor Aristides tried to allay in a speech with many similarities to Dio's; and, like Dio, Aristides spoke in vain, for the dispute continued into the third century.[23] In Nicomedia and elsewhere Dio, like Aristides, accuses unnamed persons of stoking the quarrel for their own ends.[24]

As he often does, Dio tries to prove the futility of the quarrel by contrasting it with the classic rivalry of Athens and Sparta. Even if Nicomedia were to gain the primacy it would not also gain the "tribute" (*phoroi*) now paid to its rival, summon the cities that now belong to its court, install harmosts there, or cease to pay Nicaea "the tithes from the Bithynians" (26). Dio's word "tribute" is chosen to recall the levy imposed by Athens on its allies; but the same word also means "rents," and thus designates the revenues drawn by Nicaea from public land. The "court" again recalls disputes between Athens and its allies, but here refers to the system of assizes already discussed by Dio in the *Apamean* and the second *Tarsian*: little is known of this system in Bithynia, but neither Nicaea nor Nicomedia can have lacked the privilege of receiving the assizes.[25] It has been seen, and will be again, that the boundaries of the judicial districts could be altered: here Dio means that such an alteration would not necessarily follow if Nicomedia had sole right to be called "first." His reference to "tithes" is less clear. He has been taken to mean some otherwise unknown rent paid by the native population of Bithynia and collected by Nicaea or by Roman officials resident there.[26] A simpler explanation is that "the Bithynians" are merely the inhabitants of Bithynia, and that the "tithes" are the direct tax, or "tribute," paid annually by all provinces to the Roman government.[27] Each city was responsible for raising its own share: and it is not surprising that in Bithynia they had to forward it to Nicaea, for this had earlier been the headquarters of the tax-farmers.[28] Although the emperors are usually thought to have abolished the old system of assessing tribute by fixed quotas, the evidence is not decisive.[29]

A single word, according to Dio, is at the bottom of the whole dispute, since the Nicomedians wish to be "inscribed" (*epigraphesthai*) as first (28): he simplifies the issue for effect, since it was not the title itself that Nicomedia wanted, but the exclusive right to it. His "inscribed" probably refers to the carving of the city's titles on its public monuments. A vivid illustration of the jealousy such inscriptions awakened in other cities is given by the east gate of Nicaea, on which the words "the first of the province" have been erased: after the defeat of Pescennius Niger, Nicomedia was at last able to have the offending phrase erased from its rival's monuments.[30] Dio may also, however, refer to the "inscribing" of Nicomedia's titles in letters and decrees, for this too could provoke bitter controversy.

Dio follows the destructive part of his speech with more positive advice. As at Tarsus, he reminds Nicomedia that it is the "mother-city" (*metropolis*) of the province, and should not oppress its inferiors (31).[31] Its position as a port gives it the means to benefit them all. The text is partly corrupt, but Dio seems to indicate that Nicomedia at present restricts the flow of goods through its port: this restriction may have been achieved by requiring that certain of these must be sold to the city. The other cities are thus reduced to "smuggling" these goods, or to the indignity of having to beg the "necessary commodities" from Nicomedia. Although Nicomedia always complies with such requests, Dio urges the city to relax its controls and extend its favors to all alike (32). If this is right, the passage is not concerned with harbor dues, even though Nicomedia may have been entitled to levy them.[32] Apamea similarly restricted goods passing through its port on the way to Prusa.

From the subject of the other cities it is a logical step to that of the governors. As one of the chief cities of Bithynia, Nicomedia had great weight in the regional council; and since this body expressed the collective will of the Bithynians, Nicomedia's attitude toward the governors might affect their administration of the whole province. Dio, therefore, urges it to make them cautious by showing that it will stand up for other cities, and not be content with favor toward itself (33). If it settles its feud with Nicaea, their combined influence will be irresistible, and the rewards of concord even greater (34). That Dio is not talking of possibilities is clear from his later description of certain bad governors and their tactics (36–37).

Dio contrasts the present situation with this desirable outcome of concord. Far from defending the lesser cities, the two cities are now induced by their quarrel to bow to them (34–35). In these competitions for titles and privileges the provincial council gradually came to occupy a position between the cities and the emperors, so that the council and not the petitioning city forwarded the request for a new title and received the imperial reply.[33] Thus, rivalry between the greater cities profited the lesser ones, since Nicaea and Nicomedia needed their votes if either was to win a majority in the council. Aristides in his speech on concord, which was actually delivered at a session of the Asian council, appeals to the three chief cities not to debase themselves before the others.[34]

The governors too profit from these disputes. They side either with the Nicomedians and their party (*hetaireia*) or with the Nicaeans and theirs, and so have the support of one side (*meros*) or the other (36). They have only to address one of the cities in speech or writing as "first," and they are free to commit every kind of outrage (37). Again, Dio refers to the provincial council. By siding with either of the two cities, a governor could count on all the votes it controlled if the question arose of his prosecution: in Dio's own time, a shift in the balance of the council probably caused Bithynia to withdraw the charges against Varenus Rufus.[35] The sensitivity of cities to forms of address is illustrated equally by the rivalry among the first three of Asia. These insulted one another by failing to use the proper titles in letters and decrees, so that the emperor himself had to intervene.[36] Dio reminds the Nicomedians of the vanity of such contests (38–40): in the same way a Roman official writes to Phrygian Laodicea condemning "vain competitiveness" in the struggle for "primacy."[37]

Dio depicts the advantages that concord will bring. At present the two cities face each other like armed camps, and those who do wrong in one of them can take refuge in its rival. When they are reconciled, however, each will draw on the advice, wealth, and generosity of the other's citizens: it will be as if the inhabitants had two cities, as they already have common ancestors, gods, customs, and festivals. Dio would gladly bring Ephesus or Smyrna, let alone Nicaea, into "fraternity" with Nicomedia (44–47). This passage is the chief evidence for the view that by promoting concord Dio aimed at an exchange of citizenship between the two cities.[38] In fact, he is painting in rhetorical colors the results that will follow from the end of strife. Normally the wealthy men of one city might act as magistrates or benefactors in another,[39] and this custom, suspended in times of discord, will resume when harmony is reestablished. Though there seems no other evidence, it is easily understood that during faction a city would provide a haven to wrongdoers from the other and extradite them in time of peace. Dio's reference to common ancestors is flattery of Nicomedia. At its foundation it had absorbed the Megarian colony of Astakos, and informally even affected its name.[40] This gave it the Hellenic pedigree essential to self-respect and put it on a level with Nicaea, which boasted descent from "the first of Greeks." [41]

Dio's speech *On Concord in Nicaea* (*Or.* 39) is much simpler and shorter than the *Nicomedian*. It differs from it, and from the other two speeches on the same subject, in that it celebrates concord already achieved rather than advising how to achieve it; moreover, here the concord is between different bodies in one city, and not between different cities. The speech appears, however, to be from the same period as the other speeches on the same topic, and like them it was presumably delivered before the assembly.

Nicaea had been founded in the late fourth century by one of Alexander's generals, Antigonus, and was soon destroyed and refounded by his rival Lysimachus, king of Thrace: one or both of these settled Macedonian colonists there.[42] In due course the city discovered more truly Hellenic origins. It had been settled by citizens of its namesake in Locris who had served in Alexander's army: better still, it had been founded by the god Dionysus and named after a beloved nymph, or by Heracles on his travels with the ship *Argo*.[43] These myths, celebrated on the coins and inscriptions of Nicaea,[44] were to serve Dio well. The city's chief material advantages were its territory, which was especially fruitful in olives, its proximity to the sea, and its communications with the interior. Following a period in the late republic and early empire when it had prospered by

Italian enterprise, by Dio's time it had fallen below Nicomedia, though still large and wealthy: the finely preserved walls still convey past grandeur.[45]

Dio begins, as at Nicomedia, by thanking Nicaea for honoring him: it is a privilege to be distinguished by a city of such "prosperity and size," of such large population and distinguished ancestry, "where the most glorious of races mingled, not a few wretches from here and there, but the first of Greeks and Macedonians"; best of all, its founders were gods and heroes (1). It is not known what honor Dio had received, but it is likely that, now or earlier, he was made a citizen of Nicaea as of Nicomedia: some connection with the city is shown by the fact that the historian Cassius Dio, a native, appears to be his descendant.[46] "Size" was a usual ingredient in laudations of cities,[47] though Nicaea's claim to it was justified. So also was "nobility," which allows Dio to allude to the various legends of Nicaea's origins: the reference to other cities founded by "a few wretches" may be a glance at the humble beginnings of Rome. The coins and inscriptions show the pride which it took in the same "nobility."[48] It was a claim especially valuable in a province where most of the cities were founded or refounded by native kings; in particular, it was a useful weapon in the war of words against Nicomedia, whose very name betrayed less glorious origins. Nonetheless, so Dio reminds his hearers, all these advantages—prosperity, divine favor (theophileis),[49] and fortune—are worth nothing unless conjoined with moderation and virtue (2).

Dio does not say explicitly what has caused the recently ended faction. He congratulates the city, however, on having "a single appearance and single voice" (3), compares its recent state to that of a ship without a pilot or a chariot without a driver (6), and prays that it may continue to "agree in wish and thought" (8). All this suggests that there had been disagreement between the council and assembly, as at Tarsus:[50] later dissension between the two bodies in Nicaea is implied by coins which proclaim their "concord."[51] Beneath these struggles lay a deeper division between the rich, who controlled the council, and the comparatively poor, who had access only to the assembly. These struggles were probably more widespread even than rivalry between cities, just as the conditions for their growth were; Plutarch is eloquent on the topic of internal discord, but practically ignores that between rival cities.[52] In Nicaea the faction may have been exacerbated by corrupt proconsuls, since Dio praises concord for making a city respected by good governors and safe from wicked ones (4). Just as governors could exploit the hostility between cities, so they could profit from the tensions within them: Apollonius of Tyana is supposed to have warned Syrian Antioch against the divisive tactics of the governor.[53] Dio ends by praying to "Dionysus the forefather of this city, Heracles its founder," and a whole litany of other gods including Concord, all of whom are known to have been worshiped there.[54] He begs them to preserve the city's unity and banish strife, "so that in future it may be among the best and most blessed of cities" (8): he thus attempts to make Nicaea's Hellenic pride into a source of concord, as he used the pride of Tarsus and Nicomedia in their title of "mother-city."

Dio's two speeches on concord between Prusa and Apamea (Or. 40, 41) are of interest in that they reveal the disagreements, not between great and famous cities like Nicomedia and Nicaea, but between comparatively insignificant ones: there must have been many neighboring cities in east and west whose quarrels resembled those of Prusa and Apamea. These speeches also show how far one man with contacts in both cities could intervene to effect a reconciliation.

Apamea was only about twenty kilometers from Prusa, and their territories were contiguous. Originally a colony of Colophon with the name Myrleia, it had been refounded by Prusias I, also the founder of Prusa. Under the Triumvirs it became a Roman colony, Colonia Julia Concordia Apamea, and by Dio's time it was the only colony in Bithynia and correspondingly insistent on its privileges. It owed such significance as it had mainly to its port, which also served Prusa, though it was rich enough in olive trees to export its oil.[55]

Again, Dio does not say what had caused the dispute, but hints that it concerned territory (Or. 40.30): this is consistent with his mention of "money and advantage" (23), since a city's material wealth was related to the amount of land attached to it. The quarrel began during his exile, and on his return he urged his citizens to settle it: in order not to lose his influence over them, he declined an invitation to visit their rivals (16). While he was away on his embassy to Trajan, the two cities began to be reconciled (17). The present speech was delivered in Prusa immediately after his return and is addressed to the assembly (6). Since Dio claims to speak in support of the chief magistrate and "the mover" (20), a motion in favor of concord had presumably passed the council and was now being presented to the people for its agreement. If that is right, it confirms the impression given by Plutarch and in other speeches of Dio that the popu-

lar assembly was still far from impotent, even though it could only approve or reject motions of the council.[56]

Not all of the speech is directly concerned with concord, and many of
the arguments are theoretical: some, however, are drawn from the circumstances. Thus, Dio reminds his audience that Apamea is "no small
city," and that it has "a special constitution and a kind of honor and influence with the governors": the citizens of the two communities meet
almost every day, very many are connected by marriage with each other's
city, "and certain of our citizens, virtually all the most influential among
us, have attained to office there" (22). Though Dio elsewhere calls Prusa
"not the largest of cities" (*Or.* 44.9), its more favorable situation and extensive territory suggest that it was larger than its neighbor. Apamea's
"special constitution" derived from its status as a Roman colony, which
probably exempted it from the Pompeian law of the province. This may
have been one of the irritants in the feud with Prusa, the Prusans claiming to be the truer Hellenes, the Apameans to enjoy a privileged status.
The "most influential citizens" of Prusa honored at Apamea must include
Dio and his forebears on both sides, since his maternal grandfather and
his mother had been made citizens of Apamea by the emperor and his
father directly by the city (*Or.* 41.6).[57] The word translated "office" probably refers to the position of "duovir," one of the two chief magistrates of
every Roman colony.[58]

It would be cowardice, Dio argues, to yield to the Apameans if they
were the aggressors: but since they have taken the first steps toward
peace, Prusa must "transfer the rivalry from the quarrel to this more
honorable arena" (23–24). Dio uses the same argument in the second
Tarsian, and the Roman authorities urged quarreling cities to "take the
first step" toward reconciliation and make themselves "more respected":[59] like the appeal to a city's nobility, this was an argument intended
to recruit a force for discord to the side of harmony.

When meeting for joint fairs, feasts of the gods, and spectacles, it is
far better that the cities should pray together than curse: their acclamations in the stadia and the theater should contain praise, not insult, for cities reviling one another are like harlots trading obscenities from their
brothels (28–29). Dio's image is appropriate to the scene he has in mind.
He has already referred often to the acclamations of the assembly: his
choice of words here—"spectacles," "theaters," "stadia"—reveals that he
is referring to gladiatorial shows, probably given by the imperial priests
in the two cities.[60] By their violent nature these might readily fuel rival-

ries between cities, as the chariot races of Alexandria fueled those between inhabitants of a single city. It was a gladiatorial show at Pompeii, attended by the citizens of the neighboring Nuceria, that provoked bloodshed between the two colonies.[61] Plutarch advised politicians to ban every kind of spectacle that excited the "murderous and bestial" instincts of the mob.[62]

Prusa's quarrel with Apamea has yet another evil consequence. Their geography "compels them to have relations, even if they do not wish it": the Apameans need Prusa's timber and many other things, and Prusa cannot import through any other harbor, or export its own products (30). This suggests that the quarrel, even if originally territorial, had led to economic warfare, in which Apamea refused to handle Prusa's exports and imports, and Prusa to sell its neighbor the goods it needed: timber was the chief of these, for while Prusa had an inexhaustible supply, Apamea had none. Such reprisals, repeated in every dispute, apparently led Apamea to look to Perinthus on the opposite shore of the Propontis as an outlet for its goods.[63] Dio now anticipates that the very ambassadors due to be sent to Rome will either have to "use the harbor of a hostile city" or "go round about, as if the sea near us is difficult of approach" (33).

The speech delivered on the same subject in Apamea (*Or.* 41) is obviously contemporary. Since Dio claims to address "the council and the most reasonable of the others present here" (1), he seems to be speaking to a joint meeting of the council and assembly such as is attested in other Greek cities of the period:[64] his language suggests that, as at Prusa, the opponents of concord were in the assembly and not among the upper class.

As he did at Nicomedia and Nicaea, Dio first mentions honor paid to him by the city: when he returned from exile the Apameans had passed a decree whereby they congratulated him on his restoration and invited him to visit (1, cf. *Or.* 40.16). Other cities he has seen, which include "most of those equal in honor" to Apamea, have granted him citizenship, membership of the council, and their highest privileges: but Apamea honored him as its own citizen, not as a stranger (2). Dio had recently become a citizen of Nicomedia and Nicaea; but the cities referred to here appear not to be in Bithynia. The honors were probably granted after his return from exile, and perhaps during his travels of 100 and 101, when he visited Athens and Olympia.[65] The cities "equal in honor" to Apamea should be Roman colonies, though he is not known to have visited any.

Dio is aware that certain of his hearers, "as is to be expected in an assembly," distrust him as a citizen of Prusa (1). But it would be more like a tyrant than a benefactor to expect no opposition, and he hopes to persuade his critics that he considers Apamea his second ancestral city (*patris*, 3). This profession of loyalty to two or more cities is a feature of the age. Thus, a son of Dio's pupil Polemo acknowledged on coins a double devotion to his native Laodicea and his adoptive Smyrna; Artemidorus of Ephesus loyally signed his *Oneirocritica* as a son of the less famous Daldis.[66] Dio further recalls to the Apameans that he has friends "neither few nor without influence" through whom he might long since have reconciled the two cities. These obviously are well-placed Romans; it was expected that a Greek politician would have friends "among the most influential" at Rome, and use them for the advantage of his city.[67]

Dio appeals, as he did at Nicomedia and Nicaea, to the ancestry of the city he addresses. The Apameans must prove by their behavior their descent from "that fortunate city by which you were sent here to live as friends among friends"; just as that excels all mankind in fortune and power, so also it is of boundless goodness and generosity; it gives to all its franchise, its laws, and its magistracies, considers no worthy man a stranger, and preserves justice for all (9). Apamea must be "gentle" in dealing with a neighbor so close and having so many common ties, "marriages, children, citizenships, sacrifices to the gods": in fact the two cities are virtually one, since Apamea has chosen many Prusans to be its own citizens, councillors, and magistrates "and given them a share in those solemn privileges that belong to a city of Romans" (10). Though these praises of Rome are again conventional, they need not be insincere. Dio does not imply that Apamea could grant citizenship of its own accord: those whom it made citizens must either have had the Roman franchise already, or like Dio's grandfather received it simultaneously with that of Apamea.[68]

Dio's four speeches on concord are the fullest evidence that survives for the meaning of a word central to Greek political life. They presumably resemble hundreds of addresses on the same topic now lost, or never written down, for every right-thinking politician was expected to strive for harmony within and between cities.[69] In this matter, as in his services to Prusa, Dio's speeches survive not because of the originality of the subject matter but of the limpidity of the style in which it is discussed. By default, he becomes the spokesman for a class and time.[70]

11
Local Politics

With the political treatises of Plutarch, Dio's Bithynian speeches are the
best literary source for the city politics of the principate. Of the two, Plutarch is more concerned with the general laws of political life in widely
different cities of the empire: Dio discusses particular problems in a comparatively small area. The picture which he gives is, therefore, full, but
not necessarily typical. The Pompeian law which regulated the constitu-
tions of the Bithynian cities was valid only for the province. The cities
differed in their status before Rome, free or subject, Greek city or Roman
colony. Moreover, in Dio's time Bithynia was exceptionally turbulent and
had moved Trajan to rule it through legates responsible to himself.[1]
On more abstract issues than those of the moment, for example, in his
respect for the city council, Dio's evidence is less prone to be distorted
by regional differences. His attitudes cannot always, however, be assumed to represent those of a whole class: it is clear, for example, that
not all shared his abhorrence of faction or of gladiatorial shows. Men
like Dio and Plutarch view political life as members of the wealthy class,
but also as thinkers and philosophers.

Prusa was the city in whose politics Dio was most deeply involved.
Here at least it is possible to observe through him the political machinery,
in its normal operation and when it was disrupted by stress and faction.
Prusa's constitution has been sketched earlier in this book;[2] here some
details may be added from speeches already considered and from others.

In theory the city was a democracy, even if not like that of classical Athens, "where they gave the greatest weight to the many and the commoners."[3] This was now given to the council, which must have numbered several hundred even before an extra hundred were gained by Dio.[4] There was probably a property qualification of one hundred thousand sesterces for membership, so that a man who had bankrupted himself would lose his status unless rescued by the city or the emperor.[5] By the law of Pompey a councillor had to be thirty years old and to have held a magistracy or been enrolled by the censors, who revised the roll every fifth year: an edict of Augustus allowed men to hold the lower magistracies of the city probably from the age of twenty-five, and in Dio's time these too were admitted to the council.[6] Besides enrolling new members, the censors presumably were able to strike unqualified ones from the roll, like their counterparts at Rome; Dio mentions the arbitrary inclusion and exclusion of councillors as the mark of a factious city.[7] Membership of the council became a matter of caste, like the consulship of republican Rome, so that there was a prejudice against admitting such as were not themselves the sons of councillors.[8] Similarly, the offices of the city tended to be engrossed by certain families: both Dio and his son were chief magistrates,[9] and many of his relatives were active in Prusa's affairs.[10]

The council thus acquired an aura of prestige and wealth. "When you censure the council, the eminent, the select," Dio tells the assembly, "are you not censuring yourselves?" For the councillors were not only of superior birth, but included the benefactors on whom the poor depended for many of their pleasures.[11] When speaking before the councillors, Dio compares them to the most solemn buildings and sanctuaries of the city, while all others are like the houses or the shops; the council is the eyes of the city, the people its feet.[12] Over two centuries later, Libanius expresses the same reverence for the council of Antioch and equates the members with the city's benefactors: despite the intervening period, the values of the Greek city had not greatly changed.[13]

The second place in the political structure of the city was held by the assembly. This too was no doubt regulated by the law of Pompey, though no evidence of his dispositions for it survives. Presumably only citizens could vote, though as at Tarsus and in Dio's Euboean city noncitizens could attend.[14] The list of citizens was maintained by a special magistrate distinct from the censors, the *politographos*:[15] those newly enrolled may have had to pay a fee, like the five hundred drachmae required at Tarsus.[16] The right to vote may have been further restricted, not only to those who could pay the fee, but to those with a certain property qualification.[17]

Acting independently, the council conducted the routine administration of the city; hence Dio advises the assembly to turn a financial question over to it, "so that it may take thought for the city, as it usually does."[18] However, the vote of the people was still necessary for proposals that involved public expense, such as preliminary approval for Dio's portico.[19] But though a proposal might be broached in the assembly, it had to be framed in the council before being formally presented for the people's ratification: to omit the step was "demagogic," and probably illegal.[20] If the council approved, the motion could be presented either by a magistrate or by someone whom he delegated: the proposal to make peace with Apamea was presented in the latter way.[21] Thus, the assembly, though circumscribed, was not impotent. It could no doubt express its desires by shouting, and by this or other means force the council to bring motions that it wished. If it was wary of a proposal, its approval might sometimes only be extracted by lengthy persuasion. Most of Dio's civic speeches were given before the assembly, not the council: Plutarch too evidently regarded guidance of the assembly as a formidable task.[22] Only the wealthy were expected to speak, since they had special claims on the people's attention: but others could be invited, as Dio was at Tarsus.[23] When the council was not unanimous, those addressing the people may have dissented, like the two chief speakers at the Euboean assembly: Plutarch recommends that politicians should only pretend to disagree on major issues, but could safely do so with sincerity on minor ones.[24] The divisions between the council and the assembly mentioned by Dio in Tarsus, Nicaea, and Prusa may often have been caused by the council's refusing to present motions desired by the people, or the people's refusing to accept motions from the council: it need not be assumed that it was always the assembly that yielded. In both the council and the assembly, voting seems theoretically to have been by show of hands. In fact, a shout of "It is decided" or the like was often enough: in the *Euboean* the "good" man needs only to be "praised," and his proposal is immediately executed.[25]

The procedure for election to office resembles that for decrees. At least in Prusa, and no doubt generally, the council again had the controlling voice. It drew up a list of candidates and presented it to the assembly: at both stages, the traditional ballot (*psephos*) was apparently still used.[26] Thus again, though the council limited the options available to the people, the latter's vote was still necessary, and Dio can still talk as if the people were responsible for electing magistrates.[27]

The speech in which Dio declines the office of chief magistrate was spoken in the council while it was drawing up the list of candidates. The last sentences reveal certain details of the process.[28] "I know," Dio says, "that I would not have required scrutiny, and that you would have done the same now as you did before, when you assumed I was willing, and you all voted for me openly. However, I am no longer in the same position; and I feel no embarrassment in asking you to release me, just as I know I would not have had to ask you in order to be made chief magistrate." If the text is sound, the "scrutiny" (*exetasis*) must be some examination required of candidates for office, which had previously been waived for Dio; in one of the Flavian charters for a western city, a candidate is required to give sureties for the money he would handle if elected.[29] However, Dio may be referring to some technicality of the voting; the secret ballot had recently been introduced to elections in the Roman senate.[30]

The procedure for election in the assembly is illustrated by the voting for Dio's supernumerary councillors.[31] The council seems to have made a preliminary selection of the hundred new members: these were then presented to the assembly by their backers. Dio claims that the previous councillors made their selection and gave their support for political expediency; though he could have denounced the procedure to the assembly or the governor, or written to the emperor, he preferred not to cause trouble. He refrained from participating in the election and stayed away from the assembly.

A mysterious speech of Dio's, *Against Diodorus* (*Or*. 51), was apparently delivered just after an election. Diodorus (who is not named in the speech) had previously held a position in which he "improved the ephebes and the youth" (8), evidently as the gymnasiarch who supervised the public exercise grounds (*gymnasia*).[32] This was a position which gave scope for ambitious generosity, since the holder was expected to distribute free or cheap oil.[33] Diodorus seems to have taken his opportunity, and in return to have been elected as chief magistrate: for that must be the office indicated when Dio refers to "the supreme control [*megiste arche*] of moderation, temperance, and general upright living" (6).[34] Dio now comes forward and, after protesting against those who praise insincerely, proceeds to praise Diodorus for his public spirit and the assembly for its election of such a magistrate. The speech may be sincere: but like the *Apamean* it seems rather to be lightly ironic and to reproach the Prusans for electing their chief magistrate for his wealth alone.[35] That would explain, again as in the *Apamean*, the note of exaggeration in the speech, especially when Dio compares Diodorus to Pericles and Socrates (7).

Politics were not conducted only in the council and assembly, but spilled over into another area of public life, the courts. Though the power of the city courts was limited, they were an arena for political rivalries: in this as in other respects the politics of Prusa, and by analogy of other Bithynian cities, recall those of republican Rome, perhaps because the Pompeian law preserved in the province practices that had disappeared in Rome. In his speech on the bread riot, Dio claims never to have "betrayed" anyone by collusion as an advocate; later he counts it to his credit that, apart from a single case which he could not humanly refuse, he never appeared in court.[36] So again he prides himself for not going to the Roman authorities when the assizes were first held in Prusa.[37]

In his speech on the bread riot Dio had reminded the Prusan assembly that nothing escaped the attention of the Roman authorities.[38] It is clear that Rome was always a presence which the Greek politician had to keep in mind: it is less clear how far Roman authority was passive, responding when invoked by its subjects, and how far it actively encroached on their affairs. In some matters a governor was bound to intervene. He seems regularly to have examined a city's public accounts, as Varenus Rufus was expected to do at Prusa.[39] He was expected to tour the sacred and public buildings of the cities and promote necessary repairs: it was presumably on such tours that proconsuls had inspected the tumbledown structures of Prusa, to the embarrassment of the citizens.[40] Proposals for new buildings, since they involved the financial health of a city and so the Roman tribute, had to be approved by the emperor, no doubt through the mediation of the governors: presumably the proconsul who promoted Dio's portico at Prusa did so in the knowledge that it had Trajan's support.[41]

In general, however, the role of the Roman authorities was essentially passive (though far from inactive), and they intervened in civic affairs only when requested or obliged. Though proconsuls or their legates could attend meetings of the assembly, or even convene it,[42] they cannot have attended regularly. Dio's eagerness that the assembly of Prusa not bring serious matters to the proconsul's attention implies that he would otherwise not have learned of them.[43] The old view that all decrees of a city had to be ratified by the governor is not plausible: rather, the city chose to submit them.[44] As Plutarch complained, the Greeks invoked Roman power, often because they could not settle their differences otherwise.[45] In the same spirit Dio takes pride in not drawing the proconsul's attention to the misdeeds of his fellow councillors; it was only when his project for a portico had become mired in dispute that he threatened to call in the proconsul.[46]

Theoretically, therefore, the machinery of local government was meant to run of its own accord, with the Roman authorities correcting defects. In practice, disruptions were frequent and had two main causes. One was faction in the ruling class. Despite ties of intermarriage and common interest, this group was easily divided by the competition for honors and popularity. Especially when one citizen became unusually influential, "envy" (*phthonos*) was always at hand to mark him as a "tyrant," dangerously popular with the mob, oppressive to those nominally his equals.[47] This tendency to faction led to the formation of "parties" (*mere*), which do not represent ideological divisions but alliances built on influence and interest. Thus, Dio represents those who tried to bring their friends into the council as "conspirators" (*synomotai*), "doing politics by cabals" (*hetairiai*) and "dividing the city by parties."[48] All these words, especially "cabal" and "conspiracy," were current in the politics of this age as much as of the classical one. A citizen of Flavian Cibyra is praised for ending "a great conspiracy that did the greatest harm to the city";[49] Bithynia was so prone to "cabals" that Trajan banned all organizations which might be used to form them.[50]

The other main cause of disturbance was division between rich and poor. Again in large part this resulted from envy, and again it was embodied in political units, the council and the assembly. In a food shortage the poor suspected the wealthy of exploiting them, especially those like Dio who flaunted their wealth in grandiose and profitable building. When money for Dio's portico ran short, the poor suspected the rich of embezzlement or default on their subscriptions; these suspicions were translated into hostility between the assembly and the council.[51]

A third source of trouble can sometimes be glimpsed in the sources, but its importance is not easy to assess: Rome. Just as governors could side with one city in its competition with another, so they could with one citizen or party in a city. Disgraced emperors or governors might involve their favorites in their own ruin. Dio became vulnerable when a proconsul whose friend he had been was accused of maladministration; another philosopher at Prusa who had been favored by Domitian nearly lost his civil status under Trajan.[52]

Dio's later speeches reveal a series of disturbances at Prusa. Because the chronology of these speeches is so uncertain, it is difficult to put these incidents in the right order, and any reconstruction must be tentative. In a speech delivered before the assembly, Dio claims that his enemies want him away from Prusa, "so that if there is another crisis [*kairos*] such as certain persons pray for, like the previous one . . . I may not help the people, and those falsely accused may not have an intercessor or sympathizer."[53] It is probable that this "crisis" is an occasion which Dio describes rather differently when addressing the council. Here he admits to having pitied the common people and tried to alleviate their sufferings: but the surgery they underwent was for their own good.[54] There must, therefore, have been some disturbance in which Dio had done as the wealthy were sometimes tempted to do, and had sided with the commons against his own class:[55] later, he tried to make amends with his peers and recover his lost influence.

The speech entitled *On His Works, in the Council* (*Or.* 50) seems to be spoken in this period of uneasy reconciliation between Dio and the council. Dio reassures the members of the council that he has always cherished their interests (1–3) and is not trying now to win control of it (7). He defended himself before, when accused of betraying their interests (9): now too he wishes to dispel an unpleasant rumor. His son is chief magistrate, and Dio has been suspected of using his fatherly influence to prevent the council from meeting: really he has given his son no advice and has deliberately stayed away from several sessions (10). Such attempts to halt the political machinery of the city may not have been uncommon: one of the Flavian charters prescribes a heavy fine for anyone who tries to hinder the holding of elections.[56] "Tyranny" is not too strong a term for the power wielded by some local magnates.

Another chain of events, some of which may be identical to those just considered, involves the proconsul Varenus Rufus. In his speech delivered on the occasion of Rufus' visit (*Or.* 48) Dio urges the people to show their gratitude to him for permitting them to meet again: "for of course nobody piles up green logs on a fire . . . and no sensible governor convokes a disaffected populace" (1). The disturbance which had led to the suspension of the assembly may be the "crisis" already discussed; and just as that was followed by reconciliation between Dio and the council, so now he defends the council before the assembly, relying on the effect of his own popularity (9–11).

The next stage in this history is perhaps represented by the affair of the "wicked governor." In one of his bitterest speeches, again spoken before the assembly (Or. 43), Dio denounces "weak, envious creatures," who attack him for his popularity (1) and accuse the people before "the tribunal" (2). Dio represents the charges against him as a modern counterpart of the trial of Socrates, and, as often, it is not easy to tell how much is fact and how much is invention. He had allegedly persuaded a "wicked governor" to torture persons of Prusa and to send many of them into exile,[57] while others had committed suicide. Now he was helping the "tyrant of the province" to "argue his case successfully" (11); he was harming his own citizens by his accusations, and bribing the commons in order to win immunity for his plot (12); and he was preparing to leave Prusa (8). Apparently through his influence with this governor Dio had had certain of his enemies exiled; though he pretends that his foes called him an enemy of "the people," he seems not to mean the "commons," but the city generally.[58] The governor was now about to undergo trial, with Dio active on his behalf.

Two men in this period are known to have been accused of maladministration as proconsuls of Bithynia: Julius Bassus, who governed about 101, and Varenus Rufus, who did so about 105.[59] Provided that the governor is one of these, he ought to be Rufus rather than Bassus:[60] Dio's conduct on the occasion of Rufus' visit shows that they were friends, while no connection between him and Bassus is known.[61] Eventually, perhaps because of a shift of votes in the provincial council engineered by Dio, Bithynia attempted to withdraw the charges against Rufus.[62] Trajan undertook to find out what the province really wanted: it is not known, but is likely, that the case never came to trial.[63] The "tribunal" before which the city was being accused may be that of the emperor; and the purpose of the journey to which Dio alludes may have been to speak before Trajan at Rome.

This unhappy affair illustrates not only the well known laxity of provincial government under Trajan but also the overwhelming influence that provincial magnates could acquire. A wealthy Cretan under Nero boasted that his own word determined whether the provincial council thanked retiring proconsuls; such a motion of thanks would have precluded the possibility of prosecuting them later.[64] So also in the third century members of the council of the Three Gauls attempted to have charges preferred against a governor, but were thwarted by the opposition of a magnate friendly to him.[65]

The last notice of Dio's feuds is given by Pliny. Visiting Prusa for the assizes, Pliny was called upon to arbitrate between a philosopher called Flavius Archippus and his adversaries: these may have included Dio, since Archippus later appears as one of Dio's enemies. Archippus' opponents argued that he had been sentenced to hard labor some thirty years before, while he assembled an elaborate dossier to prove that he had been honored by Prusa and Domitian. Pliny referred the matter to Trajan, who decided in Archippus' favor, though without prejudice to any further charges which might be brought against him.[66] Archippus and others later accused Dio of impropriety in the construction of his portico and of treason against the emperor's majesty.[67] This must be another round in the same long struggle; and though the two incidents are fitfully lighted by the correspondence of Pliny, the vendetta may have begun long before. The intensity with which it was conducted is shown by the charge of treason: found guilty under another emperor, Dio might have been sentenced to exile, or death.

It is hazardous to draw large conclusions from the politics of one city in a brief period. At first the picture of Greek faction and Roman intervention suggests a decline in the quality of civic life. Yet the cities still had strength and resilience. Aided by the emperors, they had the means to build grandiosely; for their wealthy citizens the rewards in glory and honor still compensated for the expense of liturgies and benefactions; the assemblies continued to participate effectively in city life and had not yet yielded all power to the councils. Faction, whether in Flavian Sardis,[68] Trajanic Prusa, or Antonine Athens,[69] is not a sign of decadence, but of the stubborn vitality of an old tradition.

12
Benefactions

For a Greek city under the emperors local benefactors remained as vital as they had been under the Hellenistic kings and the republic. Prominent citizens bore the expense of office, paid for public buildings, and used their influence with eminent Romans: the rewards varied from a simple acclamation or decree to public burial and even deification. The compensation was not excessive, since generosity cost dear: not only was there expenditure and the physical dangers of travel, but today's hero might be accused tomorrow before governor or emperor, and perhaps stripped of his property or banished from his province.

Dio's benefactions in his last years, therefore, conform to a known pattern: but they also reveal many details of it. The physical monuments, above all, the inscriptions, tend to display only the bright side of benefaction, its honors and privileges: it is mainly the literary record that supplies the shadows. Nothing, for example, in the numerous inscriptions concerning Claudius Aristio of Ephesus shows that he was denounced to Trajan for his dangerous popularity: that is known only because Pliny was present at the hearing.[1] Dio's early speech on the bread riot at Prusa has shown the dangers that beset the wealthy in difficult times. His later Bithynian speeches reveal a progression from the acclaim of his first years after exile to the litigation and discord of his last.

Dio's initial popularity is shown by the *Speech of Greeting* (*Or.* 44), probably delivered on his return from the embassy to Trajan. The embassy had brought several benefits to Prusa, and the whole journey had enhanced his reputation in Rome and Greece. On his return Prusa expressed its public gratitude, and this speech, spoken before the assembly (10), is his reply. Dio begins with a refusal, or at least the polite show of one, of the honors offered by his citizens (1). Etiquette demanded that benefactors decline or moderate the rewards offered by grateful beneficiaries: the ritual whereby emperors deprecated measures for their own deification is merely the most conspicuous instance.[2] Dio affirms that his greatest pleasure is to see and hear the people (evidently chanting their acclamations), or to receive their honors and praise, even if he is praised by all the Greeks and the people of Rome (1): this last seems to allude to the success of his own recent journey. Nonetheless, he professes already to have every honor if he has the goodwill of his compatriots: so the emperor Tiberius had declined a temple by affirming that he already had temples in the hearts of his subjects.[3] Dio has no need of portraits (*eikones*),[4] proclamations, seats of honor, or even a "gold" statue placed "in the most distinguished sanctuaries" (2): it is implied that all these were now being offered to him by Prusa. The first three are comparatively common marks of honor. "Gold" statues, which were actually of gilded bronze, are much rarer:[5] however, it was customary to place an honorific statue in a distinguished shrine or temple.

If Dio must have such rewards, those granted to his forebears are enough. His father had received due thanks for guiding the city justly all his life, and his mother was granted a sacred image (*agalma*)[6] and shrine (*hieron*, 3). Deification, the highest honor a city could bestow, had become rare under the empire, when divine honors had largely been engrossed by the imperial family.[7] That it was granted to Dio's mother need not have been due to her father's eminence alone, for women too could be active in office and generosity: thus, Junia Theodora, a wealthy Lycian lady roughly contemporary with Dio's mother, performed many services for her compatriots and received half-divine honors at her death.[8] Like his mother and grandfather, other relatives of Dio received "many statues, public burial, commemorative games, and many other valuable things" (4). A public burial was a high privilege, characteristically granted to benefactors:[9] commemorative games are much rarer, since they recurred annually and thus committed the city to a permanent expense.[10] This whole passage reveals how single families, through many branches and generations, maintained traditions of public generosity.

Prusa was grateful even for what could not be attained. Dio's grandfather (presumably, his mother's father) would gladly have used his friendship with the reigning emperor to gain freedom for the city, but had too little time (5). The practice whereby Greeks used their influence with eminent Romans for the good of their city went back to the republic, and Dio's efforts for Prusa are in the same tradition:[11] here his emphasis on his grandfather's good intentions may have a personal motive, since for his own part he seems to have failed to win freedom for Prusa. Even now, however, the city has so many excellent citizens that it should not despair: Dio declines to name them, for almost all are his relatives and he does not wish to seem simply to be doing them a good turn (5). Again, his words suggest a society in which interrelated families were accustomed to control local politics, though the later opposition to him shows that his was not the only influential clan in Prusa.

Dio now turns to praising the city. It is no wonder that he prefers to live there than in one of the chief cities of Greece; though frequently invited, he has never thought of living elsewhere (6), just as bees never desert their hive, however unfavorable the situation and difficult the work (7). A slight flick of reproof is audible, as if Dio were threatening to abandon the city for another more welcoming. But he congratulates Prusa on its many fine young members, including his own son (8). It has long been reputed for the excellence of its citizens,[12] despite its small size and comparatively recent foundation (8–9): some of these have acquired fame elsewhere, others not at all inferior have remained to serve it (9). Here again Dio seems to suggest the possibility of his own departure.

He ends with an exhortation. The people should hope to receive from the emperors such gifts as only they can bestow, while striving to excel all others in discipline (eutaxia),[13] modesty, "obedience to good men," and all the other virtues (10). Such qualities are worth more than material goods, a large number of councillors, holding the assizes, new sources of income, and even freedom (11): for so-called freedom is given by Rome only sparingly, while the true kind, the conduct worthy of a free man, depends on the agent. To show that he has not neglected the city's interests, he reads the letter that he sent to Trajan when he was summoned, no doubt before his embassy, and the emperor's reply (12).[14] Once more there are undertones: Dio seems to have tried unsuccessfully to obtain Prusa's freedom, and his failure appears to have muted the elation of his return.

One of Dio's greatest benefactions to Prusa was the embassy that produced the other concessions mentioned in his speech. The employment of eminent men, especially cultured ones, as ambassadors was a common and ancient practice.[15] This embassy seems to have been prompted not only by the emperor's invitation but also by the city's gratitude for some favor, probably his support of Dio's new building. His enemies later charged that the emperor had met the deputation coldly and granted less than it asked; he had given Smyrna endless money and many gifts, including statues of the local goddesses, the twin Nemeseis; if someone other than Dio had led the delegation, he would have obtained "number-less councillors, a stream of gold . . ., and countless myriads" of drachmas. Dio retorts that the emperor had given him all that he asked.[16] Smyrna's success, which Dio's enemies used against him, may have resulted from the eloquent advocates it had as a capital of the Second Sophistic: a contemporary of Dio, the sophist Scopelian, was noted for the success of his embassies to emperors undertaken on its behalf.[17] The worship of twin Nemeseis was peculiar to Smyrna, and one of its principal cults: Trajan probably honored the goddesses by dedicating new statues of them.[18]

Dio does not deny that the ambassadors of Smyrna were more successful than he was: yet elsewhere he claims that only one city received benefactions equal to Prusa, and from his description it appears to be Miletus. If that is right, and he is not exaggerating, that is a measure of what was granted to Prusa: for Trajan undertook to rebuild the Sacred Way, which stretched for more than ten miles from Miletus to Didyma, and he also appears to have constructed a great fountainhouse for the city, the Nymphaeum.[19]

One of the benefits obtained by Dio's embassy concerned Prusa's council. Hitherto it had been restricted by the law of Pompey to a size which is not known, although it must have been in the hundreds: Trajan now permitted a further hundred councillors to be enrolled.[20] Though Dio is concerned only with his own benefactions, other cities of Bithynia were also allowed extra councillors, though not necessarily so many as Prusa.[21] This concession had a double effect: it increased a city's consequence, since size of council was an index of prosperity; and it increased its revenues, since Trajan evidently required that the new members pay a sum of money for the honor of election. When Antoninus Pius increased the council of a Macedonian city to eighty members, he required them to pay five hundred drachmas each for admission, so that the city would gain further prestige from the size of the council and further income from the money paid by the newly enrolled.[22] These payments for office (*summae honorariae*) or for membership of the council (*honoraria decurionatus*) were a common feature of the city life of the Roman empire: a man elected to a position like the eponymous magistracy, or enrolled in the council, was expected either to perform a service for the city, such as repairing a public building, or to pay cash for the city to put to a similar use.[23] It is a striking testimony to the attractive power of "reputation" that men were still willing to pay for office (though they might also hope to be compensated by the perquisites).

Another privilege, apparently only granted after the embassy had returned to Prusa, concerned the assizes. Hitherto Prusa had been "like a village," assigned to the district of another city: Dio's words are exaggerated, since Prusa had not been subjected to the other city, but they show how keenly the lack of this privilege was felt.[24] Prusa had tried to obtain it once before, but to the delight of its neighbors had been rebuffed by one of the "leaders" (*hegemones*); although this term may designate a proconsul, who would have refused to support the city's petition, it probably refers to an emperor.[25] Trajan now made Prusa the head of an assize-district, and a few years later Pliny dispensed justice there.[26] The benefits were several and immediate. Like the new councillors, the assizes caused "the people's prestige to be greater and the city to receive greater honor from visitors and from the government."[27] No more important, but more tangible, were the material advantages. The Prusans now "judged for themselves, and were not judged before others": as in the *Apamean*, Dio refers to the custom whereby governors or their deputies sat in judgment with an advisory panel of provincials: since these might naturally be drawn mainly from the assize-city, citizens of it had an advantage in litigation.[28] In addition, the city's revenues were increased:[29] the *Apamean* gave a vivid tableau of the crowds that thronged to the assizes and swelled the city's income. There, however, Dio spoke with an irony which is naturally not audible here.[30]

Just as Dio reminded the Apameans that this privilege was jealously contested, so he warns his citizens that their elevation "irks everybody else."[31] This competitiveness, together with considerations of convenience, tended to increase the number of assize-districts under the principate: not only Prusa, but several cities in neighboring Asia are known to have received assizes between the reigns of Augustus and Caracalla.[32] Dio does not say to which city the Prusans had previously gone for justice, and little is known about the Bithynian districts: but it may have been

Apamea.[33] Even if Apamea was a smaller city than Prusa, its status as a colony may have been enough to win it the assizes; and if it had now lost Prusa from its district, that would explain why Dio anticipated trouble for the ambassadors sent to thank Trajan when they sailed from Apamea.[34]

Dio may have obtained yet another favor for Prusa, though, if so, he does not mention it. Between Nero and Trajan, Prusa had issued no coins: it now began to do so again for a brief while, before relapsing into silence.[35] The emission of coinage, because it was coveted and expensive, was a privilege only granted by imperial permission, and one that an influential subject would request for his city.[36] It may not be coincidental that one of the types issued by Prusa under Trajan honors Olympian Zeus:[37] this, the chief god of the city, was also Dio's eponym, whom he celebrated in one of his most exalted speeches, the *Olympian*. So also Lucian alleges that the prophet Alexander of Abonuteichos, after obtaining permission from Marcus Aurelius for his city to issue coins, stamped on them the image of his own favorite gods.[38]

One privilege may have been denied. Freedom for a city remained as coveted under the empire as it had been under the republic, even though the rights it entailed were severely circumscribed.[39] The emperors continued to grant it down to the third century, but (with the exception of Nero) not very liberally. When Dio claims that his grandfather had tried to win it for Prusa and warns his audience of the difficulty of obtaining it, his words suggest that he had tried, or been expected, to do the same.[40] Trajan did not care for cities in so troubled a province as Bithynia to have more rights than necessary;[41] he may have felt that relaxation of Roman control in Prusa would only encourage faction and civic extravagance. If Dio made the request, it was refused.

By contrast, another project that Dio mentions was perhaps never meant to be carried out. He claims that he would have liked to unite other communities with Prusa, not only the villages within its territory but some cities as well: but knowing the obstacles, he had refrained from anything so ambitious.[42] By his comparison with Epaminondas and Theseus, Dio implies that his measure would have entailed the physical displacement of the surrounding population: he is not talking about a mere extension of Prusa's citizenship,[43] or an attempt to allay antagonism between the city and the surrounding villages.[44] Even in the imperial period so drastic a step is not inconceivable, though it would have required the emperor's support.[45] This vague ambition probably should be taken no more seriously than Dio's wish to join Ephesus and Smyrna in a "fraternal" bond with Nicomedia.[46]

One class of benefactions is conspicuously absent from the Prusan speeches: there is no word of gladiators, athletes, performing artists, and the like. This is not accidental. In the *Rhodian* Dio denounced the gladiatorial shows of Athens and Corinth; in the *Alexandrian* he mocks the addiction of his hearers to mimes, dancers, and tricksters.[47] One of his moral essays, the first *On Glory* (*Or.* 66), satirizes those who use such amusements to win renown in their cities. The temptation that incites them is some worthless "bait," a branch (*thallos*),[48] a crown, or a headband (*taenia*, 2): all three are well known compensations of civic benefactors.[49] Though Dio elsewhere prides himself on his grandfather, who had bankrupted himself in public service,[50] here he mocks those who do so for such paltry honors (2–3). Such is the power of glory that the same purple robe costs two or three minae (eight or twelve hundred sesterces) from the dyers, but many talents (one talent was worth twenty-four thousand sesterces) from the people; a headband costs a few drachmas (five would be twenty sesterces) in the market, while in the assembly it often costs a man's whole estate; the benefactor and the bankrupt are alike "proclaimed," the one in the theater, the other by the auctioneer (4). Dio mocks athletes who died in competition for the worthless wild-olive, the prize at the Olympic games (5): the same contest is mentioned with more respect in the *Rhodian*.[51] He reproves those who spend extravagantly to win the crown of pine at the Isthmia (5): here the reference is doubtless to the musical competitions which were now so important at this festival.[52] A man seeking the people's favor has to buy endless food and wine for public feasts, to assemble "pipers, mimes, cithara-players, tricksters, and in addition boxers, pancratiasts, wrestlers, runners and such like, if he is to feast the people without shame or meanness"(8). The contemporary passion for such entertainers is shown by the honors they received in so Hellenic a city as Delphi;[53] like Dio's benefactor, a citizen of Priene obtained entertainers from abroad and a famous pantomime for a public dinner.[54] Dio's lover of glory has to spend five talents on "an Amoebeus or a Polus" (respectively a citharode and an actor of proverbial fame)[55] or on an Olympic victor. This sum, just under a quarter of a million sesterces, is well within the upper range attested by inscriptions for the price of shows.[56]

As often, Dio expresses a taste common at least to the more reflective members of his class. Plutarch voices the same aversion for those benefactors who "drag the people by the belly" with their gifts of food or cash, and who assemble dancers of the pyrrhic (an elaborate ballet) or gladiators.[57] Similar sentiments are expressed by fourth-century Christian bishops who deplore the "vainglory" of the rich.[58] But while educated taste abhorred benefactions intended solely to glorify the donor and amuse the mob, it approved those which brought honor to a man's city: that was patriotism, not selfish ambition. Thus, Plutarch praises the magistrate who supervises building projects for his city:[59] the emperor Antoninus Pius commends an Ephesian who chose "not the usual way of politicians, who for the sake of immediate glory squander their generosity on spectacles, distributions, or the giving of games, but a means whereby he hopes to make the city more august."[60]

It is not, therefore, surprising that the benefaction which recurs most frequently in Dio's speeches is his gift of a portico. The cities of the empire depended heavily on their wealthy for the provision of their public buildings, and the long tale of Dio's portico reveals much about this aspect of civic life. On returning to Prusa from exile, he determined to advertise his public spirit with an ambitious project. His immediate impulse was in a letter of Trajan which he brought with him expressing the emperor's desire for the improvement of Prusa.[61] The emperors frequently gave such encouragement to benefactors, either by approval and goodwill,[62] or more practically by donations of money.[63] The fact that Prusa immediately sent an embassy to "thank" Trajan suggests that his support was more than passive; and the embassy, led by Dio, obtained new revenues for the city, which may also have been intended to further new construction.[64] Later Dio was to compare Trajan's gifts to Prusa with his generosity to Miletus; and his benefactions to Heraclea by Salbace in Caria, made in honor of his doctor and chronicler, are another index of what Prusa may have received.[65]

The motives that impelled Dio to his proposal were various. A primary one must have been the desire to make Prusa the equal of other cities and a more suitable setting for himself: hitherto it had been ugly, and continued to be despite his efforts.[66] There was also the stimulus of competition. Antioch and Tarsus, Smyrna and Ephesus were building rapidly; so were Nicomedia, Nicaea, and, nearer to Prusa, even the minor city of Caesarea.[67] Emulation of other cities was frequently a spur to public construction,[68] and, despite his Stoicism, Dio was not immune.

Because the erection of public buildings readily led to extravagance or malpractice, it was closely controlled by the Roman authorities, and Dio's proposal was duly submitted to the proconsul even before it was mentioned in public. By Dio's account, the proconsul gave not only permission but encouragement, and summoned a meeting of the assembly to which he read out the plan: though taken by surprise, Dio spoke up in support.[69] It is striking to observe a proconsul so closely involved in civic affairs, and even convening an assembly: at a later stage another proconsul attended one of its meetings and was expected to examine the accounts of the construction.[70]

Dio's benefaction took a form well known from legal texts and inscriptions, that of an official "promise" (*hyposchesis*).[71] A citizen undertook to construct or repair a public building, sometimes gratuitously, often on condition of his election to office. He thus became liable to an obligation of which the terms were precisely defined in Roman law: one of these, which was to affect Dio, stipulated that a promised building once begun must be completed.[72] Dio's promise does not seem to have been conditional on any reward for himself, but there were several other terms.[73] He was to contribute from his own funds and be the official curator; but there was also to be support from other subscribers and from public funds.[74] Though he gave the citizens every opportunity to decline the scheme by bringing it forward in the council house and theater, it was fully ratified by the city and by the Roman authorities.[75]

As curator of the project, Dio was directly involved in all the details of its construction, and he even "made a laborious journey to the mountains," no doubt to select marble; so also Plutarch performed menial tasks for Chaeronea.[76] Soon the work became entangled in petty politics, and opposition grew as old buildings were swept away. Dio at first claimed to have knocked down only an old smithy.[77] Later he rebuts the imputation of having destroyed "monuments and sacred buildings": the same had been done in other famous cities, and in Nicomedia a certain Macrinus, "whom you inscribed as a benefactor of the city," had displaced the monuments of King Prusias.[78] At one point the resistance became so strong that subscriptions and construction temporarily ceased, and the people clamored that the building should be either completed or torn down: so also in Thera, when a public stoa began to go to ruin, "there were often clamors from the whole people" for its repair.[79]

By the time of the speech delivered when Varenus Rufus was proconsul (*Or.* 48), so about 105, the city was in crisis. The cause was evidently Dio's portico, which was still incomplete (11–12). The people clamored for the subscribers to pay what they had promised (11); and there were suspicions that some of those in charge of the work had embezzled public moneys (9). Such peculation was evidently common, since public building was usually entrusted to the wealthy few.[80] This bred resentment in the lower classes, which were usually denied access to office and could only express themselves by outcry. At Prusa the assembly had become so turbulent that it had been forbidden to meet, perhaps, though not certainly, by Varenus himself: Dio's speech was given just when the ban had been lifted. He urges the people to be grateful to the governor for restoring the assembly: "you should put off the other things you were shouting about since he will inspect the public accounts himself, even if you wish to prevent him" (2). It would be better if the people made their own attempt to recover the public moneys, and not resort to the proconsul unless they fail (3): Plutarch expresses similar dislike of resort to outside authority.[81]

Dio's chief arguments, as is natural in a society so concerned with reputation, are aimed at the city's self-respect. Mutual recrimination lowers the citizens in the eyes of their neighbors (4) and the authorities (5). The attack on the wealthy had inevitably pitched the assembly against the council, as in Tarsus and Nicaea: Dio's retort eloquently expresses the difference in the social composition of the two bodies. The members of the council are the leaders of the city: "if your superiors are bad, what must one think of the rest?" (9). "Is it not you who often praise us for the whole day, calling some 'excellent,' others 'Olympians,' others 'saviors,' others 'nourishers'?" (10). All these titles of benefactors are independently attested on inscriptions, some of them from Bithynia;[82] it was still customary in the fourth century for these acclamations to continue from morn till night.[83]

It is unclear whether another speech of Dio before the assembly (*Or.* 47) is earlier or later than the previous. Here he is less conciliatory and speaks with little reserve of his disappointment and fatigue. He invokes the example of Aristotle, who used his influence with Philip and Alexander to rebuild his native village and yet was accused by his enemies before "the king and the visiting satraps" (9): this suggests that Dio's opponents had gone to the proconsuls and the emperor.[84] Instead of trying to shield his colleagues and calm the mob, Dio now points to others who have erected public buildings without giving an account, or have taken money from the magistrates "like a bottomless jar" for interminable projects; he is even ready to approach the proconsul and ask him to compel the subscribers to pay their share (19).

It is the younger Pliny, and not Dio, who gives the last information about his building. On arriving in the province Pliny immediately set to inspecting Prusa's accounts, and as Trajan had anticipated found that much public money was held by citizens: it is not known if Dio was one of the guilty, though some of those involved with his portico had been suspected of embezzlement earlier.[85] The next year citizens of Prusa accused Dio before Pliny on two charges concerning a building which must be his portico.[86] Having completed it on the city's behalf, he was accused of attempting to terminate his responsibility before the accounts were inspected; moreover, he had allegedly included in the building a statue of the emperor and tombs of his wife and son, thus exposing himself to a charge of treason.[87] The latter Trajan dismissed with contempt, but he insisted that Dio's accounts be inspected. It is clear that Dio had at last finished his portico, and that his enemies, having failed to halt it, tried to make one last use of it in their vendetta. It is not known what the results of Pliny's investigation were, but it is hard to believe that they did not favor Dio. The emperor had encouraged his gifts, summoned his embassy, and already dismissed one of the charges against him: the emperor's legate was not likely to find him guilty. The culture of the age lifted the eloquent and the clever to a position from which they could defy Roman governors: Dio's position with Trajan is exactly parallel to that of Philostratus' sophists, who "conversed with gods as their equals."[88]

13
Trajan

The presence of the emperor Trajan can be felt in many of Dio's works, especially the Prusan speeches. Trajan looms largest, however, in the four pieces *On Kingship*, which an ancient editor placed at the head of the collection. As this position implies, late antiquity considered them Dio's masterpieces, and they influenced Julian,[1] Themistius,[2] Synesius,[3] and others.[4]

These works raise several problems. In none of them is Trajan or any other emperor named; it is only an inference, though a virtually certain one, that they were written in his reign. Only two of the pieces, the first and third, are in the form of addresses to an emperor, while the second and fourth recount imaginary dialogues between historical figures. On the one hand, it is possible that those which purport to have been spoken before the emperor were not really so: on the other, though Dio's second and fourth pieces are cast as narratives of dialogue, they may yet have been spoken, and even spoken before the emperor.[5] The greatest problem raised by these works concerns their purpose. On one view, they simply adopt traditional Greek ideas to conform with the prevailing circumstances:[6] on another, they are "not only a registration of existing facts but, first and foremost, an exposition of eternal norms which must be accepted or rejected by Trajan."[7]

The real Trajan is elusive.[8] Before the general eye he paraded an image of bluff practicality, a pleased but uncomprehending patron of the gentle, and especially the Greek, arts. This is the Trajan who, in Philostratus' anecdote, "took Dio in the golden chariot in which the emperors lead the processions returning from war, and often turning to him said, 'What you are saying I do not know, but I love you as myself.' "[9] The historian Cassius Dio was nearer to the truth when he called Trajan a man "not highly cultured as far as words went, but who thought and acted like a person of culture."[10] The real Trajan evidently spoke Greek;[11] he knew the Greek lands from his earlier service in Syria and (probably) in Asia. The key to his character is perhaps that yearning for "glory," which, as Dio's speeches show, was still a powerful force in the thought and manners of the ancient world.[12] This desire led him, as it led many others, to adopt historical models for imitation: among Romans, Julius Caesar, among Greeks, one whom Caesar had himself emulated and been compared to, Alexander of Macedon. As emperor, Trajan conducted wars in Dacia and Parthia: Alexander had begun his conquests by a campaign on the lower Danube and went on to conquer Persia, while Caesar died contemplating the same conquests made by Trajan.[13] So far from regarding literature with amused tolerance, Trajan ensured that his reign and conquests would be celebrated directly or indirectly by a flourishing of Greek and Latin letters. For a Tacitus or a Pliny, favor and freedom were a sufficient inducement: for others, especially Greeks, the rewards were more material. Trajan promoted Dio's native Prusa as he promoted the little Heraclea of southeastern Caria, the home of his doctor and chronicler Crito; and it may also be argued that he benefited the shrine of Delphi, where Plutarch was a priest.[14]

On the question of whether these four works are ceremonial or convey positive advice, the first, (*Or.* 1), is particularly eloquent. Dio begins by comparing himself to the musician Timotheus, who played before Alexander (1–8); he then undertakes to describe "the customs and the disposition of the good king" (9–36); next he portrays "the first and greatest of kings and rulers, Zeus" (37–47); he ends by recounting a myth of Heracles which is evidently modeled on a famous story about the hero told by the sophist Prodicus:[15] given the choice between Kingship and Tyranny, Heracles chooses Kingship and will favor the emperor and his empire as long as he too remains a king (48–84).

In the opening section the reference to Alexander flatters Trajan's devotion to him, and by comparing himself to Alexander's favorite musician, Dio artfully suggests his own influence with the emperor. When Dio begins to describe the "good king," this ideal figure again turns out to have a distinct resemblance to Trajan. This king calls his soldiers "comrades" (22): so Pliny in his *Panegyric* praises the emperor for being both "commander and comrade" to his troops.[16] Dio's king is a fathe. to his subjects, who "does not like to be called master of his own slaves, let alone of free men" (22): so too Pliny avers that all speak of Trajan not as their master, but as their father.[17] Dio's king does not corrupt his soldiers with idleness (28): Pliny congratulates Trajan on "rekindling the lapsed fire of military discipline."[18]

Because rulers were so commonly equated with Zeus, the description of the god which follows might not seem fitted to Trajan in particular. Nevertheless, this was the god with whom Trajan was most commonly identified.[19] A conspicuous monument of this assimilation is found at Pergamum, where a splendid temple was built for Trajan and the Zeus of Friendship (*Philios*), and a new festival founded in their joint honor.[20] In this same section of Dio's speech the appellation "Philios" is heavily emphasized, and the theme of the good king's reliance on friends and advisers recurs throughout the work.[21] It is not by chance that Dio's words seem to find an echo in Pergamum, or that Pliny's *Panegyric* also praises Trajan's reliance on his friends;[22] all are inspired by the wishes of the emperor.

The last section of the speech, containing the myth of Heracles' choice, is equally designed to gratify the ruler. Trajan had a personal attachment to Heracles: the hero starts to appear on his coins in the year 100, and about the same time he became the emblem of a new legion, the Second Traiana, probably raised for the first Dacian war.[23] The reason for this attachment is revealed by the legend on the coins, *Hercules Gaditanus*, since the hero had a famous temple at Gades (modern Cadiz), the religious capital of Trajan's native Baetica.[24] Trajan's adoption of Heracles as his "helper" also asserted his own proximity to Zeus, the hero's father and king of the gods; it honored Alexander, who was supposedly descended from Heracles; and generally it symbolized the emperor's program of arduous toil and selfless devotion to the good of mankind.

Dio's Heracles is more, however, than a symbol of Trajan's rule, but is also his prototype and avatar. The orator zealously corrects the view that Heracles was a mere king of Argos, or that he traveled the world unaccompanied: rather, he ruled the whole world from sunrise to sunset, visiting every place where there are now temples to him. Dio's audience knew that Roman emperors claimed the same world-rule;[25] and they could not have failed to think of a temple of Heracles in the far west, in which stood a statue of Alexander once admired by Julius Caesar.[26] Dio's Heracles was simply educated, not trained by sophists and other such wretches; so too Trajan affected a Roman simplicity, though prepared to listen to a Greek who saw himself as the enemy of sophists. In the same vein Dio explains Heracles' lionskin and club as symbols of self-denial and his generosity to his friends; he carefully demonstrates that he cannot have traveled alone, but can only have taken cities and overthrown tyrants with an army (59–63). It is evident that the figure with the club and lionskin is Trajan, just as a famous bust shows Commodus in the same dress.[27]

Another way in which Dio covertly praises Trajan is by his implicit criticism of another emperor, Domitian. The many references to the emperor's friendliness are meant as a contrast to his predecessor's reserve. When Dio and Pliny praise Trajan for refusing the name of "master," they think of Domitian, who gave offence by claiming the title as his due.[28] When Dio observes that a bad man cannot be king, "even if the birds of the air and the beasts of the mountains" obey him (14), that is another hit at Domitian, for whom his flatterers had made this very claim.[29] The criticism of monarchs who abuse the power delegated to them by Zeus (46) is aimed at Domitian, who had been hailed as the earthly Jupiter.[30] Above all, the closing myth of Heracles' choice symbolically contrasts the reigns of the two emperors. For Dio and others Domitian was "the tyrant" personified;[31] Trajan is a king, and will have Heracles' protection so long as he remains one (84). Once more Pliny and Dio form a chorus: in the *Panegyric*, Trajan's services for Domitian strike the same chill into his lord as did Heracles' into Eurystheus, and, like Dio's Heracles, Pliny's Trajan is benevolently protected by Jupiter.[32]

These coincidences between Pliny and Dio, and especially their references to Heracles, suggest that they are prompted by more than common friendship with Trajan. There is no evidence that one influenced the other; rather, they express the ideology of a particular time.[33] Pliny's *Panegyric* was originally delivered in 100; the same year appears, for independent reasons, to be that of Dio's first visit to Trajan's Rome.[34] It may be inferred that Dio's speech is likewise of this year[35] and that its similarity to Pliny's *Panegyric* reflects the time of its delivery. This was Trajan's third consulate; at the end of the previous year he had entered Rome for the first time as emperor; at the beginning of the next he was to set out for Dacia. There he was to encounter the formidable Decebalus, whom

Domitian had fought in vain.[36] The era of "tyranny" was over and a new "age" had begun. The pretended sloth of the previous era was to be shaken off, as Rome stirred at last from its slumbers.[37] One result of that sloth had been a disgraceful compromise with Decebalus, for it was natural for a tyrant to tolerate a tyrant; now a "king" was to go forth like a new Heracles, ridding the world of terrors. Trajan was not receiving directions from Dio and Pliny: by their coincidences, among them their coinciding claims to frankness and spontaneity, they are revealed as the servants of his wishes.

The second piece *On Kingship*, (*Or.* 2), recounts an imaginary dialogue between Philip and Alexander of Macedon, in which the young prince maintains that Homer is the best, or rather the only, poet for kings. Much of the argument turns on Homer's portrayal of Achilles (14–32); the last main section expounds his comparison of Agamemnon with a bull (66–74). The exaltation of Alexander and the discussion of kingship show that the work was intended for Trajan, whether or not it was delivered as a speech before him; the date is indeterminable.[38]

This ingenious piece does not seem to formulate "eternal norms." The notion of Homer as a tutor of princes was an old one: Dio has cleverly combined it with another tradition, Alexander's worship of Homer, which he was supposed to have expressed by his emulation of Achilles.[39] As in the prologue to the first piece, Alexander is introduced out of compliment to Trajan; and just as Dio made his way in there disguised as the musician Timotheus, so here he appears as the Aristotle on whose behalf Philip and Alexander rebuilt Stagira (79).[40] As Kingship and Tyranny in the first piece symbolized the contrast between Trajan and Domitian, so it is probably not fanciful here to see the same contrast implied in Dio's discourse on the bull. Domitian seems to be the bad bull, which "despises and savages its own herd, yields to the attacks of outsiders, and sacrifices the helpless multitude" (73): Trajan is the good bull, "bold and fearless against beasts, majestic, able to defend and lead the herd" (74).

The third piece, (*Or.* 3), is the most remote of the four from actual circumstances, though even here certain details can have been meant only for Trajan. Like the first, it is a speech purportedly delivered before the emperor; from the degree of intimacy with him which Dio claims, it seems to be the later of the two in date, but again no precision is possible.[41] The speech begins with what is in effect an encomium of Trajan (1–11); Dio pauses to defend himself against the suspicion of flattery (12–24); when he returns to the subject, he pretends to protect himself against such suspicions by devoting the rest of the speech to the ideal king (25–138). The first section scarcely conceals its flattery of the emperor; and the defensiveness of the second, perhaps prompted by the criticism of rivals, suggests that Dio's earlier addresses to the emperor had been understood in the same way. Even when Dio speaks generally of the ideal king, however, he gives him features curiously like those of the real Trajan. Two of these are especially notable. One is the description of the good king's toils on behalf of his subjects and his empire (55–85): so also in the first speech Trajan's Herculean image was meant to convey the same notion of a hero toiling endlessly for the good of all mankind. Within this same section, Dio makes a striking comparison between this man of sorrows and the ever-watchful, ever-traveling sun, whose power and philanthropy the good ruler must imitate (73–82). The comparison of rulers with the sun was very old, and more commonly used as a metaphor for their glory or justice: it is characteristic that Dio has adapted the traditional idea to the Trajanic ideology of Herculean toil.[42] The other feature of the good king that particularly resembles the official Trajan is his dependence on friends (86–122), which was also emphasized in the first of these works and in Pliny's *Panegyric*. Here too, therefore, is "a registration of existing facts," or at least of the approved version of the facts; Dio is not holding out to the emperor "eternal norms." It is the existing emperor, not an ideal one, of whom Dio is thinking when he declares, "The good king considers hunting an excellent institution, and takes the greatest pleasure in it; it makes his body stronger, his soul braver, and trains him in every martial art" (135). This same item turns up in Pliny's *Panegyric* as an attribute of Trajan; actually hunting was a favorite sport in Spain, particularly in Baetica, and Trajan and Hadrian were notorious devotees.[43] Thus, even in an apparently trifling detail the model king is himself modeled on Trajan.

The fourth piece *On Kingship*, (*Or.* 4), like the second, is a dialogue of which one partner is Alexander of Macedon: the other, however, is the Cynic Diogenes. This time Alexander is the newly crowned king, about to undertake his expedition to Persia: and the burden of Diogenes' discourse is that the true king must be his own ruler and gain mastery over his impulses before attempting to conquer other men. The latter part of the work consists of Diogenes' depiction of three spirits, the voluptuary, the miser, and the lover of glory; he promises to tell of a fourth spirit, which combines true education and reason and must be that of the perfect monarch, but before this promise is fulfilled the piece breaks off.

The work may not originally have ended so abruptly, but these enigmatic endings are of a piece with Dio's studiously unstudied style.[44]

Besides the peculiar close, the date of the work raises a difficulty. Once more, the introduction of Alexander suggests Trajan's reign.[45] It has been argued that the reference to Alexander's eastern campaign covertly alludes to Trajan's Parthian war, and that the whole work indirectly criticizes it; if so, it cannot have been delivered before the emperor, but rather before an audience of Greeks.[46] The love of glory criticized by Dio's Diogenes was thought by some to have been Trajan's chief motive for undertaking his expedition; and the emperor was conscious of traveling in Alexander's path.[47] However, since the subject of Alexander inevitably evoked that of his most notable campaign, it is not necessary to suppose that Dio refers to contemporary Parthia; the question of his intention must be answered from the speech.

On inspection the contents do not appear very different from those of the other three pieces, except that this one defines the ideal king negatively rather than positively. The first main section argues that the true king does not go to war simply for his own glory; he is a shepherd of his flock, and "a shepherd's task is the safety and preservation of his sheep" (44). This is not far from the good bull of the second piece, "able to defend and lead the herd." With his present disposition Alexander will not be made a true king by conquering Babylon (53): this is the Stoic doctrine that "only the wise man is king," which was also implied in the tale of Heracles' choice in the first piece. Just as Domitian was covertly criticized there in the figure of Tyranny, so several aspects of him appear to be embodied in the three "spirits" here: for sensuality, avarice, and vaingloriousness are all vices which the later tradition ascribed to him.[48] Even if in the published version Dio did not proceed to describe the fourth "spirit," which combined "culture and reason," it may be guessed that this figure was meant to suggest Trajan, just as the same two qualities are ascribed to the unnamed emperor in the *Alexandrian*. The Alexander of this work, boyish and impulsive, is not a portrait of Trajan: rather, Trajan is an Alexander grown to maturity, and led by a wise mentor in the paths of "culture and reason."

Two other brief works of Dio are relevant to the purpose of the pieces *On Kingship*. In the dialogue called *Agamemnon* (*Or.* 56) the main speaker argues that true kings are not irresponsible, but take advice as Agamemnon did from Nestor. It might be supposed that Dio criticizes the Roman emperors, if not Trajan in particular, for their lack of responsibility.[49] Most of the emperors, however, made a show of deferring to the senate and their advisers; Trajan's reliance on his friends has been seen to be one of his most conspicuously advertised virtues.[50] Like the first and third speeches *On Kingship*, this seems artfully to praise Trajan by assimilating him to a Homeric king; and just as Dio appeared earlier in the guise of Timotheus and Aristotle, so here he may be present in the guise of Nestor.

The next piece in the collection is actually entitled *Nestor* (*Or.* 57), and here Dio unequivocally compares himself with the Homeric sage. His text is a sentence spoken by Nestor, "In my time I have talked with better men than you." Dio's listeners (probably fellow citizens) must be patient when he recites his own speeches given before the emperor; they should not think him boastful, but be eager to know whether his words were beneficial to mankind (11). From this claim it does not follow, however, that the discourses *On Kingship* were intended to convey serious advice. The speeches of course express the pious hope that the emperor will be guided by them: Dio's myth in the first is a "holy and beneficial tale," and his discourse on the ideal king is as appropriate for an emperor as a discourse on health would be for a doctor or on the stars for a pilot.[51] It suited Trajan to be ostentatiously attentive to learned Greeks: "what you are saying I do not know, but I love you as myself." Dio was not going to question the etiquette, especially when his listeners chafed at hearing about his influence with the emperor.

It was not without reason that an ancient editor followed the pieces *On Kingship* and the connected *Libyan Tale* with the five "Diogenes speeches" (*Or.* 6–10). They may belong to the same period;[52] and the first of them, which is concerned with tyranny, recalls the myth of Heracles' choice. Just as Tyranny there seemed to represent Domitian, so the same emperor is suggested by Dio's picture of the Persian king, trembling in ceaseless dread of assassination; like Tyranny, and unlike Trajan, Dio's tyrant "cannot hope for goodwill or friendship from anyone."[53]

Other works now lost seem from their titles to have resembled the pieces *On Kingship* and may have been written to gratify Trajan. One was an *Encomium of Heracles against Plato*, evidently reproving the philosopher for the levity with which he often treats the hero.[54] The other was a work in eight books *On the Virtues of Alexander*; this too may be connected with Trajan, though the character of Alexander had long been a matter of learned dispute.[55]

Another work, the lost *Getica*, or *Getic History*,[56] might have told much about Dio's relations with Trajan. This traced the history of the people more usually known as Dacians, apparently from their earliest beginnings to the author's own day. It appears to have been written, or at least completed, after Domitian's death in 96, for a passage that may be derived from it speaks of him unflatteringly.[57] It is not necessary, however, to suppose that it was published soon after that date.[58] Whether or not Dio accompanied Trajan to the front in 101, the natural conclusion for a *Getic History* composed under Trajan was, not Domitian's inglorious compromise, but the new monarch's victory and triumph.

If that is right, Dio's *Getica* belong to a whole harvest of literature produced by the Dacian wars. The emperor set the example with his own account, written like the *Commentaries* of Julius Caesar in a style that was military and spare.[59] A friend of Pliny's began to struggle with a Greek epic on the subject.[60] As Dio may have done, Trajan's doctor Crito accompanied him to the front and chronicled the campaigns in a work with the same title as Dio's, *Getica*.[61] Both men were part of the literary flowering of the new age; and the benefactions that Trajan made to their cities advertised his celebrated friendship and rewarded their services on his behalf. It may even be true that, as Philostratus alleges, Dio traveled with Trajan in one of his two Dacian triumphs: a closer connection between the emperor's military glory and his patronage of literature could not have been devised.[62]

Dio's last years saw him restored to a position seemingly higher even than the one he had enjoyed under Vespasian and Titus; and as he had then praised an athlete favored at court, so now he praised the emperor. His works exemplify the way a benevolent monarchy can mold opinion. Largely through Dio, Trajan transmitted to posterity a picture of himself as the ideal king. How far Dio expressed his true sentiments of the emperor is beyond investigation: but it will not readily be assumed that so sedulous a supporter of the ruling monarch was a covert critic of the empire he ruled. Dio's view of Trajan is, therefore, relevant to his view of Rome.

14
Rome

In all of Dio's major speeches, even the frivolous-seeming *Trojan*, there is always in the background the presence of Rome. His attitude toward Rome unites all of his works which concern his age; but it is also a topic with many aspects. There is the actual city, which might be regarded as the acme of beauty and convenience or the sink of vice.[1] As the capital of an empire, it stood for the power that governed much, or by a frequent conceit all, of the known world. Without ever having been there, many had attained the franchise for service in the army or by other means, so that Rome was the badge of the upper layers of society. It was inseparable from the constitutional system whereby one man was simultaneously first citizen and supreme commander: Rome was the seat of the emperors, and was often worshiped beside them. Finally, Rome was characterized by its own history and culture, and for the Greeks even the language and literature of the ruling power was "Roman," not "Latin."

Rome was conventionally contrasted with Greece, as conqueror, rival, or partner. Yet Greece too was many things. As a geographical term it embraced every land in which Greek was the predominant language.[2] Like Rome, Greece also stood for a history and a culture. Unlike the Romans, however, the Greeks had to look far back into the past for their political supremacy, and even for their greatest art; they did so with such persistence not just from resentful pride, but because their achievements gave them a unity and spiritual nationhood that compensated for their

dispersion in space and time. Rome and Greece were not mutually exclusive, but as the two major cultures within a single empire, they could
not but attract and repel each other. On the Greek side a spectrum of attitudes towards Rome ranges from ill-concealed hostility to uncritical ac-
ceptance. Like other writers of his time, Dio's position falls between the
two extremes.

The most vocal center of exclusive Hellenism was the city which
ranked second to Rome in size and importance, Alexandria. The Alexandrians remembered that theirs was the last of the Hellenistic kingdoms
to fall before Rome, and even those who were not hostile to Rome could
talk proudly of the Ptolemies as "their" kings.[3] Others were led by this
spirit of independence to open contumacy, and their devastating ex-
changes with Roman prefects and emperors were recorded (or embel-
lished) in widely circulating pamphlets.[4] In one, a hearing before Trajan
is terminated by a miracle that throws Rome into panic; in another, a
victim of Roman tyranny is led to execution in the crown and white shoes
of a Greek gymnasiarch.[5] This literature does not overtly inculcate rebellion or apostasy, though it comes as close as a mere narrative can; to
come closer would have been unsafe, and was unnecessary in a city that
traditionally resisted the legitimate emperors or supported their rivals. In
addition, it was a favorite haunt of Cynics, and the extreme edges of this
school readily shaded into hatred of Rome; it was an Alexandrian who
taught Peregrinus Proteus, an ardent Hellene and advocate of rebellion.[6]
Alexandria was not the only center of such views, but is made notable by
the preservation of papyri: Antioch may have been similar, and Athens
may occasionally have toyed with rebellion.[7]

Other Greeks embraced the institutions and ways of Rome without
hesitation: these were perhaps the majority of the wealthy and the mod-
erately wealthy, eager for fortune and position. The lone Olbian who
shaved in order to display his friendship with the Romans may be a creature of Dio's fancy;[8] but Dio would not have pretended that he was
unique in Olbia unless his type was commoner in less old-fashioned cities.
Greeks eager for "repute" were inevitably drawn to Rome and the ca-
reers it offered, and as inevitably incurred the censure of their less worldly
compatriots. Dio mocks the vanity of those who paraded as Asiarchs, the
provincial priests of the emperor; but he mocked in vain, for this was a
step that could raise a man's descendants to senatorial status.[9] Plutarch
deplores the Greeks who scrambled for positions as Roman senators or
administrators: but he too opposed an ever-rising tide.[10] If this was the

attitude of the "first" people, it was not surprising that the cities they had guided should abandon their Hellenic traditions, as Rhodes defaced its antique statues and Athens defiled the theater of Dionysus with the blood of gladiators.

There are three Greeks of the reign of Trajan whose attitudes toward Rome can be compared, Dio, Plutarch, and Epictetus. They do not represent one school of thought, and even when they are in accord are not necessarily typical of one class; all three are philosophers, and philosophers may disagree among themselves and with even the educated views of the day. The ex-slave Epictetus might be thought likely to be the most sympathetic to Cynicism of the three, and the least influenced in his view of Rome by material benefits received from the emperors. Like Dio, he lightly mocks those who paraded in the trappings of their imperial priesthood; like Plutarch, he criticizes those who cannot resist the lure of office at Rome.[11] But though he censures many aspects of Roman life, for example, the exaltation of material wealth,[12] he affirms the necessity of Roman rule: a man born "in the ruling city" and of the ruling class has public obligations which he must fulfill.[13] Though Epictetus is theoretically closer to Cynicism than either Dio or Plutarch, he is also less ardently Hellenic. In a Cynic like Peregrinus, Hellenism could be a call to rebellion; but in Dio and Plutarch, one or probably both of whom were Roman knights, it is a mark of high education, and this was the property of those who derived the most advantages from Roman rule.

By contrast with Epictetus, Plutarch comes the closest of the three to a positive enthusiasm for Rome. It is true that he deplores many aspects of it: the inhumanity, tastelessness, or vulgar opulence which were the result of excessive riches. But his interest in Roman institutions and history, and his goodwill toward the Rome of the present, are evident. At the same time he feels an intense pride in the past of Greece and a keen consciousness of his country's decline. His Hellenism is more contemplative and less vocal than Dio's, though that may be because he is an essayist and not a speaker. Like one another, they could reconcile their Greek patriotism with goodwill toward Rome, and received the favor of Trajan.

Dio is more mercurial than Plutarch, and it is not easy to penetrate to his real views; for example, he assures the Rhodians that theirs "exceeds all cities but one," and the Alexandrians that theirs is "the second under the sun."[14] Addressing the proudly Hellenic Nicaea, he seems to allude to Rome as a city founded by outcasts; when in Ilion, Rome's mythical ancestor, or Apamea, one of its colonies, he eulogizes its history and institutions.[15] It is best, therefore, to assess his view of Rome from those works in which it is not adjusted to please an audience.

In the speech on the bread riot (*Or.* 46), he claims never to have accused others of occupying property belonging to Caesar (8); and to bring his compatriots to order, he reminds them of the watch kept on the cities "as over naughty children" by the emperor and his agents (14). Here at least there is nothing offensive or subversive. The Roman watch on the cities was welcomed by right-thinking citizens as a check on the unruly mob; and when Dio or Plutarch compares the cities to children, they reprove the Greeks for their childishness, not the Romans for paternalism.[16]

The *Rhodian* oration (*Or.* 31) has been thought to express hostility, or at least coldness, toward Rome; but, overtly at least, the speech contains nothing that could not have been spoken by a supporter of the ruling power.[17] Dio's exaltation of Hellenic culture might, however, suggest a deeper purpose, a desire to fan the embers of Greek resistance to barbarism. His aim is not to assimilate culture and politics, but to distinguish them. The Rhodians will not earn disfavor by being Hellenes, but by the opposite, abandoning the freedom and fearlessness of their ancestors.[18] Conversely, Dio mocks the unlucky philhellenism of Nero, his Olympic ambitions (110) and the passion for Greek art which made him plunder the great shrines (148–150). If the *Rhodian* has a deeper message, it is not anti-Roman. Philhellenism in an emperor was no virtue if it led to excess or vice; but Greeks who abandoned their traditions deserved only scorn, especially those who should have been the most Hellenic of all, the Athenians.

In the *Alexandrian* (*Or.* 32), which is perhaps contemporary, Dio's sympathies are with Rome. The Romans are the benevolent guardians of the city, the Alexandrians are unruly "children." Once more Nero is contrasted unfavorably with the present emperor: the citizens' passion for citharody and chariot-racing will do them as little good as Nero's did him, and the present ruler's "culture and reason" are a better model. Acquiescence in Roman rule is not treachery toward the Hellenic past; a morbid passion for Greek arts is no substitute for virtue, either in Greeks or Romans.

In the dialogue *On Beauty* (*Or.* 21), which may belong to the period of Dio's exile,[19] he speaks more harshly of Rome than anywhere else. "Whenever they have to choose a king, they choose the wealthiest person and the one from whom they expect the most money"(8): they only reluctantly deposed Nero (9), and even now they all wish he were still alive (10). In part this is a position assumed for the sake of argument, since the speaker is accused of "always trying to disparage humanity" (10). Nevertheless, it may for once represent a sincere, if only temporary, view of Dio's: it would not be surprising if poverty and exile had made him contemptuous of Roman greed, and he later claims to have spoken out against the vices of Domitian's rule.[20] Dio's dislike of Nero, however, is not a passing mood: unlike other Greeks, Plutarch, for example, he never speaks of the emperor except to condemn him.[21]

The topic of materialism recurs often in Dio's late speeches, but here Rome is not his only target. The parable of the gold-digging ants in the *Apamean* seems to glance at Rome:[22] but it occurs in a speech whose greater part condemns the materialism of Apamea. When, in the second *Tarsian*, Dio fulminates against the general "increase of greed and incontinence" (*Or.* 34.53), he has Rome in mind, but is mainly concerned with Tarsus. In his speech *On Wealth* (*Or.* 79), which appears to have been delivered in Rome, his theme is that material values are relative, and persons conventionally regarded as "fortunate" are not really so. Two of the arguments with which he supports his position have political implications: to pay foreign nations for luxury goods is in effect to pay them tribute (5), and for nations to acquire them is to incite the depradations of others (6). The second argument is illustrated by the conventional chain of empires, Assyria, Media, Persia, Macedonia: since it is implied that each had fallen to the next because of its wealth, and since Macedonia had been conquered by Rome, Dio suggests that Rome too may be crushed by its burden of luxury. But he does not speak as an outsider gloating at the prospect: it is "our folly" (5) that he is concerned to uproot. Like Plutarch, he contemplates with dismay the possibility of Rome's fall.[23]

A similar message is implied in his speech *On Exile* (*Or.* 13), which was probably spoken in Athens.[24] After recounting how he was sent into exile, and how people came to him for advice, Dio repeats the speech which he had given on such occasions, ascribing it to "a certain Socrates" (14).[25] When he was in Rome (evidently after his exile), he had been asked for moral guidance, and this time he summarizes his reply. The message is essentially the same. "If they despised gold, ivory, delicacies, myrrh, and sex, they would live contentedly and govern themselves, first of all, and thus all others too: 'then,' I said, 'your city will be great, strong, and truly supreme, for at present its greatness is unsound and none too firm' " (33–34): the wealth accumulated at Rome is like a pyre awaiting the torch (36). Even though Dio may have sharpened his attack on Roman decadence to please his Athenian audience,[26] it is aimed at Rome's morality, not at its power: when it is free of its vices, it will be better able to rule the world. So far from exalting Greece above Rome, Dio regards the culture of the classical Athenians as unlucky, since it had not made them better men (26, 28). There is no need to suspect him of irony: this position follows from two of his most cherished views, that strength comes only from virtue, and that the art of virtue is worth more than all the fine arts.

The *Euboean* (*Or.* 7) has been considered for its information about Dio's exile, and its contrast between an ideal rustic community and the evil city.[27] It is also relevant, if only indirectly, to his view of Rome. The last part is concerned to prove that virtue is possible even "in the suburbs and city" (104).[28] It would do no harm if the "virtuous poor" were all re-settled in the country (107–108): but, since that cannot be, Dio's argument demands that he point out which professions may be pursued in the city without moral or physical harm. In the end, he names very few (114): the demonstration becomes largely negative, and in the last part of the speech he inveighs against city life and its demoralizing professions, especially pandering and prostitution. It seems clear that Rome is intended as the chief object of this indictment, as it was the city which epitomized urban vice in the eyes of the Romans as well as their subjects.[29] But there is no ground for supposing that Rome is Dio's sole target, and that "the city" stands for one city only,[30] and not others such as Alexandria or Antioch: when the context requires it, Dio makes clear that he means all cities, at least all that aspire to virtue.[31]

Moreover, even if Rome is primarily meant, Dio's attack does not imply a desire for the city's fall. As *On His Exile* and *On Wealth* showed, he finds nothing inconsistent in deploring Roman decadence and desiring the preservation of Roman rule. He speaks as a Greek and regrets that "Greeks were previously not often slaves, but now are generally and abjectly so" (134): though even here the context shows that he is talking about literal slavery, not enslavement to Rome.[32] His Hellenism is not blind. Just as he maintained elsewhere that Athens' culture accelerated its political decline, so here he mocks the Greek cities which take pride in the great artists they produced in the past, and the actors and mimes they produce today: even when Alexander had sacked Thebes, and all its past greatness was in ruins, the citizens' only concern was to reerect a monument commemorating their pipers (119–121).

The *Euboean* does not show Dio politically unsympathetic to Rome, but rather, like the works *On Kingship*, reveals his conformity with approved views. When the "good man" proposes a scheme for emptying the city of its idle poor, he reflects contemporary schemes of Nerva and Trajan:[33] the same ideal inspires Dio's wish that the "virtuous poor" might be moved from the city to the countryside. His diatribes against the prevailing immorality breathe the spirit of the "new age" of Trajan, in which the extravagance and vice of other eras were to vanish in the bracing atmosphere of resurgent Rome. No longer was the Palace to be a house for concubines, but the residence of a chaste empress:[34] Dio called for prostitution to be banned as a threat to the home, and the letters of a respectable senator duly celebrated the blessings of married felicity.[35] Mimes were banished as a "taste unworthy of the age": Dio chastised the Greeks for honoring such trash, and Pliny gently satirized an old lady who continued to maintain a troupe.[36] The new emperor, if he did not take up farming, was at least devoted to the hunt: Dio held up the huntsman's life as the pattern of rustic virtue, and dutiful senators uneasily joined the newly fashionable sport.[37]

Dio does not show the warmth for Rome that a Plutarch does, or speak of it with the enthusiasm of an Aristides. He nowhere talks explicitly of the blessings of Roman peace, of Roman support of right-thinking politicians in the subject cities, of the security of travel or the beauty of refurbished monuments. But Dio was not by nature warm or enthusiastic. Usually sharp, dry, and abrupt, he can occasionally glow when his subject is of a kind to give intellectual pleasure to a Stoic: the chariot of the cosmos, the omnipotence of Zeus, the labors of Heracles. Such a man could not be expected to panegyrize the shadowy goddess Roma, or (like Aristides) to grow lyrical over the frontier defenses or the Roman citizenship.

The views of a Dio or a Plutarch, or even an Epictetus, the ex-slave preaching comfortably to knights and senators, may not be representative of more than part of a thin layer of society in a small space of time. In a world that measured by wealth and education, however, theirs was a class influential far beyond its numbers; and the Roman world was at the peak of its political and military power. It may also be true that the same authors, like their Roman contemporaries, speak for an age in which "freedom and the principate" were in brief and happy equilibrium, and literature was guided by a touch neither rigid nor lax. Later emperors such as Hadrian were probably less judicious; and later circumstances—

famine, increased taxation, or the wars of rival pretenders—were sometimes to reawaken old grievances and a spirit of opposition.

The central tradition of Hellenism, however, proud of its own culture and yet open to the merits of Rome, persisted from the era of Dio and Plutarch until the disruptions of the late third century. In the first part of that century Cassius Dio of Nicaea, probably Dio's descendant, became a Roman consul and wrote the history of all Rome in language modeled on Thucydides. A little later, another historian and Roman citizen organized the defense of his native Athens against barbarian marauders.[38] When order had been restored in the next century, the old opposition between Greece and Rome was transformed: Hellenism had a more deadly rival than the material values of Rome, the spiritual ones of the newly triumphant Christianity. Just as Greece had once fallen beneath the might of Rome, then "captured its untamed captor" with its arts, so now its spoils went to create a Christian culture. Ever adaptable, Dio survived by his Stoic virtue and beguiling style.

Chronology

/

BIRTH   ca. A.D. 40–50   There is no secure evidence beyond the fact that Dio was already active in the 70s (below, on *Or.* 31, 32), and still alive ca. 110 (Pliny, *Ep.* 10.81–82). In his *Olympian* oration, perhaps delivered in 101, he refers to himself as "past my prime" (τῇ ἡλικίᾳ παρηκμακώς, *Or.* 12.15), which might imply an age between about fifty and sixty: cf. Plut. *Aem. Paull.* 10.2, ἡλικίας ἤδη πρόσω καὶ περὶ ἑξήκοντα γεγονὼς ἔτη. W. Schmid, *RE* 5 (1905) 849–850, proposed a date not later than 40 for Dio's birth, but his argument rested on an erroneous identification of two homonymous athletes: see L. Robert, *Hellenica* 11/12 (1960) 338 n. 4.

Or. 71   68 or later   Nero is "one of the emperors of our time" (9).

Or. 77–78   68 or later (?)   The reference to castration (36) might allude to Nero and Sporus, cf. *Or.* 21.6, though the practice was common: there is no need to see an allusion to Domitian's banning of it, Suet. *Dom.* 7.1.

Or. 31 (Rhodian)   ca. 70–75 (?)   Rhodes is free (112–113): this must be either before its freedom was taken away by Vespasian, probably near the beginning of the reign (Suet. *Vesp.* 8.4), or after it had been restored, probably by Titus (cf. Chapter 4, n. 17). The earlier date is made preferable by the fact that Nero's reign is "very recent" (110).

Or. 46   ca. 70–80   According to the manuscript title, the speech was delivered "before he was a philosopher," and Dio has only a wife and small child (13), whereas in late speeches he talks of an adult son (*Or.* 40.2, 44.8, 50.5, 10) and several children (*Or.* 41.6). The speech should therefore belong approximately in the reign of Vespasian: thus H. Dessau, *Hermes* 34 (1899) 83–84, accepted by Arnim, ibid. 374–376 (Arnim had previously argued for a Domitianic date, *Dio* 205–207).

Praise of a Fly, Praise of a Gnat, Tempe, Memnon   ca. 70–80? Chapter 2 at n. 54.

To Musonius, Against the Philosophers   ca. 70–80?   Chapter 2 at nn. 62–63.

Or. 32 (*Alexandrian*)   ca. 71–75?   The chief evidence is the reference to a "Conon" who commanded Roman troops in quelling a riot, apparently not long before (72). Such a person should have been the prefect of Egypt, as on similar occasions in 38 (Philo, *in Flaccum* 44 ff.) and 66 (Jos. *BJ* 2.494). Moreover, by qualifying him as ὁ βέλτιστος Dio suggests a Roman of high rank: cf. *Or.* 45.2, τὸν βέλτιστον Νέρβαν, *Or.* 48.1, τῷ κρατίστῳ Οὐαρηνῷ. No prefect of Egypt was ever called Conon: but one in Dio's lifetime had a very similar name, L. Peducaeus Colonus (possibly "Colo"), whose last name is transcribed in documents as Κόλων. He should be Dio's "Conon"; and since he governed from 70 to 72, or possibly 73, the speech should belong in those years or not long thereafter. For this argument, *Historia* 22 (1973) 302–309; for new evidence about Colo(nus), J. D. Thomas, *ZPE* 21 (1976) 153–156.

J. F. Kindstrand, *Historia* (in press), defends the usual dating of the speech to the reign of Trajan, mainly on the ground that Dio advances Cynic ideas in it: but this cannot be reconciled with his attack on the Cynics in sect. 9, and it is very doubtful whether Dio sympathized with Cynicism, especially in his last period.

Or. 11 (*Trojan*)   ca. 71–80   Apparently an early speech (Chapter 2 at n. 83); perhaps subsequent to the *Alexandrian* (Chapter 5, n. 4).

Or. 29, 28   probably not much later than 74 or 78   One of these two years seems to be the date of the Neapolitan *Sebasta* during which the athlete Melancomas died: Chapter 2 at n. 71.

Or. 30   ca. 75 or later   This is a dialogue concerning a deceased pupil of Dio: it seems unlikely that he would have had pupils until the age of thirty or so.

Or. 80   ca. 83 or later   Dio depicts himself as a wanderer unburdened by ordinary human cares. This suggests a date after the beginning of his exile, and thus after 83 or so: above, Chapter 6 at n. 3. However, he continues to speak of himself as a wanderer even after his restoration: cf. *Or.* 7.1, 12.16, 47.8.

Or. 72   ca. 85 or later   Dio speaks of himself as a philosopher (13): he claims not to have accepted this appellation until going into exile (*Or.* 13.11), cf. on *Or.* 80.

Or. 21 (*On Beauty*)   88 or later?   Dio's statement that all the Romans wish that Nero were alive (10) might conceivably refer to the false Nero who appeared about this time; the mood of the piece suggests a date during his exile; cf. Chapter 6 at n. 45, Chapter 14 at n. 20.

Or. 66   shortly before 96?   The reference to a great house in danger (6) might allude to the Flavian dynasty; cf. Chapter 6 at n. 48.

Or. 7 (*Euboean*)   probably 96 or later   Dio refers to himself as a πρέσβυς, 1; his tale of the huntsman (1–66) seems to be drawn from his experiences in exile; for possible references to measures of Nerva and Trajan, Chapter 7 at nn. 19–21, Chapter 14 at n. 33.

Or. 19   probably 96 or later   Apparently, though not certainly, after Dio's exile (1).

Or. 13 (*On His Exile*)   after 96 and probably after 100; perhaps 101 After Dio's exile (1); apparently after a subsequent visit to Rome (29); perhaps contemporary with *Or.* 12, cf. Chapter 6 at n. 75.

Or. 36 (*Olbian*)   ca. 98 or later   Dio mentions "the summer after my exile" (1), presumably that of 97 (cf. Chapter 6 at n. 61). According to the title, he recited the work in Prusa: he seems not to have reached home until some time had passed since his recall (*Or.* 45.2).

Or. 38 (*Nicomedian*)   ca. 98 or later   Nicomedia and Nicaea are both the "first" cities of Bithynia (35, 39): Nicomedia did not gain this title until the reign of Domitian (Chapter 10 at nn. 13–14). Since Dio was banished from Bithynia during his exile, the speech must be later than his return.

Or. 39 (*Nicaean*)   ca. 98 or later   Dio complains of ill-health (7). He elsewhere claims to have fallen ill when in exile (*Or.* 19.1, 40.2, 45.1), and so far as can be told only mentions his illness in late speeches (in addition to those cited, *Or.* 12.12, presumably *Or.* 52.1). Since he is in Bithynia, the speech should be later than his return.

Or. 42   ca. 98 or later   Dio speaks of himself as a philosopher (1) and of his speeches as widely known (4). If the manuscript title is right in saying that the speech was delivered in Prusa, it must be later than his return from exile.

Or. 52   ca. 98 or later   Dio is ill, and in his own house (1): the work should therefore be later than his return from exile, cf. on *Or.* 39 above.

Or. 1 (*On Kingship I*)   probably 100   Chapter 13 at nn. 33–37 and below, discussing *Or.* 40.

Or. 2 (*On Kingship II*)   ca. 100 or later   Chapter 13 at n. 38.

Or. 3 (*On Kingship III*)   ca. 100 or later   Probably later than *Or.* 1; Chapter 13 at n. 41.

Or. 4 (*On Kingship IV*)   ca. 100 or later; conceivably ca. 115   Chapter 13 at nn. 45–48.

Or. 5 (*Libyan Tale*)   ca. 100 or later; conceivably ca. 115   Probably contemporary with *Or.* 4; Chapter 13, n. 44.

Or. 6–10 ("Diogenes speeches")   ca. 100 or later?   Chapter 6 at nn. 40–43, Chapter 13 at nn. 52–53.

Or. 33 (*First Tarsian*)   ca. 100 or later?   Dio implies that he is not young (14), and seems to consider himself a philosopher (16), cf. above, on *Or.* 72. Otherwise there is no clear evidence of date, but see below, on *Or.* 34.

Or. 34 (*Second Tarsian*)   ca. 100 or later?   Again, Dio talks of himself as a philosopher (3, 52). The reference to the emperor (25) is neutral, and yet slightly unfavorable to the reign of Domitian, when Dio was in exile (cf. *Or.* 45.1). Similarly, the hint that governors of Cilicia were often guilty of maladministration (9, 38–42) is more suitable to Trajan's reign than Domitian's (cf. Suet. *Dom.* 8.2). *Or.* 34 should therefore be a late speech; if so, *Or.* 33 will probably also be, since they seem likely to have been spoken on a single visit (cf. *Or.* 33.51 with *Or.* 34.14, 47). In a speech that is certainly late, Dio refers to Athens, Sparta, Rome, Antioch, and Tarsus as cities in which he can be sure of a welcome (*Or.* 47.17). This may suggest that he had recently been an honored guest in Tarsus.

D. Kienast, *Historia* 20 (1971) 74–75, has proposed putting the speech in 112 or 113 on the evidence of sect. 11. After referring to injuries inflicted on Tarsus by its neighbors, Dio observes, "if you had done something of the sort, you would have been thought to be sacking the cities and beginning revolt and war, and to need an army to quell you." This army, it is argued, is the one which Trajan was soon to lead through Tarsus on his way to the Parthian war. But there was a Roman army regularly stationed in neighboring Syria; and in any case Dio's point is that the Tarsians do not need to be checked by force.

Or. 35 (*Apamean*)   ca. 100 or later?   There is no clear evidence, but see Chapter 8 at n. 2.

Or. 51 (*Against Diodorus*)   ca. 100 or later?   Evidently spoken when Dio had a leading part in the politics of Prusa, and so probably in his last period.

Or. 53   ca. 100 or later?   Sections 11–12 are very similar to parts of the works *On Kingship*, especially *Or.* 2.

Or. 54   ca. 100 or later?   In this contrast between Socrates and the sophists Dio seems to be thinking of his own battles with his de-tractors: in late speeches he frequently compares himself with Socrates (e.g. *Or.* 43.8–12) and makes sustained attacks on "sophists" (cf. *Or.* 4.28–38, 12.1–12): earlier jibes at them are more transitory (cf. *Or.* 11.6, 14, 32.11).

Or. 55   ca. 100 or later?   As in *Or.* 54, the exaltation of Socrates suggests a late date.

Or. 56 (*Agamemnon*)   ca. 100 or later?   The content of this dia-logue connects it with the works *On Kingship*, cf. Chapter 13 at n. 50.

Or. 57 (*Nestor*)   ca. 100 or later   Dio refers to his speeches given before the emperor: he must mean at least *Or.* 1 and *Or.* 3, cf. Chapter 13 at n. 51.

Or. 62   ca. 100 or later   Addressed to an emperor (1); the similarity of the content to the works *On Kingship*, especially *Or.* 1, strongly suggests that Trajan is the addressee. The picture of Sardanapalus "lurking in the women's quarters" might glance at Domitian: cf. Chapter 13 n. 48.

Or. 12 (*Olympian*)   101?   Chapter 6 at nn. 70–74.

Or. 13 (*On His Exile*)   101?   After the end of Dio's exile (1) and after a subsequent visit to Rome (29); probably contemporaneous with *Or.* 12, cf. Chapter 6 at n. 75.

Or. 40   101   Dio has just returned to Prusa for the second time since his exile (1, 5); this second absence cannot have lasted more than a year, since an event which occurred before his departure belongs to "last year" (18). Since he vehemently defends the achievements of his embassy to Trajan (13–15), this is evidently the cause of his recent absence. It in turn can be at least plausibly dated by circumstantial evidence. It is not certain that the embassy met Trajan in Rome (in 13, Dio talks of the emperor "meeting us at the gate," but this might be the gate of another city or a camp: I retract the relevant part of *Chiron* 5 [1975] 403 n. 1). It is, however, clear that the embassy was sent to "thank" the emperor (*eucharistountes*) for benefits already conferred, which appear to be those mentioned in a letter which Dio carried with him on his return to the city from exile (5); it, therefore, is unlikely that this was an embassy sent to congratulate the emperor on his accession (as supposed by Millar, *Emperor* 414), since some time must have elapsed since that event.

The dating of *Or.* 1 now becomes relevant. There are good, though again circumstantial, reasons for supposing that that speech was delivered before Trajan in about 100, and that Dio proceeded with him to the Danube in early 101 before returning to Prusa later in the same year (Chapter 6 at nn. 69–74). The evidence is most simply combined by supposing that Dio returned to Prusa for the first time since his exile in about 98, left it again when the city sent an embassy of thanks to Trajan in 100, and returned for the second time only in 101; if so, this speech should belong to 101.

Or. 41   101   The contents make this contemporaneous with *Or.* 40; and like that speech they presuppose that some time has elapsed since Dio's exile (1, 7–8').

Or. 44 (*Speech of Greeting*)   101?   Dio has just returned to Prusa after an absence (1). This cannot be his exile, since he speaks as if Prusa had already been granted a larger council, the assizes, and increased revenues (11): yet the enlarged council and new revenues were gained by his embassy (*Or.* 40.14–15), and the assizes were granted soon after it (*Or.* 40.33). As in *Or.* 40, therefore, he must have returned from his embassy, not from exile; for a contrast between these two returns, cf. *Or.* 40.1, 5.

Or. 45   ca. 101–103   Certainly after the death of Nerva (2), and soon after Dio's embassy, since the privileges gained by it are still recent (3). The reference to departure (1) need not refer to his departure of ca. 106 (below, on *Or.* 43), since these threats recur in the Prusan speeches, including the early *Or.* 46 (*Or.* 46.12, 47.2, 19, 49.15; note esp. *Or.* 50.7).

Or. 47   ca. 102 or later   Spoken when Dio's stoa had aroused strong opposition (8–25). This project was aired soon after his return from exile (*Or.* 40.5–6), and had already become controversial by 101 (above, on *Or.* 40); this speech should therefore be somewhat later. Dio's reference to an imminent departure need not be taken seriously, cf. on *Or.* 45 above.

Or. 49   ca. 102 or later?   Dio speaks of himself as a philosopher (13), and since the speech is spoken in Prusa it must be subsequent to his return from exile. The reference to an impending departure, even if only a bluff (above, on *Or.* 45), suggests a time when his popularity had waned.

Or. 48   ca. 105   Delivered when Varenus Rufus was proconsul (1); on this date, Chapter 11 at n. 59. The reference to "cursed Getae" (5) is appropriate to a time when Rome was at war with them, cf. Arr. *Epict.* 2.22.22.

Or. 50   after ca. 105   Spoken after an occasion on which Dio had "pitied the common people" (3). This seems to be the "crisis" mentioned in *Or.* 43.7, and this in turn may be connected with the proconsulate of the "wicked governor," apparently Varenus Rufus (Chapter 11 at nn. 53–63).

Getica   after 106?   The work seems likely to have commemorated one, and probably both, of Trajan's two Dacian wars in 101–102 and 105–106; cf. Chapter 13 at nn. 56–58.

Or. 43   ca. 106–107?   Dio is under attack for having abetted a "wicked proconsul," apparently Varenus Rufus (Chapter 11 at n. 60). Here his departure is a real one, since his enemies allege that he is going to help the governor "win his case" (8, 11): the reference seems to be either to Rufus' expected trial, or to the investigation by Trajan which replaced it (Chapter 11 at n. 63).

DEATH   110 or later   Dio was still alive at the time of Pliny, *Ep.* 10.81–82, in the second year of Pliny's administration, which began no earlier than 109 (Syme, *Tacitus* 659).

Bibliography
Abbreviations
Notes
Index

Bibliography

This bibliography lists all books and articles mentioned in the notes and Appendix, except for the following: articles in works of reference (except for ones in *RE* which have been especially useful), handbooks, editions of literary texts, coins, inscriptions, and papyri (except when I have drawn on the accompanying discussion). I have partly supplied the less well known abbreviations of journals, e.g., *AAT* appears as *Atti Acc. Sc. Torino*, but *HSCP* remains; for other abbreviations, see Abbreviations.

Arnim, H. von. *Leben und Werke des Dio von Prusa.* Berlin, 1898.

———. "Zum Leben Dios von Prusa," *Hermes* 34 (1899) 363–379.

Arundell, F. V. J. *Discoveries in Asia Minor, Including a Description of the Ruins of Several Cities, and Especially Antioch of Pisidia.* London, 1834.

Asmus, J. R. *Julian und Dio Chrysostomus.* Tauberbischofsheim, 1895.

———. "Synesius und Dio Chrysostomus," *Byz. Zeitschr.* 9 (1900) 85–151.

Aytug Taşyürek, O. "Cilician Excavations and Survey, 1973," in "Recent Archaeological Research in Turkey," *Anat. Stud.* 24 (1974) 26–29.

Barnes, T. D. *Tertullian: A Historical and Literary Study.* Oxford, 1971.

Beaujeu, J. *La religion romaine à l'apogée de l'Empire. 1: La politique religieuse des Antonins.* Paris, 1955.

Belin de Ballu, E. *Olbia: Cité antique du littoral nord de la mer Noire.* Leiden, 1972.

Bernhardt, R. *Imperium und Eleutheria: Die römische Politik gegenüber den freien Städten des griechischen Ostens.* Hamburg, 1971.

Bidez, J., and F. Cumont. *Les mages hellénisés: Zoroastre, Ostanès et Hystaspe d'après la tradition grecque.* Paris, 1938.

Birley, A. R. *Marcus Aurelius.* London, 1966.

Blanck, H. *Wiederverwendung alter Statuen als Ehrendenkmäler bei Griechen und Römern.* Studia Archaeologica 2. Rome, 1969.

Boethius, A. "*Et crescunt media pegmata celsa via* (Martial's De Spectaculis 2.2)," *Eranos* 50 (1952) 129–137.

Bogaert, R. *Banques et banquiers dans les cités grecques.* Leyden, 1968.

Bonhöffer, A. *Epictet und die Stoa: Untersuchungen zur stoischen Philosophie.* Stuttgart, 1890.

Bonner, C. "A Tarsian Peculiarity (Dio Prus. Or. 33)," *Harv. Theol. Rev.* 35 (1942) 1–11.

Borthwick, E. K. "Dio Chrysostom on the Mob at Alexandria," *CR* 22 (1972) 1–3.

Bouché-Leclerq, A. *Histoire de la divination dans l'antiquité.* Paris, 1879–1882.

Bowersock, G. W. *Augustus and the Greek World.* Oxford, 1965.

———. "Some Persons in Plutarch's *Moralia*," *CQ* 15 (1965) 267–270.

———. *Greek Sophists in the Roman Empire.* Oxford, 1969.

———. Introduction to *Philostratus: Life of Apollonius of Tyana.* Translated by C. P. Jones. Harmondsworth, 1970.

———. "Greek Intellectuals and the Imperial Cult in the Second Century A.D.," in *Le Culte des Souverains dans l'empire romain.* Entretiens Hardt 19. Geneva, 1973, 177–206.

———. "The Greek-Nabataean Bilingual Inscription at Ruwwafa, Saudi Arabia," *Le monde grec: Hommages à Claire Préaux.* Brussels, 1975, 513–522.

Bowie, E. L. "Greeks and their past in the Second Sophistic," *Past and Present* 46 (1970) 3–41 (*Studies in Ancient Society.* Edited by M. I. Finley. London and Boston, 1974, 166–209).

Broughton, T. R. S. "Roman Asia" in *An Economic Survey of Ancient Rome.* Edited by Tenney Frank, 4. Baltimore, 1938, 499–918.

Brückner, A. "Geschichte von Troja and Ilion," in W. Dörpfeld, *Troja und Ilion.* Athens, 1902, 549–593.

Brunt, P. A. "Charges of Provincial Maladministration under the Early Principate," *Historia* 10 (1961) 189–227.

———. "Aspects of the Social Thought of Dio Chrysostom and the Stoics," *Proc. Camb. Phil. Soc.* 19^2 (1973) 9–34.

Burckhardt, J. "Über den Wert des Dio Chrysostomus für die Kenntnis seiner Zeit," *Gesamtausgabe XIV: Vorträge.* Berlin and Leipzig, 1933, 86–109.

Burton, G. P. "Proconsuls, Assizes, and the Administration of Justice under the Empire," *JRS* 65 (1975) 92–106.

Cadoux, C. J. *Ancient Smyrna: A History of the City from the Earliest Times to 324 A.D.* Oxford, 1938.

Callu, J.-P. *La politique monétaire des empereurs romains de 238 à 311.* Bibl. des éc. fr. d'Ath. et de Rome 214. Paris, 1969.

Cameron, A. *Porphyrius the Charioteer.* Oxford, 1973.

———. *Circus Factions: Blues and Greens at Byzantium.* Oxford, 1976.

Castritius, H. "Ein bisher unbekannte Statthalter Kilikiens?," *Historia* 20 (1971) 80–83.

Charlesworth, M. P. "The Refusal of Divine Honours: An Augustan Formula," *Pap. Brit. Sch. Rome* 15 (1939) 1–10.

Cohn-Haft, L. *The Public Physicians of Ancient Greece.* Smith College Studies in History 42. Northampton, Mass., 1956.

Colin, J. *Les villes libres de l'Orient gréco-romain et l'envoi au supplice par acclamations populaires.* Collection Latomus 82. Brussels, 1965.

Coster, C. H. *Late Roman Studies.* Cambridge, Mass., 1968.

Crimi, C. U. "Sull'orazione *Agli Alessandrini* di Dione Crisostomo," *SicGymn* 26 (1973) 356–362.

Day, J. "The Value of Dio Chrysostom's Euboean Discourse for the Economic Historian," *Studies in Roman Economic and Social History in Honor of Allan Chester Johnson.* Princeton, 1951, 209–235.

Deininger, J. *Die Provinziallandtage der römischen Kaiserzeit.* Munich, 1965.

Desideri, P. "Il *Dione* e la Politica di Sinesio," *Atti Acc. Sc. Torino* 107 (1973) 551–593.

Dessau, H. "Zum Leben Dios von Prusa," *Hermes* 34 (1899) 81–87.

Dörner, F. K. "Prusa ad Olympum," *RE* 23 (1957) 1071–1086.

Downey, G. *A History of Antioch in Syria from Seleucus to the Arab Conquest.* Princeton, 1961.

Duncan-Jones, R. P. *The Economy of the Roman Empire: Quantitative Studies.* Cambridge, 1974.

Eck, W. *Senatoren von Vespasian bis Hadrian: Prosopographische Untersuchungen mit Einschluss der Jahres- und Provinzialfasten der Statthalter.* Vestigia 13. Munich, 1970.

Fiechter, E., and R. Herbig. *Das Dionysos-Theater in Athen.* Ant. griech. Theaterbauten 5 and 6. Stuttgart, 1935.

Flacelière, R. "Hadrien et Delphes," *CRAI* 1971, 168–185.

Forbes, C. A. *NEOI: A Study of Greek Associations.* Amer. Philol. Assoc., Philol. Monogr. 2. Middletown, Conn., 1933.

Fowler, H. N., and R. Stillwell. *Corinth 1: Introduction: Topography, Architecture.* Cambridge, Mass., 1932.

Fraenkel, E. *Horace.* Oxford, 1957.

Francotte, H. "Le pain à bon marché et le pain gratuit dans les cités grecques," *Mélanges Nicole.* Geneva, 1905, 135–157.

Fraser, P. M., and G. E. Bean. *The Rhodian Peraea and Islands.* London, 1954.

———. *Ptolemaic Alexandria.* Oxford, 1972.

Friedländer, L. *Darstellungen aus der Sittengeschichte Roms.*[10] Leipzig, 1921–1923.

Fritz, K. von. "Musonius, 1," *RE* 16 (1933) 893–897.

Fuchs, H. *Der geistige Widerstand gegen Rom in der antiken Welt.* Berlin, 1938.

Gaertringen, H. von. "Rhodos," *RE* Suppl. 5 (1931) 731–840.

Gallavotti, C. "Sopra un opuscolo perduto di Dione Crisostomo," *Riv. Fil. Istr. Class.* 59 (1931) 504–508.

Garnsey, P. D. *Social Status and Legal Privilege in the Roman Empire.* Oxford, 1970.

———. "Honorarium Decurionatus," *Historia* 20 (1971) 309–325.

Garzya, A. "Il *Dione* di Sinesio nel quadro del dibattito culturale del IV secolo d. C.," *Riv. Fil. Istr. Class.* 100³ (1972) 32–45.

Gawantka, W. *Isopolitie: Ein Beitrag zur Geschichte der zwischenstaatlichen Beziehungen in der griechischen Antike.* Vestigia 22. Munich, 1975.

Gelder, H. van. *Geschichte der alten Rhodier.* The Hague, 1900.

Georgoudi, St. "Problèmes de transhumance dans la Grèce ancienne," *REG* 87 (1974) 155–185.

Geytenbeek, A. C. van. *Musonius Rufus and Greek Diatribe.* Assen, 1963.

Gigon, O. "Antike Erzählungen über die Berufung zur Philosophie," *Mus. Helv.* 3 (1946) 1–21.

Graindor, P. *Athènes sous Auguste.* Cairo, 1927.

———. *Athènes de Tibère à Trajan.* Cairo, 1931.

Gren, E. *Kleinasien und der Ostbalkan in der wirtschaftlichen Entwicklung der römischen Kaiserzeit.* Uppsala, 1941.

Grimal, P. "Deux figures de la *Correspondance* de Pline: Le philosophe Euphratès et le rhéteur Isée," *Latomus* 14 (1955) 370–383.

Grosso, F. "La *Vita di Apollonio di Tiana* come fonte storica," *Acme* 7 (1954) 333–532.

Habicht, Ch. *Altertümer von Pergamon VIII 3: Die Inschriften des Asklepieions.* Berlin, 1969.

———. *Gottmenschentum und griechische Städte².* Zetemata 14. Munich, 1970.

———. "Die augusteische Zeit und das erste Jahrhundert nach Christi Geburt," in *Le Culte des Souverains dans l'empire romain.* Entretiens Hardt 19. Geneva, 1973, 41–88.

———. "New Evidence on the Province of Asia," *JRS* 65 (1975) 64–91.

Helm, R. "Hieronymus' Zusätze in Eusebius' Chronik und ihr Wert für die Literaturgeschichte," *Philologus* Suppl. 21, 2 (1929).

Henrichs, A. "Vespasian's Visit to Alexandria," *ZPE* 3 (1968) 51–80.

———. "*Monumentum aere perennius* (Zu P. Oxy. 2435)," *ZPE* 4 (1969) 150.

Herrmann, P. "Zwei Inschriften von Kaunos und Baba Dağ," *Opuscula Atheniensia* 10 (1971) 36–39.

Hertzberg, G. *Die Geschichte Griechenlands unter der Herrschaft der Römer.* Halle, 1866–1875.

Highet, G. "The Huntsman and the Castaway," *GRBS* 14 (1973) 35–40.

———. "Lexical notes on Dio Chrysostom," *GRBS* 15 (1974) 247–253.

Hirschfeld, G. "Kelainai-Apameia Kibotos," *Abh. Akad. Berlin* (1875) 1–26.

Höistad, R. *Cynic Hero and Cynic King: Studies in the Cynic Conception of Man.* Uppsala, 1948.

Holleaux, M. "Une inscription de Séleucie-de-Piérie," *Études d'épigraphie et d'histoire grecques* 3. Paris, 1942, 199–254.

Howell, P. "The Colossus of Nero," *Athenaeum* 46² (1968) 292–299.

Humphrey, J. H. "Prolegomena to the Study of the Hippodrome at Caesarea Maritima," *Bull. Amer. Sch. Or. Research* 213 (1974) 2–45.

Imhoof-Blumer, Fr. "Coin-types of Some Kilikian Cities," *JHS* 18 (1898) 161–181.

———. "Fluss- und Meergötter auf griechischen und römischen Münzen," *Revue Suisse de Numismatique* 23 (1923) 173–421.

Jones, A. H. M. *The Greek City from Alexander to Justinian.* Oxford, 1940.

———. *Cities of the Eastern Roman Provinces*². Oxford, 1971.

———. *The Roman Economy: Studies in Ancient Economic and Administrative History.* Edited by P. A. Brunt. Oxford, 1974.

Jones, C. P. *Plutarch and Rome.* Oxford, 1971.

———. "The Date of Dio of Prusa's Alexandrian Oration," *Historia* 22 (1973) 302–309.

———. "The Reliability of Philostratus," in *Approaches to the Second Sophistic.* Edited by G. W. Bowersock. University Park, Penn., 1974, 11–16.

———. "An Oracle Given to Trajan," *Chiron* 5 (1975) 403–406.

Jouguet, P. "Les Assemblées d'Alexandrie à l'époque ptolémaïque." *Bull. Soc. Arch. Alex.* 37 (1948) 71–94.

Jüthner, J. "Zu Dio Chrysostomus XXVIII," *Wiener Studien* 26 (1904) 151–157.

———. *Hellenen und Barbaren: Aus der Geschichte des Nationalbewusstseins.* Leipzig, 1923.

Kahrstedt, U. *Das wirtschaftliche Gesicht Griechenlands in der Kaiserzeit: Kleinstadt, Villa und Domäne.* Diss. Bernenses 1, 7. Bern, 1954.

Kienast, D. "Die Homonoiaverträge in der römischen Kaiserzeit," *Jahrb. f. Num. u. Geldgesch.* 14 (1964) 51–64.

———. "Ein vernachlässigtes Zeugnis für die Reichspolitik Traians: Die zweite tarsische Rede des Dion von Prusa," *Historia* 20 (1971) 62–80.

Kindstrand, J. F. *Homer in der Zweiten Sophistik.* Studia Graeca Upsaliensia 7. Uppsala, 1973.

———. *Bion of Borysthenes.* Studia Graeca Upsaliensia 11. Uppsala, 1976.

———. "The Date of Dio of Prusa's Alexandrian Oration: A Reply," *Historia.* In press.

Kroll, W. "Randbemerkungen," *RhM* 70 (1915) 591–601.

Labriolle, P. de. *La réaction païenne: Étude sur la polémique antichrétienne du Ier au VIe siècle.* Paris, 1942.

Lacombrade, Ch. *Synésios de Cyrène: Hellène et Chrétien.* Paris, 1951.

Laet, S. J. de. *Portorium: Étude sur l'organisation douanière chez les romains, surtout à l'époque du haut-empire.* Rijksuniversiteit te Gent, Werken uitgeven door de Fakulteit van de Wijsbegeerte en Letteren 105. Bruges, 1949.

Larsen, J. A. O. "Roman Greece," in *An Economic Survey of Ancient Rome.* Edited by Tenney Frank, 4. Baltimore, 1938, 259–498.

Latte, K. "Textkritische Beiträge zu Synesios," *Class. et Med.* 17 (1956) 91–97 (*Kleine Schriften.* Munich, 1968, 606–611).

Levick, B. M. *Roman Colonies in Southern Asia Minor.* Oxford, 1967.

Lévy, I. "Études sur la vie municipale de l'Asie Mineure sous les Antonins," *REG* 12 (1899) 255–289.

Lewis, N. "Dio Chrysostom's 'Tyrant of Syria,'" *CP* 44 (1949) 32–33.

Liebenam, W., *Städteverwaltung im römischen Kaiserreiche* (Leipzig, 1900).

Lutz, Cora E. "Musonius Rufus, 'The Roman Socrates,'" *Yale Class. Stud.* 10 (1947) 3–147.

Maass, M. *Die Prohedrie des Dionysostheaters in Athen.* Vestigia 15. Munich, 1972.

MacMullen, R. *Enemies of the Roman Order: Treason, Unrest, and Alienation in the Empire.* Cambridge, Mass., 1966.

Magie, D. *Roman Rule in Asia Minor.* Princeton, 1950.

Maricq, A. "Une influence alexandrine sur l'art augustéen? Le Lageion et le Circus Maximus," *Rev. Arch.* 37[6] (1951) 26–46.

Marshall, A. J. "Pompey's Organization of Bithynia-Pontus: Two Neglected Texts," *JRS* 58 (1968) 103–109.

Marrou, H.-I. *Histoire de l'éducation dans l'antiquité*[4]. Paris, 1958.

———. "Synesius of Cyrene and Alexandrian Neoplatonism," in *The Conflict between Paganism and Christianity in the Fourth Century.* Edited by A. Momigliano. Oxford, 1963, 126–150.

Mason, H. J., and M. B. Wallace. "Appius Claudius Pulcher and the Hollows of Euboea," *Hesperia* 41 (1972) 128–140.

———. *Greek Terms for Roman Institutions.* American Studies in Papyrology 13. Toronto, 1974.

Mazon, P., J. Carcopino, P. Roussel, and P. Collart. [discussion of Dio's *Euboean*], *CRAI* 1943, 85–87.

Mendel, G. "Catalogue des monuments grecs, romains et byzantins du Musée Imperial Ottoman de Brousse," *BCH* 33 (1909) 245–435.

Millar, F. "The *Fiscus* in the First Two Centuries," *JRS* 53 (1963) 29–42.

———. *A Study of Cassius Dio.* Oxford, 1964.

———. "Epictetus and the Imperial Court," *JRS* 55 (1965) 141–148.

———. "The Emperor, the Senate, and the Provinces," *JRS* 56 (1966) 156–166.

———. "Local Cultures in the Roman Empire: Libyan, Punic and Latin in Roman Africa," *JRS* 58 (1968) 126–134.

———. Review of Sherwin-White, *Pliny, JRS* 58 (1968) 218–224.

———. "P. Herennius Dexippus: The Greek World and the Third-Century Invasions," *JRS* 59 (1969) 12–29.

———. *The Emperor in the Roman World.* London, 1977.

Milne, H. J. "Papyri of Dio Chrysostom and Menander," *Journ. Eg. Archaeol.* 16 (1930) 187–193.

Minns, E. H. *Scythians and Greeks.* Cambridge, 1913.

Moles, J. L. "The Career and Conversion of Dio Chrysostom," *JHS* 98 (1978).

Momigliano, A. D. Review of Lepper, *Trajan's Parthian War, Riv. Stor. Ital.* 61 (1949) 124–127 (*Quinto Contributo* 2.1003–1007).

———. Review of Wirszubski, *Libertas, JRS* 41 (1951) 146–153 (*Quinto Contributo* 2.958–975).

———. "Dio Chrysostomus," *Quarto Contributo* 257–269.

Mommsen, Th. *Römisches Staatsrecht*[3]. Leipzig, 1887–1888.

———. *Römische Geschichte 5: Die Provinzen von Caesar bis Diokletian*[4]. Berlin, 1894.

———. "Die Einführung des Asianischen Kalenders," *Ath. Mitt.* 24 (1899) 275–288 (*Gesammelte Schriften* 5. Berlin, 1908, 518–529).

————. *The Provinces of the Roman Empire.* Translated by W. P. Dickson. London, 1909.

Montevecchi, O. "Nerone e l'Egitto," *Par. del Pass.* 160 (1975) 48–58.

Mordtmann, A. D. *Anatolien: Skizzen und Reisebriefen aus Kleinasien 1850– 1859.* Hannover, 1925.

Morr, J. *Die Lobrede des jüngeren Plinius und die erste Königsrede des Dio von Prusa.* Troppau, 1915.

Mras, K. "Die προλαλιά bei den griechischen Schriftstellern," *Wien. Stud.* 66 (1949, publ. 1950) 71–81.

Münsterberg, R. "Die Münzen der Sophisten," *Num. Zeitschr.* 8² (1915) 119– 124.

Murray, O. "Philodemus on the Good King according to Homer," *JRS* 55 (1965) 161–182.

Musti, D. "Sull'idea di συγγένεια in iscrizioni greche," *Annali Sc. Norm. Pisa* 32 (1963) 225–239.

Musurillo, H. A. *The Acts of the Pagan Martyrs: Acta Alexandrinorum.* Oxford, 1954.

Nock, A. D. "ΣΥΝΝΑΟΣ ΘΕΟΣ," *HSCP* 41 (1930) 1–62 (*Essays* 1.202–251).

————. *Conversion: The Old and the New in Religion from Alexander the Great to Augustine of Hippo.* Oxford, 1933.

————. "The Emperor's Divine *Comes,*" *JRS* 37 (1947) 106–116 (*Essays* 2.653– 675).

————. "*Soter* and *Euergetes,*" *The Joy of Study: Papers . . . F. C. Grant.* Edited by S. L. Johnson. New York, 1951, 127–148 (*Essays* 2.720–735).

Nörr, D. *Imperium und Polis in der hohen Prinzipatszeit.* Munich, 1966.

Oertel, Fr. *Die Liturgie: Studien zur ptolemaischen und kaiserlichen Verwaltung Ägyptens.* Leipzig, 1917.

Oliver, J. H. *The Sacred Gerousia.* Hesperia Suppl. 6. Baltimore, 1941.

————. "The Roman Governor's Permission for a Decree of the Polis," *Hesperia* 23 (1954) 163–167.

————. *Marcus Aurelius: Aspects of civic and cultural Policy in the East.* Hesperia Suppl. 13. Baltimore, 1970.

Palm, J. *Rom, Römertum und Imperium in der griechischen Literatur der Kaiserzeit.* Skrifter utgivna av Kungl. Humanistiska Vetenskapssamfundet i Lund 57. Lund, 1959.

Pease, A. S. "Things Without Honor," *CP* 21 (1926) 27–42.

Peterson, E. ΕΙΣ ΘΕΟΣ. Forschungen zur Religion und Literatur des Alten und Neuen Testaments, N.F. 24. Göttingen, 1926.

————. "Die Bedeutung der ὠκεανέ-Akklamation," *RhM* 78 (1929) 221–223.

Petriconi, H. "Spenglers *Untergang des Abendlandes* als Werk der schönen Literatur," *Ant. u. Abendl.* 7 (1958) 47–61.

Pflaum, H.-G. *Le marbre de Thorigny.* Bibl. Éc. Hautes Études 292. Paris, 1948.

Philippson, A. *Reisen und Forschungen im westlichen Kleinasien III. Das östliche Mysien und die benachbarte Teile von Phrygien und Bithynien.* Petermanns Mitteilungen, Ergänzungsheft 177. 1913.

Pohlenz, M. *Die Stoa*[4]. Göttingen, 1970–1972.

Poland, Fr. *Geschichte des griechischen Vereinswesens*. Leipzig, 1909.

Pritchett, W. K. *Studies in Ancient Greek Topography*. University of California publications, Classical Studies 1, 4. Berkeley, 1965–1969.

Ramsay, W. M. *Cities and Bishoprics of Phrygia*. Oxford, 1895–1897.

———. *The Cities of St. Paul: Their Influence on His Life and Thought*. London, 1907.

Reuter, D. "Untersuchungen zum Euboikos des Dion von Prusa." Dissertation, Leipzig, 1932.

Rey-Coquais, J.-P. *Arados et sa Pérée aux époques grecque, romaine et byzantine*. Bibl. arch. hist. Inst. fr. Beyrouth 97. Paris, 1974.

Riewald, P. *De imperatorum romanorum cum certis dis et comparatione et aequatione*. Diss. philol. Halenses 20, 3. 1912.

Robert, L. "Études épigraphiques, Première série," *BCH* 52 (1928) 407–425 (*OMS* 2.878-896).

———. "Trois inscriptions de l'Archipel," *REG* 42 (1929) 20–38 (*OMS* 1.530–548).

———. "Epigraphica," *REG* 42 (1929) 426–438 (*OMS* 1.214–226).

———. "Nouvelles remarques sur l'édit d'Eriza," *BCH* 54 (1930) 262–267 (*OMS* 2.966–971).

———. "Pantomimen im griechischen Orient," *Hermes* 65 (1930) 106–122 (*OMS* 1.654–670).

———. "Sur des inscriptions de Chios," *BCH* 57 (1933) 505–543 (*OMS* 1.473–511).

———. "Études d'épigraphie grecque," *Rev. Phil.* 8[3] (1934) 267–292 (*OMS* 2.1166–1191).

———. "Notes d'épigraphie hellénistique," *BCH* 59 (1935) 421–437 (*OMS* 1.178–194).

———. "Études sur les inscriptions et la topographie de la Grèce centrale VI: Décrets d'Akraiphia," *BCH* 59 (1935) 438–452 (*OMS* 1.279–293).

———. "Études épigraphiques, Deuxième série," *BCH* 60 (1936) 190–207 (*OMS* 2.897–914).

———. *Études anatoliennes*. Paris, 1937.

———. "Inscriptions grecques d'Asie Mineure," in *Anatolian Studies Presented to William Hepburn Buckler*. Manchester, 1939, 227–248 (*OMS* 1.611–632).

———. "Hellenica," *Rev. Phil.* 13[3] (1939) 97–217 (*OMS* 2.1250–1370).

———. *Les Gladiateurs dans l'Orient grec*. Paris, 1940.

———. "Un édifice du sanctuaire de l'Isthme dans une inscription de Corinthe," *Hellenica* 1 (1940) 43–53.

———. "Épitaphe de Tripolis de Lydie," *Hellenica* 1 (1940) 149–153.

———. "Voyages épigraphiques en Asie Mineure," *Rev. Phil.* 16[3] (1943) 170–201.

———. "Sur un type monétaire de Prousa de l'Olympe et sur des épigrammes," *Hellenica* 2 (1946) 94–102.

————. "Épigramme d'Égine," *Hellenica* 4 (1948) 5–34.

————. "Épigrammes relatives à des gouverneurs," *Hellenica* 4 (1948) 35–126.

————. "Deux textes inutilisés sur Pergè et sur Sidè," *Hellenica* 5 (1948) 64–76.

————. "Sur une monnaie de Synnada: ΤΡΟΦΕΥΣ," *Hellenica* 7 (1949) 74–81; with additions, *Hellenica* 11/12 (1960) 569–576.

————. "Inscription honorifique de Tarse," *Hellenica* 7 (1949) 197–205.

————. "Le culte de Caligula à Milet et la province d'Asie," *Hellenica* 7 (1949) 206–238.

————. "Contribution à la topographie des villes d'Asie Mineure méridionale," *CRAI* 1951, 254–259.

Robert, J. and L. *La Carie II: Le plateau de Tabai et ses environs.* Paris, 1954.

Robert, L. Review of A. Rehm, *Didyma, Gnomon* 31 (1959) 657–674 (*OMS* 3.1622–1639).

————. "Sur un papyrus de Paris: Glossaire latin-grec," *Hellenica* 11/12 (1960) 5–15.

————. "Épitaphes et acclamations byzantines à Corinthe," *Hellenica* 11/12 (1960) 21–52.

————. "ΑΙΤΗΣΑΜΕΝΟΣ sur les monnaies," *Hellenica* 11/12 (1960) 53–62.

————. "Circulation des monnaies d'Histiée," *Hellenica* 11/12 (1960) 63–69.

————. "Décret d'Andros," *Hellenica* 11/12 (1960) 116–125.

————. "Inscriptions d'Asie Mineure au Musée de Leyde," *Hellenica* 11/12 (1960) 214–262.

————. "Épigrammes," *Hellenica* 11/12 (1960) 267–349.

————. "Prêtres de Cyrène," *Hellenica* 11/12 (1960) 542–555.

————. "Recherches épigraphiques," *REA* 62 (1960) 276–361 (*OMS* 2.792–877).

————. "Voyage en Grèce et en Cilicie," *CRAI* 1961, 173–179 (*OMS* 3.1460–1466).

————. "Sur des lettres d'un métropolite de Phrygie au Xe siècle," *Journ. Savants* 1961.97–166, and 1962.5–74.

————. *Villes d'Asie Mineure*[2]. Paris, 1962.

————. *Noms indigènes dans l'Asie Mineure gréco-romaine.* Paris, 1963.

————. *Hellenica* 13: *D'Aphrodisias à la Lycaonie.* Paris, 1965.

————. *Documents de l'Asie Mineure méridionale: Inscriptions, monnaies et géographie.* Paris, 1966.

————. "Inscriptions d'Aphrodisias: Première partie," *Antiquité Classique* 35 (1966) 377–432.

————. "Encore une inscription grecque de l'Iran," *CRAI* 1967, 281–296.

————. "Sur des inscriptions d'Éphèse: Fêtes, athlètes, empereurs, épigrammes," *Rev. Phil.* 41[3] (1967) 7–84.

————. "Enterrements et épitaphes," *Antiquité Classique* 37 (1968) 406–488.

————. "Trois oracles de la Théosophie et un prophète d'Apollon," *CRAI* 1968, 568–599.

————. "Les inscriptions," in *Laodicée du Lycos: Le Nymphée.* Québec and Paris, 1969, 247–389.

————. "Inscriptions d'Athènes et de la Grèce centrale," Ἀρχ. Ἐφ. 1969, 1–58.

————. "Théophane de Mytilène à Constantinople," *CRAI* 1969, 42–64.

————. "Les épigrammes satiriques de Lucillius sur les athlètes: Parodie et réalités," *L'épigramme grecque.* Entretiens Hardt 14. Geneva, 1969.

————. "Deux concours grecs à Rome," *CRAI* 1970, 6–27.

————. "Les colombes d'Anastase et autres volatiles," *Journ. des Savants* 1971, 81–105.

————. "Épigraphie et antiquités grecques," *Annuaire du Collège de France, 73ᵉ Année* (1973) 473–492.

————. "Sur des inscriptions de Délos," *Études déliennes.* BCH Suppl. 1. Paris, 1973, 435–489.

————. "De Cilicie à Messine et à Plymouth avec deux pierres errantes," *Journ. des Savants* 1973, 161–211.

————. "Un citoyen de Téos à Bouthrôtos d'Épire," *CRAI* 1974, 508–529.

————. "Les inscriptions de Thessalonique," *Rev. Phil.* 48³ (1974) 180–246.

————. "Des Carpathes à la Propontide," *Studii Clasice* 16 (1974) 53–88.

————. "Documents d'Asie Mineure," *BCH* 101 (1977) 43–132.

————. "La titulature de Nicée et de Nicomédie: La gloire et la haine," *HSCP* 81 (1977) 1–39.

Romilly, J. de. "Vocabulaire et propagande, ou les premiers emplois du mot ὁμόνοια," *Mélanges . . . Pierre Chantraine.* Études et commentaires 79. Paris, 1972.

Rossner, M. "Asiarchen und Archiereis Asias," *Studii Clasice* 16 (1974) 101–142.

Rostovtzeff, M. I. "Frumentum," *RE* 7 (1910) 126–187.

————. *Studien zur Geschichte des römischen Kolonates,* Arch. f. Papyrusf. Beih. 1. Leipzig and Berlin, 1910.

————. "Pontus, Bithynia and the Bosporus," *Ann. Brit. Sch. Athens* 22 (1916–1918) 1–22.

————. *Iranians and Greeks in South Russia.* Oxford, 1922.

————. *The Social and Economic History of the Hellenistic World.* Oxford, 1941.

————. *The Social and Economic History of the Roman Empire².* Edited by P. M. Fraser. Oxford, 1957.

Ruge, W. "Tarsos," *RE* 4 A (1932) 2413–2419.

————. "Nicaia 7," *RE* 17 (1936) 226–243.

————. "Nicomedia," *RE* 17 (1936) 468–492.

Ruggini, L. Cracco, "La vita associativa nelle città dell'Oriente greco: tradizioni locali e influenze romane," in *Assimilation et résistance à la culture gréco-romaine dans le monde ancien.* Bucharest and Paris, 1976, 463–491.

Russell, D. A. Review of Jones, *Plutarch, JRS* 62 (1972) 226–227.

Şahin, S. "Neufunde von antiken Inschriften in Nikomedia (Izmit) und in der Umgebung der Stadt." Dissertation, Münster, 1973.

————. "Ein Stein aus Hadrianoi in Mysien in Bursa," *ZPE* 24 (1977) 257–258.

Sautel, G. "Aspects juridiques d'une querelle de philosophes au IIᵉ siècle de notre ère: Plin., ad Traian., ep. 81–82," *Revue internationale de droits de l'antiquité* 3³ (1956) 423–443.

Scharold, J. *Dio Chrysostomus und Themistius.* Burghausen, 1912.

Schmid, W. *Der Atticismus in seinen Hauptvertretern.* Stuttgart, 1887–1897.

――――. "Dion 18," *RE* 5 (1903) 848–877.

Schmitt, H. H. *Rom und Rhodos: Geschichte ihrer politischen Beziehungen seit der ersten Berührung bis zum Aufgehung des Inselstaates im römischen Weltreich.* Münch. Beitr. z. Papyrusf. 40. Munich, 1957.

Schneider, A. M., and W. Karnapp. *Die Stadtmauer von Iznik (Nicaea).* Istanbuler Forsch. 9. Berlin, 1938.

Sherwin-White, A. N. *The Letters of Pliny: A Historical and Social Commentary.* Oxford, 1966.

Stadter, P. A. "Xenophon in Arrian's *Cynegeticus,*" *GRBS* 17 (1976) 157–167.

Stanton, G. R. "Sophists and Philosophers: Problems of Classification," *AJP* 94 (1973) 350–364.

Starr, C. G. "Epictetus and the Tyrant," *CP* 44 (1949) 20–29.

Stotz, C. L. "The Bursa Region of Turkey," *Geographical Review* 29 (1939) 81–100.

Strack, P. L. *Untersuchungen zur römischen Reichsprägung des zweiten Jahrhunderts I: Die Reichsprägung zur Zeit des Traian.* Stuttgart, 1931.

Syme, R. *Tacitus.* Oxford, 1958.

――――. "People in Pliny," *JRS* 58 (1968) 135–151.

Szarmach, M. "Les discours Diogeniens de Dion de Pruse," *Eos* 65 (1977) 77–90.

Tcherikover, V. A., and A. Fuks. *Corpus Papyrorum Judaicarum.* Cambridge, Mass., 1957–1964.

Thomas, J. D. "L. Peducaeus Colo(nus), Praefectus Aegypti," *ZPE* 21 (1976) 153–156.

Touloumakos, J. *Zum Geschichtsbewusstsein der Griechen in der Zeit der römischen Herrschaft.* Göttingen, 1971.

Tréheux, J. "'Ἐπ' ἀμφότερα," *BCH* 77 (1953) 155–165.

Trisoglio, F. "Le idee politiche di Plinio il Giovane e di Dione Crisostomo," *Il Pensiero Politico* 5 (1972) 3–43.

Turner, E. A. "The Gerousia of Oxyrhynchus," *Arch. f. Papyrusf.* 12 (1937) 179–186.

Vatin, Cl. "Damiurges et épidamiurges à Delphes," *BCH* 85 (1961) 236–255.

――――. "Une inscription inédite de Delphes," *BCH* 86 (1962) 57–63.

Vaux, R. de. *Archaeology and the Dead Sea Scrolls.* London, 1973.

Vidman, L. *Étude sur la correspondance de Pline le jeune avec Trajan.* Rozpravy Československé Akademie Věd 70, 14. Prague, 1960.

Vielmetti, C. "I 'Discorsi bitinici' di Dione Crisostomo," *Stud. Ital. Filol. Class.* 18 (1941) 89–108.

Vittinghoff, F. *Römische Kolonisation und Bürgerrechtspolitik unter Caesar und Augustus.* Abh. Akad. Wiss. Mainz, Jahrg. 1951, 14. Wiesbaden, 1952.

Wasowicz, A. *Olbia pontique et son territoire.* Ann. litt. de l'Univ. de Besançon 168. Paris, 1975.

Weber, E. "De Dione Chrysostomo Cynicorum sectatore," *Leipz. Stud. zur kl. Philol.* 10 (1887) 77–268.

Weingärtner, D. G. *Die Ägyptenreise des Germanicus.* Papyrolog. Texte u. Abh. 11. Bonn, 1969.

Weinreich, O. *Studien zur Martial.* Tüb. Beitr. zur Altertumswiss. 4. Stuttgart, 1928.

Welles, C. B. "Hellenistic Tarsus," *Mél. de l'Univ. Saint-Joseph* 38, 2 (1962) 41–75.

Wilcken, U. "Kaiser Nero und die alexandrinischen Phylen," *Arch. für Papyrusf.* 5 (1909) 182–184.

Wilhelm, A. *Beiträge zur griechischen Inschriftenkunde.* Österreich. Arch. Inst., Sonderschr. 7. Vienna, 1909.

———. "Neue Beiträge zur griechischen Inschriftenkunde. Dritter Teil," *Sitzungsb. Akad. Wien* 175, 1 (1913) (*Akademieschriften zur griechischen Inschriftenkunde* 1.125–176).

Williams, W. "The *Libellus* Procedure and the Severan Papyri," *JRS* 64 (1974) 86–103.

Wilmes, E. "Beiträge zur Alexandrinerrede (Or. 32) des Dion Chrysostomos," Dissertation, Bonn, 1970.

Wirszubski, Ch. *Libertas as a political idea at Rome during the late Republic and early Principate.* Cambridge, 1950.

Zablocka, J. "Über die Pacht von Gemeindeland in kleinasiatischen Städten der frühen Kaiserzeit," *Eos* 54 (1954) 166–180.

Abbreviations

Abbreviations of journals follow the practice of *L'Année Philologique*. Greek authors are cited in accordance with Liddell-Scott-Jones, *A Greek-English Lexicon*, Latin in accordance with *The Oxford Latin Dictionary*, with these exceptions: Philostratus' *Vitae Sophistarum* are cited by book, chapter, and section followed by the Olearius page (e.g. *VS* 1.8.4, p. 492), Synesius' *Dio* is cited by page and line of von Arnim's edition of Dio, 2.313–319. Epigraphical and papyrological publications are cited in accordance with Liddell-Scott-Jones.

The following special abbreviations have been used (for bibliographical details, see the Bibliography):

Ann. épigr.	*L'Année Épigraphique*
Arnim, *Dio*	H. von Arnim. *Leben und Werke des Dio von Prusa*
BMC	*Catalogue of the Greek Coins in the British Museum*
Bowersock, *Augustus*	G. W. Bowersock. *Augustus and the Greek World*
Bowersock, *Sophists*	G. W. Bowersock. *Greek Sophists in the Roman Empire*
Bull.	J. and L. Robert. "Bulletin épigraphique" appearing annually in *REG*, numbered by year of publication and item
Burckhardt, "Dio Chrysostomus"	J. Burckhardt. "Über den Wert des Dio Chrysostomus für die Kenntnis seiner Zeit"
Culte des Souverains	*Le Culte des Souverains dans l'Empire romain* Entretiens sur l'Antiquité classique 19. Geneva, 1973

Daremberg-Saglio	Ch. V. Daremberg, ed., and Edm. Saglio. *Dictionnaire des antiquités grecques et romaines.* Paris, 1877–1919
Deininger, *Provinziallandtage*	J. Deininger. *Die Provinziallandtage der römischen Kaiserzeit*
Duncan-Jones, *ERE*	R. P. Duncan-Jones. *The Economy of the Roman Empire: Quantitative Studies*
ESAR 4	Tenney Frank, ed. *An Economic Survey of Ancient Rome* 4. Baltimore, 1938
Friedländer, *Sittengeschichte*	L. Friedländer. *Darstellungen aus der Sittengeschichte Roms*[10]
Habicht, *Inschriften des Asklepieions*	Ch. Habicht. *Altertümer von Pergamon VIII 3: Die Inschriften des Asklepieions*
IOlb	T. N. Knipovitch and E. I. Levi. *Inscriptiones Olbiae (1917–1965).* Leningrad, 1968
Jones, *CERP*[2]	A. H. M. Jones. *Cities of the Eastern Roman Provinces*[2]
Jones, *GC*	A. H. M. Jones. *The Greek City from Alexander to Justinian*
Jones, *Plutarch*	C. P. Jones. *Plutarch and Rome*
Le Bas-Waddington	Ph. Le Bas and W. H. Waddington. *Inscriptions grecques et latines recueillies en Asie Mineure.* Paris, 1870
Liebenam, *Städteverwaltung*	W. Liebenam. *Städteverwaltung im römischen Kaiserreiche*
LSJ	H. G. Liddell and R. Scott. *A Greek-English Lexicon.* Revised by Sir H. Stuart Jones, with a Supplement. Oxford, 1968
Magie, *RRAM*	D. Magie. *Roman Rule in Asia Minor*
Migne, *PG*	J.-P. Migne. *Patrologiae Cursus Completus: Series Graeca*
Millar, *Cassius Dio*	F. Millar. *A Study of Cassius Dio*
Millar, *Emperor*	F. Millar. *The Emperor in the Roman World*
Momigliano, *Quarto Contributo*	A. D. Momigliano. *Quarto Contributo alla Storia degli Studi classici e del Mondo antico.* Rome, 1969
Momigliano, *Quinto Contributo*	A. D. Momigliano. *Quinto Contributo alla Storia degli Studi Classici e del Mondo antico.* Rome, 1975
Mommsen, *Staatsrecht*	Th. Mommsen. *Römisches Staatsrecht*[3]
Nock, *Essays*	A. D. Nock. *Essays on Religion and the Ancient World.* Oxford, 1972

Nörr, *Imperium und Polis*	D. Nörr. *Imperium und Polis in der hohen Prinzipatszeit*
PIR	*Prosopographia Imperii Romani*
RE	*Real-Encyclopädie der classischen Altertumswissenschaft*
Robert, *Ét. anat.*	L. Robert. *Études anatoliennes*
Robert, *Gladiateurs*	L. Robert. *Les Gladiateurs dans l'Orient grec*
Robert, *Laodicée*	L. Robert, in J. des Gagniers et al., *Laodicée du Lycos: Le Nymphée*
Robert, *Noms indigènes*	L. Robert. *Noms indigènes dans l'Asie Mineure gréco-romaine*
Robert, *OMS*	L. Robert. *Opera minora selecta*. Amsterdam, 1969–1974
Robert, *Villes*[2]	L. Robert. *Villes d'Asie Mineure*[2]
Roscher, *Lexikon*	W. H. Roscher, ed. *Ausführliches Lexikon der griechischen und römischen Mythologie*. Leipzig, 1884–1937
Rostovtzeff, *SEHRE*[2]	M. I. Rostovtzeff. *The Social and Economic History of the Roman Empire*[2]
Sherk, *RDGE*	R. K. Sherk. *Roman Documents from the Greek East*. Baltimore, 1969
Sherwin-White, *Pliny*	A. N. Sherwin-White. *The Letters of Pliny: A Historical and Social Commentary*
Syme, *Tacitus*	R. Syme. *Tacitus*

Notes

Chapter 1. Prusa

1. F. K. Dörner, *RE* 23 (1957) 1077–1078; Ch. Habicht, ibid. 1103–1104.

2. For geographical descriptions of the city and its region, see A. Philippson, *Petermanns Mitteilungen, Ergänzungsheft* 177 (1913) 69–72, C. L. Stotz, *Geographical Review* 29 (1939) 81–100, Magie, *RRAM* 306; an interesting picture of nineteenth-century Bursa in A. D. Mordtmann, *Anatolien: Skizzen und Reisebriefen aus Kleinasien (1850–1859)* (Hannover, 1925) 289–302.

3. Philippson (above, n. 2) 71; Robert, *Ét. anat.* 231, *Hellenica* 2 (1946) 94–102; Dörner (above, n. 1) 1082–1083.

4. Cic. *De Or.* 1.62 (other references in Magie, *RRAM* 1188 n. 18); *ILS* 7789.

5. Robert, *Hellenica* 2 (1946) 94–102.

6. *Or.* 44.9, cf. *Or.* 48.4. These remarks may be the ultimate source of St. Byz. s.v. Προῦσα, πόλις μικρὰ Βιθυνίας, which is not accurate.

7. On this see essentially W. Ruge, *RE* 3 (1897) 508–509; E. Gren, *Kleinasien und der Ostbalkan in der wirtschaftlichen Entwicklung der römischen Kaiserzeit* (Uppsala, 1941) 15–18.

8. Robert, *Ét. anat.* 228–235 (*SEG* 16.744); on these *epistatai*, M. Holleaux, *Études d'épigraphie* 3 (Paris, 1942) 216–219.

9. Memnon, *FGrHist* 434 F 28.6, App. *Mith.* 334 (who calls the city "Prusias" by mistake). Cf. Plutarch's Chaeronea in the first Mithridatic war, Jones, *Plutarch* 6–7.

10. Cf. Strabo on the boundaries of Roman provinces, 13.629.

11. The principal texts are Pliny, *Ep.* 10.79, 80, 112, 114, 115, D.C. 37.20.2. Cf. Magie, *RRAM* 369; L. Vidman, *Étude sur la correspondance de Pline le Jeune avec Trajan* (Prague, 1960) 66–67; Sherwin-White, *Pliny* ad loc.; A. J.

Marshall, *JRS* 58 (1968) 103–109, who argues that Gai. *Inst.* 1.193 does not refer to Pompey's law, as usually supposed.

12. T. R. S. Broughton, *ESAR* 4.543–546; Magie, *RRAM* 399–401.

13. Magie, *RRAM* 400.

14. Memmius: F. Münzer, *RE* 15 (1931) 612. Brigands: Str. 12.574, Robert, *Ét. anat.* 97–98, Peek, *GVI* 1728.

15. Cf. Robert, *RPh* 16³ (1943) 201.

16. D.C. 51.20.6–7; on this enactment, Deininger, *Provinziallandtage* 16–19; Ch. Habicht in *Le Culte des Souverains* 55–64.

17. On the *koinon*, Deininger (above, n. 16) 60–64. Broughton (above, n. 12) 709 suggests that the Pontic *koinon* only became separate from the Bithynian after Dio.

18. Str. 17.840, D.C. 53.12.4. On the implications of this measure, F. Millar, *JRS* 56 (1966) 156–166.

19. On the unusual status of the Bithynian procurators, M. Rostovtzeff, *ABSA* 22 (1916–1918) 15–19.

20. Magie, *RRAM* 596, 605, 626, 662.

21. D.C. 54.7.4–5 (20 B.C.): the edict of Augustus mentioned by Pliny, *Ep.* 10.79.2, may date from this time.

22. Dörner (above, n. 1) 1081.

23. Restriction: see now Cl. Vatin, *BCH* 85 (1961) 248–250; Jones, *GC* 173–174, minimizes the frequency of such restrictions. Legislation: Liebenam, *Städteverwaltung* 247–248, 480; Jones, *GC* 177–178. Suspension: Dio, *Or.* 48.1.

24. Membership: Pliny, *Ep.* 10.79.1, 114.3. Censors: Pliny, *Ep.* 10.79.3, 112.1, 114.1. Cf. Liebenam, *Städteverwaltung* 258–259; Robert, *BCH* 52 (1928) 410–411 (*OMS* 2.881–882), Magie, *RRAM* 1505 n. 31.

25. Liebenam, *Städteverwaltung* 285–286; Jones, *GC* 174; Magie, *RRAM* 643–644, Dörner (above, n. 1) 1081.

26. On *gerusiae* generally, see Chapter 9 at nn. 73–75. Le Bas-Waddington 3.1112.

27. *Or.* 44.3, 46.2–3, 50.7.

28. Tac. *Ann.* 1.74, 12.22, 14.46.

29. Ibid. 2.54, where Pontus and Bithynia are clearly one of the provinces "worn out by internal strife or the wrongdoing of their governors" (*magistratus:* for this sense, cf. *Ann.* 4.6).

30. Cl. Bosch, *Die kleinasiatische Münzen der römischen Kaiserzeit* 2, 1, 1 (Stuttgart, 1935) 173 (council), 92 (Nicaea and Nicomedia).

31. *PIR²* L 309; Dio, *Or.* 46.3–4, with the comments of Arnim, *Dio* 123. Note the temple of Claudius at Prusa, Pliny, *Ep.* 10.70.2. Cf. Millar, *Emperor* 481–482.

32. To those mentioned by Strabo, 12.566, must be added the poet Parthenius of Nicaea.

33. *Or.* 46.3. παιδεία could indicate a man of letters, but also a profession such as medicine.

34. Viz. the two Aemiliani, G. W. Bowersock, *CQ* 15² (1965) 268–269. Another contemporary, Cassius Asclepiodotus of Nicaea, may also have been a philosopher; note συνόντων, D.C. 62.26.2.

35. Philip of Prusias: K. Ziegler, *RE* 21 (1951) 682. Archippus of Prusa: Pliny, *Ep.* 10.58.

36. However, two Stoic philosophers known from inscriptions at Prusa are from Hadriani in Mysia: S. Şahin, *ZPE* 24 (1977) 257–258.

37. Reckoning Prusa about a third of the size of Pergamum, of which the total population can be supposed about 180,000: Duncan-Jones, *ERE* 261 n. 0.

38. *Or.* 44.5.

39. Cf. Trajan on the freedom of Amisus, Pliny, *Ep.* 10.93; generally, R. Bernhardt, *Imperium und Eleutheria* (Hamburg, 1971) 229–240; G. P. Burton, *JRS* 65 (1975) 105–106.

40. Cf. Jones, *GC* 135–136; Chapter 11 at n. 41.

41. Cf. Jones, *GC* 122–123; Chapter 12 at n. 26.

42. Dio, *Or.* 46.6, 9; Pliny, *Ep.* 10.70.2.

43. Pliny, *Ep.* 10.23.1; 70.1; Dio *Or.* 47.15, 40.9.

44. Peasants: Jones, *GC* 172–173; though Dio's huntsmen of Euboea had citizen rights in the nearby city, *Or.* 7.49. Tradesmen: cf. the Linenworkers at Tarsus, *Or.* 34.21–23, and Chapter 9 at n. 79.

45. *Or.* 44.3 (for the expression προεστὼς τῆς πόλεως, cf. *Or.* 36.21, 40.18, 48.9). The name is preserved only by Phot. *Bibl.* 165A, Suda, Δ 1240.

46. *Or.* 46.5. The drift of the passage shows that the debts were owed to the estate, so that διαλέλυμαι in 6 must mean "I have been paid," not "I have paid" (thus rightly LSJ s.v. διαλύω, I 7).

47. Cf. Philostr. *VS* 2.1.4, p. 549; Duncan-Jones, *ERE* 21.

48. Duncan-Jones, *ERE* 344.

49. *Or.* 46.3; for this sense of φιλοτιμία, "benefaction," see especially Robert, *Gladiateurs* 276–280. That this is Dio's maternal grandfather is shown by *Or.* 41.6.

50. *Or.* 44.3.

51. Ibid. For public burial, Robert, *AC* 37 (1968) 413–416; for funeral games, Robert, *Ét. anat.* 48.

52. For intermarriage between Bithynian cities, *Or.* 38.22, 40.22; for Dio and Apamea, *Or.* 41.6.

53. *Or.* 46.6; siblings are mentioned in *Or.* 44.3, 8.

54. *Or.* 46.6.

55. Cf. Pliny, *Ep.* 2.4.3, with the comments of Duncan-Jones, *ERE* 18; also the decree for Agreophon of Caunus, full of parallels to Dio, P. Herrmann, *OAth* 10 (1971) 37 line 14.

56. *Or.* 46.7–8. For a map of modern land utilization in the vale of Bursa, Stotz (above, n. 2) 82, reproduced by Robert, *StClas* 16 (1974) 66.

57. The denial in *Or.* 46.8 is evasive.

58. For a survey of land values in Italy, mostly rural estates, Duncan-Jones, *ERE* 210–215.

59. For such colonnades see Broughton (above, n. 12) 800–801, 938, Robert, *JS* 1971, 91; on the ἐργασταί who traded here, Robert, *REG* 42 (1929) 33–34 (*OMS* 1.543–544).

60. *Or.* 41.6. Thus correctly explained by F. Vittinghoff, *Römische Kolonisation* (Mainz, 1951) 21 n. 3, cf. F. Millar, *JRS* 58 (1968) 222; Sherwin-White, *Pliny* 676, argues that Dio's father was a *peregrinus*.

61. Assumed by G. F. Hertzberg, *Die Geschichte Griechenlands unter der Herrschaft der Römer* 2 (Halle, 1868) 186.

62. Both Arrian, *Epict.* 1.12.13, etc., and Sextus Empiricus (ed. Mau, *Index Nominum* s.v.) use it as a stock name: cf. Plut. *Aet. Rom.* 271 E. Other Dios in Prusa: Lebas-Waddington 3.1113 a-b, G. Mendel, *BCH* 33 (1909) 411 no. 413. Cult of Zeus: Dörner (above, n. 1) 1084.

63. Perhaps Claudius, cf. Chapter 1 at n. 31: the historian Cassius Dio, probably Dio's descendant (Millar, *Cassius Dio* 11) had "Claudius" among his names, *Bull.* 1971.400 = *Ann. épigr.* 1971.430.

64. Pliny, *Ep.* 10.81.1. The notion that it derives from his friendship with Nerva (thus, most recently, Sherwin-White, *Pliny* 676), does not seem plausible, though Pliny, *NH* 33.36, might be thought to provide an analogy. Other Cocceiani in the province: *IGRR* 3.1432 (Amastris), *Bull.* 1953.193 no. 2 (Prusias ad Hypium).

65. Cf. *PIR²* D 93; Millar, *Cassius Dio* 11.

Chapter 2. Education and Youth

1. H.-I. Marrou, *Histoire de l'éducation dans l'antiquité⁴* (Paris, 1958) 359–389.

2. The younger Pliny's Comum had no *praeceptor* until about 104, *Ep.* 4.13. The grave epigram of Magnus, Prusa's first *grammaticus*, survives, but cannot be exactly dated, G. Mendel, *BCH* 33 (1909) 317–318 no. 71 (Peek, *GVI* no. 1182).

3. Cf. Marrou (above, n. 1) 360.

4. *Or.* 18.8; cf. Sen. *Ep.* 49.5.

5. For an eloquent architect, Cic. *de Or.* 61; doctors, Cic. ibid., Pliny, *NH* 29.8–9, Dio, *Or.* 33.6, Bowersock, *Sophists* 66–67.

6. Cf. esp. Arr. *Epict.* 3.23, Musonius in A. Gell. 5.1 (pp. 130 ff. Hense), Bowersock, *Sophists* 11–12.

7. On these terms, Bowersock, *Sophists* 12–14; G. R. Stanton, *AJP* 94 (1973) 350–364; C. P. Jones in *Approaches to the Second Sophistic*, ed. G. W. Bowersock (University Park, Penn., 1974) 12–14.

8. Philostr. *VS* 1.21.5, p. 519.

9. Thus apparently Dio, *Or.* 32.11.

10. Thus Musonius pp. 59, 61 Hense.

11. Cf. Pius in *Dig.* 27.1.6.7.

12. Dio, *Or.* 11.6, 14, Plut. *quaest. conviv.* 710 B, Arr. *Epict.* 2.20.23, 3.2.11.

13. Luc. *Peregr.* 13, DC. 66.15.5.

14. *VS* 1. pref., p. 484, 1.8.4, p. 492.

15. *VS* 1.7, pp. 486–488.

16. Reading τρύχεσι with Cobet.

17. The standard biography is by Ch. Lacombrade, *Synésios de Cyrène* (Paris, 1951); good surveys in C. H. Coster, *Late Roman Studies* (Cambridge, Mass., 1968) 145–182, 218–268.

18. The first part in Arnim's edition of Dio, 2.313–319; the full text in N. Terzaghi, ed., *Synesii Cyrenensis Opuscula* (Rome, 1944) 233–278; texts and translations by K. Treu (Berlin, 1959), A. Garzya (Naples, 1970); commentary by K. Treu (Berlin, 1958); English translation and notes by A. Fitzgerald, *The Essays and Hymns of Synesius of Cyrene* (London, 1930) 1.148–182.

19. 314 line 24, 317 lines 31 ff.

20. 315 lines 28 ff.

21. 316 lines 1 f., 314 line 25.

22. 316 lines 8 ff.

23. 316 lines 22 ff.

24. Cf. the useful summary by Treu in his translation (above, n. 18) 3–4.

25. On the *Dio* as a "*Streitschrift*," Lacombrade (above, n. 17) 137–149; H.-I. Marrou in *The Conflict between Paganism and Christianity in the Fourth Century*, ed. A. Momigliano (Oxford, 1963) 144–145; A. Garzya, *RFIC* 100[3] (1972) 32–45; P. Desideri, *AAT* 107 (1973) 551–593, esp. 590–591.

26. Fronto, p. 133 Hout = 2.50 Haines: "quid nostra memoria Euphrates, Dio, Timocrates, Athenodotus? quid horum magister Musonius? nonne summa facundia praediti neque minus sapientiae quam eloquentiae gloria incluti exstiterunt?" This passage has had an unlucky history. It is not mentioned in Arnim's *Dio* or included among the *testimonia* in his edition (2.311–332). Brzoska, *RE* 5 (1903) 848 no. 5, considers this an unknown Dio: Schmid, ibid. 851, correctly refers it to Dio of Prusa (thus already *PIR*[1] D 78). P. Grimal, *Latomus* 14 (1955) 373 n. 2, understands *magister* simply to indicate superiority in eloquence, but this seems impossible. Timocrates was also a pupil of Euphrates (Philostr. *VS* 1.25.5, p. 229), but a man could be taught by his teacher's teacher.

27. *PIR*[2] A 1291.

28. *Or.* 31.122, cf. Arnim, *Dio* 216. Note the many Musonii at Athens, including a Musonius Rufus, in Dittenberger's index to *IG* III.

29. On Musonius generally, K. von Fritz, *RE* 16 (1933) 893–897; Cora E. Lutz, *YCIS* 10 (1947) 3–147 (text and translation of the fragments); A. C. van Geytenbeek, *Musonius Rufus and Greek Diatribe* (Assen, 1963).

30. Tac. *Ann.* 14.59, cf. 14.22.

31. Ibid. 15.71.

32. Gyaros: von Fritz (above, n. 29) 893–894. For this island as a place of banishment, see Mayor on Juv. 1.73, and more recently *The New York Times Index 1973*, p. 929. Isthmus: Philostr. *VA* 5.19, [Luc.] *Nero*.

33. Tac. *Hist.* 3.81, 4.10, 4.40.

34. Them. 173 C; D.C. 66.13.2.

35. Jer. *Chron.* ad Ol. 214, 3, p. 189 Helm[2]; note the doubts of R. Helm, *Philologus*, Suppl. 21, 2 (1929) 85–87.

36. Pages 114 ff. Hense (beard), 57 ff. (land), 13 ff. (women), 60 f. (sophists).

37. The citations are collected by Hense, pp. 124 ff.

38. Arr. *Epict.* 2.23, esp. sect. 20.

39. Pliny, *Ep.* 1.10 (*PIR²* E 121).

40. Philostr. *VA* 7.16.

41. Thus *Or.* 21.6–10, 31.110, 150, 32.60. Cf. Jones, *Plutarch* 18–19.

42. Philostr. *VA* 5.24 ff., esp. 27 (Vespasian, Dio, Euphrates), 32–37 (debate), 37 (characterisation of Dio), 38 (reconciliation, pupil).

43. Hdt. 3.80–82. The same passage is imitated by Philostratus' contemporary Cassius Dio, 52.1–41.

44. "Narratio fide parum digna," Stein, *PIR²* D 93; it is defended by F. Grosso, *Acme* 7 (1954) 396–407, 416 n. 71.

45. *VA* 5.26. For other signs of the influence of Dio on the *VA*, cf. *Or.* 31.121 with *VA* 4.22.

46. *Or.* 7.66.

47. Dio, *Or.* 33.14, 47.19, 50.6, Luc. *Nigr.* 20, Philostr. *VS* 1.22.3, p. 524. In some of these passages, however, "king" (βασιλεύς) may simply mean "great man," like the Latin *rex*.

48. Jones, *Plutarch* 44.

49. Note the *Graeci comites* of an oriental prince educated in Rome, Tac. *Ann.* 2.2.

50. Them. 139 A, cf. Stein, *RE* Suppl. 5 (1931) 730. On Titus' love life, Suet. *Tit.* 7, Jul. *Caes.* 311 A.

51. *Or.* 28, 29.

52. *Or.* 13.1, cf. *PIR²* F 355.

53. *Or.* 45.2. For Nerva and the Flavians, Suet. *Dom.* 1.1, Syme, *Tacitus* 2.

54. Philostr. *VS* 1.7.1, p. 205, Synes. 317 lines 34 f., 319 line 22.

55. Luc. *Musc. Enc.*, Apul. *Flor.* 12. Cf. A. S. Pease, *CP* 21 (1926) 27–42.

56. Ael. *Var. Hist.* 3.1, Philostr. *VA* 6.4.

57. Note Arr. *Epict.* 3.23.11, a philosopher "describing" Pan and the Nymphs.

58. What may be a fragment of this work, *JEA* 16 (1930), 191 fr. 5 recto, suits an attack on the Cynics: note line 140, "beggars" (ἀγύρται), and line 143, perhaps "frankness" (παρρησία), a catchword of the Cynics: cf. Arr. *Epict.* 3.22.96, Aristid. 46, p. 401 Dindorf, Philostr. *VA* 6.31; J. F. Kindstrand, *Bion of Borysthenes* (Uppsala, 1976) 263.

59. Diog. Laert. 7.2.

60. D.C. 66.12.2–3; doubted by Ch. Wirszubski, *Libertas* (Cambridge, 1950), 148–149; certainly Thrasea was accompanied by a Cynic in his last hours, Tac. *Ann.* 16.34–35.

61. Pages 32 ff. Hense. Note also Musonius' political feud with a Stoic and a Cynic, Tac. *Hist.* 4.10, 4.40, cf. *Ann.* 16.32.

62. Arr. *Epict.* 3.22, esp. sect. 80.

63. Aristides: XLVII Dindorf. Synesius: *Ep.* 154, printed in Treu's translation of the *Dio* (above, n. 18).

64. Jones, *Plutarch* 14–15; but cf. D. A. Russell, *JRS* 62 (1972) 226–227.

65. Suet. *Vesp.* 18, D.C. 66.12.1a.

66. Suet. *Vesp.* 15, D.C. 66.12.2–3 (*PIR²* H 59).

67. Suet. *Vesp.* 13, D.C. 66.12–13, 15.5.

68. Synes, *Dio* 316 lines 21 f. πολιτεία clearly has its later sense, "conduct" (Lampe, *A Patristic Greek Lexicon*, s.v. F), not "the state" (as translated by Jones, *Historia* 22 [1973] 305).

69. Thus Arnim, *Dio* 150.

70. J. Jüthner, *WS* 26 (1904) 154, suggests a stroke.

71. Thus Arnim, *Dio* 143.

72. Thus Isocrates' *Evagoras,* and compare the many funerary epigrams in *Anth. Pal.* 7 which were not meant to be cut on stone.

73. *Or.* 29.19–20 (early death), 21–22 (survivors).

74. On the last two, L. Robert, *Anatolian Studies . . . Buckler* (Manchester, 1939) 230–244 = *OMS* 614–628.

75. Robert, *AC* 37 (1968) 406–417, esp. 409–411.

76. Robert in *L'épigramme grecque,* Entretiens Hardt 14 (Geneva, 1969) 193–198.

77. Courage: Robert, *AC* 35 (1966) 429. Moral qualities: Robert, *Hellenica* 13 (1965) 140.

78. Robert, *Hellenica* 11/12 (1960) 338–340.

79. Robert (above, n. 78) 336–337, (above, n. 76) 255.

80. For the situation of *Or.* 28, Jüthner (above, n. 70) 151–155; on the *epistates,* see now Robert, *CRAI* 1974, 520–528.

81. Scars: Robert (above, n. 76) 235–236. *Aleiptos:* Robert (above, n. 78) 338–340, citing this passage.

82. See the analysis of W. Kroll, *RhM* 70 (1915) 607–610; contested by J. F. Kindstrand, *Homer in der zweiten Sophistik* (Uppsala, 1973) 154–155.

83. Synes., *Dio* p. 319 line 22. Thus Arnim, *Dio* 166, Kroll (above, n. 82) 608; against, Schmid (above, n. 26) 850, Kindstrand (above, n. 82) 144–153, 161–162.

84. This point is doubted by Burckhardt, "Dio Chrysostomus" 94, cf. 105.

85. For Ilion under the Caesars, A. Brückner in W. Dörpfeld, *Troja und Ilion* (Athens, 1902) 588–593, who makes this suggestion, 590–591.

86. Thus, correctly, Momigliano, *Quinto Contributo* 258.

87. Cf. Kindstrand, (above, n. 82) 160–162.

88. Tac. *Ann.* 12.58, with Furneaux's note; Magie, *RRAM* 103, 234, 405, 542.

Chapter 3. Riot at Prusa

1. H. Francotte, *Mélanges Nicole* (Geneva, 1905) 135–157; M. I. Rostovtzeff, *RE* 7 (1910) 182–187; id., *SEHRE²* 145–147, 599–601.

2. Liebenam, *Städteverwaltung* 362–367; Francotte (above, n. 1) 140–143, 155; Jones, *GC* 215–217, esp. 217.

3. Liebenam, *Städteverwaltung* 368–369; Francotte (above, n. 1) 155–156; Rostovtzeff, *RE* 7 (1910) 185; Jones, *GC* 217–218.

4. For *agoranomoi* so doing, Rostovtzeff (above, n. 3) 183, 185, Jones, *GC* 217; for *sitonai*, Robert, *Ét. anat.* 347, Jones, *GC* 218.

5. *Epidoseis:* Francotte (above, n. 1) 148–151; Jones, *GC* 217.

6. Liebenam, *Städteverwaltung* 368; Rostovtzeff (above, n. 3) 185; Jones, *GC* 350 n. 15.

7. On the nature of liturgies generally, and the distinction between them and *archai*, Liebenam, *Städteverwaltung* 417–430; Fr. Oertel, *Die Liturgie* (Leipzig, 1917) 2–7; Jones, *GC* 167–168, 175–176; Rostovtzeff, *SEHRE*² 387–388.

8. The earliest reference in LSJ s.v. I 4 is Aeschin. 3.19; generally, and on the even more specialized meaning of "gladiatorial show," Robert, *Gladiateurs* 276–280; several examples now in P. Herrmann, *OAth* 10 (1971) 37.

9. Cf. Dio, *Or.* 46.9.

10. On acclamations generally, E. Peterson, Εἷς θεός (Göttingen, 1926), esp. 141–145; id., *RhM* 78 (1929) 221–223; J. Colin, *Les villes libres de l'orient gréco-romain* (Brussels, 1965), Ch. IV; *Bull.*, Index III s.v. acclamations; in Dio, *Or.* 7.24–26, 40.29, 48.2, 10. For τροφεύς, Robert, *Hellenica* 11/12 (1960) 569–571, with bibliography, 569 n. 2.

11. For political pressure applied by shouts, e.g. *Ev. Marc.* 15.6–15, *Acta Ap.* 19.28–34, Dio, *Or.* 40.3, 47.18–20, 48.2–3.

12. Stoning: Dio, *Or.* 46.2, 6, 11 and below, n. 19. Burning: Plut. *praec. ger. reip.* 815 D, and below, n. 19.

13. Cf. Jones, *GC* 356 n. 47.

14. *Or.* 7.25–26.

15. Rostovtzeff, *SEHRE*² 145.

16. Aspendus: Philostr. *VA* 1.15. Acraephia: Robert, *BCH* 59 (1935) 438–452 = *OMS* 279–293, esp. 446–448 = 287–289. Antioch: *Ann. épigr.* 1925.126, cf. Rostovtzeff, *SEHRE*² 599–600, B. M. Levick, *Roman Colonies in Southern Asia Minor* (Oxford, 1967) 96–97.

17. See above, n. 16. For similar action by other governors, Cic. *Att.* 5.21.8, and perhaps F. K. Dörner, *Inschriften und Denkmäler aus Bithynien* (Berlin, 1941) 53 no. 24 (Nicomedia).

18. Migne, *PG* 31.261–278, esp. 268 B.

19. Aspendus: above, n. 16. Athens: Philostr. *VS* 1.23.1, p. 526, cf. Suet. *Vesp.* 4.3 (a proconsul pelted with turnips). Late empire: R. MacMullen, *Enemies of the Roman Order* (Cambridge, Mass., 1966) 344 n. 19.

20. *Syll.*³ 780. For a similar "siege" in nineteenth-century Turkey, ending with the burning of a house and its occupants, F. V. J. Arundell, *Discoveries in Asia Minor* 1 (London, 1834) 255–256.

21. Jones, *GC* 184, with evidence, 342 n. 55. Dio: 49.

22. *IGRR* 3.1423, [τῆς ἀγορᾶς ἐπι]μελ[ησά]μενον ἐν τῇ σει[τοδείᾳ]; cf. Jones, *GC* 350 n. 15.

23. ἀποδέχεσθαι (approve), *Or.* 31.4, 8, 122, *Or.* 51.1, 9, Robert, *REA* 62 (1960) 325 n. 2 (*OMS* 841), *Hellenica* 11/12 (1960) 571 n. 2. φιλοτιμία (munificence): above, n. 8. ἐντροπή (influence), *Or.* 31.149, Robert, *REA* 62 (1960) 327

n. 3 (*OMS* 843). αἰτεῖσθαι (request): Robert, *Hellenica* 11/12 (1960) 58–62. παρέχειν (contribute), Robert, *Hellenica* 7 (1949) 76. ἡγεμόνες (leaders), *Or.* 38.33, 36, 40.6, 43.11, etc., Robert, *REA* 62 (1960) 329 (*OMS* 845), H. J. Mason, *Greek Terms for Roman Institutions* (Toronto, 1974) 148–149.

24. Jones, *Plutarch* 114, 117–118.

25. For this sense of εὐφημεῖν, Peterson, *RhM* 78 (1929) 222.

26. Cf. Jones, *Plutarch* 112, 119.

27. Thus Q. Stertinius, brother of the famous Xenophon of Cos, earned half a million sesterces a year as the imperial doctor and left a joint estate with his brother of thirty million: Pliny, *NH* 29.7.

28. Dio: Chapter 12. Alexander: Luc. *Alex.* 58.

29. Herrmann (above, n. 8) 37 lines 13–14.

30. Migne, *PG* 31.276 A, cf. 292 B.

31. Ibid., 293 A-B.

32. F. Millar, *JRS* 53 (1963) 31–32; id., *Emperor* 163–174.

33. Observed by H. Dessau, *Hermes* 34 (1899) 83–84, and accepted by Arnim, ibid. 375–376. For Vespasian and the *fiscus*, Suet. *Vesp.* 16.3, Millar, *JRS* 53 (1963) 41.

34. Migne, *PG* 31.313 B.

35. Robert, *StudClas* 16 (1974) 64–68.

36. See below, Chronology, discussing *Or.* 45, 47.

37. Jones, *Plutarch* 116; for the later empire, Jones, *GC* 192–210.

38. *Acta Ap.* 19.40.

39. Ulp. *Dig.* 1.18.13 pref., "congruit bono et gravi praesidi curare ut pacata atque quieta provincia sit quam regit," cited by Sherwin-White on Pliny, *Ep.* 10.117.

40. Banishment, execution: Plut. *praec. ger. reip.* 813 F, 825 C. Assembly: Dio, *Or.* 48.1. Congregation: Pliny, *Ep.* 10.33.3, with Sherwin-White's note.

41. Title: Sardis may have lost the title of "Caesarian" in the same disturbance mentioned by Plutarch (above, n. 40): *Bull.* 1974.528. Freedom: Tac. *Ann.* 12.58, with Furneaux's note.

42. Plut. *praec. ger. reip.* 814 A.

43. Cf. Th. Mommsen, *Römische Geschichte* 5⁴ (Berlin, 1894) 337–338 = *The Provinces of the Roman Empire*, tr. W. P. Dickson (London, 1909) 1.366–367, esp. the sentence, "An Reinheit der Gesinnung und Klarheit über die Lage der Dinge giebt der Bithyner Dion dem Gelehrten von Chaeronea nichts nach, an Gestaltungskraft, an Feinheit und Schlagfertigkeit der Rede, an ernstem Sinn bei leichter Form, an praktischer Energie ist er ihm überlegen."

Chapter 4. Rhodes

1. For the dates of these two speeches, see the Appendix. Dio alludes to Rhodes in *Or.* 32.52.

2. Cf. Pliny, *Ep.* 3.18.1.

3. For what follows, see esp. H. von Gaertringen, *RE* Suppl. 5 (1931) 787–

808; Magie, *RRAM*, esp. 70–73, 104–111, 115–117, 218–219, 423–424; H. H. Schmitt, *Rom und Rhodos* (Munich, 1957). On Rhodian economy and society, Rostovtzeff, *The Social and Economic History of the Hellenistic World* (Oxford, 1941) 676–691; on the Peraea, P. M. Fraser and G. E. Bean, *The Rhodian Peraea and Islands* (Oxford, 1954).

4. Cf. Bowersock, *Augustus* 85.

5. Str. 14.652–653.

6. On this aspect of Tiberius' stay on Rhodes, Bowersock, *Augustus* 77.

7. App. *BC* 4.66, 72–73.

8. This seems to be implied by Dio, *Or.* 31.67, 69.

9. Str. 14.652–653, cf. Rostovtzeff (above, n. 3) 684, 687, 689–690.

10. D.C. 60.24.4, cf. R. Bernhardt, *Imperium und Eleutheria* (Hamburg, 1971) 208. For a similar incident at Cyzicus under Tiberius, Tac. *Ann.* 4.36, with Furneaux's note.

11. *IG* 12, 1, 2 (*IGRR* 4.1123), Tac. *Ann.* 12.58, Suet. *Cl.* 25.3, Nero 7.2.

12. *ILS* 8794 = *Syll.*[3] 814. Bernhardt (above, n. 10) 215, assumes that Rhodes was immune from 53 on.

13. Generally, H. van Gelder, *Geschichte der alten Rhodier* (The Hague, 1900) 290–298.

14. Coins: thus *Fitzwillian Museum, McClean Collection* no. 8633, and cf. Antiphil. *AP* 9, 178 and the commentary of A. S. F. Gow and D. L. Page. *The Garland of Philip* (Cambridge, 1968), 2.119–120.

15. Pliny, *NH* 34.45, Suet. *Nero* 31.1. *Illius principis simulacro* in Pliny, and *ipsius effigie* in Suetonius, need not mean that it was intended as a portrait of Nero (as A. Boethius, *Eranos* 50 [1952] 129–137): nor does Suetonius' *staret* imply that it was not completed (as P. Howell, *Athenaeum* 46[2] [1968] 292–299), cf. Suet. *Vesp.* 18.

16. Cf. Suet. *Vesp.* 8.4.

17. *IG* 12, 1, 58 (*IGRR* 4.1129), where the mention of κάλλιστα γράμματα from Titus strongly suggests that he was the donor: cf. the εὐκταιότατα ἀποκρίματα of *IG* 12, 1, 2 (*IGRR.* 4.1123). Thus A. Wilhelm, *SAWW* 175, 1 (1913) 51 = *Akademieschriften zur griechischen Inschriftenkunde* 1.173. A. D. Momigliano, *JRS* 41 (1951) 151 = *Quinto contributo* 969–970, suggests that Titus' grant was enacted by Domitian.

18. Plut. *praec. ger. reip.* 815 D.

19. Aristid. 24 K., esp. 58 (freedom), 32–34 (hostility).

20. Dio, *Or.* 13.12; Philostr. *VA* 4.22, Aristid. 24.1–3.

21. Dio, *Or.* 31.122; cf. Chapter 2 at nn. 27–28.

22. For the value of statues, Ch. Habicht, *Gottmenschentum und griechische Städte*[2] (Munich, 1970) 207; for this sense of τιμή, bibliography in Habicht, *Inschriften des Asklepieions* 79 n. 1.

23. Cf. Dio, *Or.* 31.9 ad fin. This is very frequent in inscriptions, cf. Habicht, *Inschriften des Asklepieions* nos. 35, 53, 56.

24. *Praec. ger. reip.* 820 B-C.

25. These two are again frequent in inscriptions: Plutarch similarly names them together in the class of moderate honors, *praec. ger. reip.* 820 C. On

prohedria, M. Maass, *Die Prohedrie des Dionysostheaters in Athen* (Munich, 1972) Ch. IV.

26. Nock, *HSCP* 41 (1930) 3 n. 2 = *Essays* 204 n. 5; Robert, *Hellenica* 11/12 (1960) 124 n. 2.

27. For the destruction of statues, Mayor on Juv. 10.58; the speech of Dio's pupil Favorinus on this subject is preserved in Dio's works (*Or.* 37), no doubt because of its affinity with *Or.* 31. For the erasure of the names of private persons, e.g. *Bull.* 1974.675.

28. Cic. *Att.* 6.1.26; H. Blanck, *Wiederverwendung alter Statuen als Ehrendenkmäler bei Griechen und Römern* (Rome, 1969) esp. 77–85; *Bull.* 1973.14.

29. Ch. Blinkenberg, *Lindos II: Inscriptions* (Berlin and Copenhagen, 1941) no. 419, cf. *Bull.* 1942.112, Blanck (above, n. 28) 101–102.

30. 24.56 K.

31. *Or.* 32.42.

32. Cf. *Bull.* 1966.289. On Dio's term ἄφρακτα, Blinkenberg (above, n. 29) 1015–1016.

33. For the changes in the status of Caunus since its liberation in 167, Bernhardt (above, n. 10) 125 (returned to Rhodes by Sulla), 141–142 (freed again before 51/50); Dio's language shows that it had been subjected again, and is corroborated by an inscription, G. E. Bean, *JHS* 74 (1954) 95 no. 37b, cf. *Bull.* 1956.274c. There is no ground for thinking that Vespasian restored it to Rhodes, as Bernhardt (above, n. 10) 215; more probably Claudius or Nero.

34. *Or.* 34.43–46, 47.13.

35. 24.45 K.

36. *Or.* 33.41, 39.1.

37. For this sense of ἀπογραφαί, *Or.* 34.10, Mommsen, *Staatsrecht* 2.417 n. 1; Broughton, *ESAR* 4.889, understands them as "lists of debt," but Dio clearly means that the temple did not lend.

38. For the bank, Broughton (above, n. 37) 559–560, 889–891, R. Bogaert, *Banques et banquiers dans les cités grecques* (Leyden, 1968) 245–254, esp. 248–249. For Ephesus in this period, Broughton (above, n. 37) 719; Seneca, *Ep.* 102.21, ranks it beside Alexandria.

39. Daremberg-Saglio 4.186; other authors also call it olive (ἐλαία), but properly it was of wild olive (κότινος).

40. L. Robert in *L'épigramme grecque,* Entretiens Hardt 14 (Geneva, 1969) 199. For such a death at Olympia, Paus. 8.40.1, with Frazer's note.

41. Suet. *Nero* 23–24, D.C. 63.14.1.

42. Cf. Bernhardt (above, n. 10) 183 (Athens, Sparta), 185 (Byzantium), 187 (Mytilene).

43. P. Graindor, *Athènes sous Auguste* (Cairo, 1927) 1–11.

44. For Athens, U. Kahrstedt, *Das wirtschaftliche Gesicht Griechenlands in der Kaiserzeit* (Bern, 1954) 42–64; Sparta, ibid. 192–203; Mytilene, Broughton (above, n. 37) 717; Byzantium, Tac. *Ann.* 12.62–63.

45. Dio no doubt alludes primarily to Demosthenes' speech *Against Leptines;* for the historical difficulties raised by his testimony, J. E. Sandys' edition, pp. xxix–xxxiii.

46. *Or.* 48.10, Robert, *Hellenica* 7 (1949) 81, citing *IGRR* 3.63, 67. For Pericles, esp. Plut. *Per.* 8.2–4. Cf. Graindor, *Athènes de Tibère à Trajan* (Cairo, 1931) 56.

47. *IG* 2² 3800; Graindor (above, n. 46) 56–58.

48. *IG* 2² 3786–3789 (only 3788 lacks the erasure); cf. *Hesperia* 36 (1967) 69 no. 13 B, *AE* 1972.56. On Nicanor, Bowersock, *Augustus* 96; *PIR²* I 440 is confused.

49. See Chapter 2 at n. 29.

50. Harold N. Fowler in *Corinth I: Introduction, Topography, Architecture* (Cambridge, Mass., 1932) 91.

51. Thus E. Fiechter, *Das Dionysos-Theater in Athen* 3 (Stuttgart, 1936) 82, followed by Robert, *Gladiateurs* 247 n. 1; J. Travlos, however, *Pictorial Dictionary of Ancient Athens* (New York, 1971) 538, dates this change ca. 400.

52. Robert, *Gladiateurs* 42, 117–118, 244.

53. Luc. *Dem.* 57, Philostr. *VA* 4.22; cf. Robert, *Gladiateurs* 246 n. 6.

54. Robert, *Gladiateurs* 248.

55. As by Graindor (above, n. 46) 56.

56. App. *BC* 5.7 may suggest competition between them for control of Tenos, cf. E. Gabba's apparatus ad loc. The Rhodians may also have remembered that, unlike themselves (*Or.* 31.113), the Athenians had supported Mithradates, cf. Tac. *Ann.* 2.55.1.

57. Automedon, *AP* 11.319, cf. Robert, *OMS* 4.93; Tac. *Ann.* 2.55.

58. *Or.* 13, 44.6.

59. 24.22, 58 K.

60. πίστις καὶ πρὸς τὸν δῆμον εὔνοια. For this stock phrase precisely at Rhodes, *IG* 12, 2, 58 (*IGRR* 4.1129); cf. Octavian on Seleucus of Rhosos, Sherk, *RDGE* no. 58 II lines 12–18.

61. Again, a stock phrase: examples are collected by Robert, *AC* 35 (1966) 405–406. For another rhetorical appeal to this treaty, App. *BC* 4.67.

62. The order in Dio shows that this cannot be a reference to Julius Agricola, as von Gaertringen supposed (above, n. 3) 811.

63. Cf. the speeches of Byzantine ambassadors to the senate, Tac. *Ann.* 12.62.

64. Many of the tablets on the Capitol were destroyed in the fire of 69, Suet. *Vesp.* 8.5.

65. Probably another exaggeration: Pliny, *NH* 36.34, talks of statues in the collection of Asinius Pollio *a Rhodo advecta.*

66. αὐτῷ προσήκοντος ἐκείνου τοῦ τεμένους. Although Pergamon is the last city mentioned, ἐκείνου implies that Dio refers to Athens: cf. below, n. 68.

67. Cf. Paus. 10.7.1 (Delphi), 5.25.8, 26.3 (Olympia), Tac. *Ann.* 16.23 (Pergamon); for possible evidence at Athens, Graindor (above, n. 46), 14–16.

68. For this possibility, cf. Graindor (above, n. 46) 13; for the inscription of Nero on the Parthenon (*IG* 2² 3277), see now S. Dow, *Cornell Alumni News,* December 1972, 13–21 (*Bull.* 1976.204).

69. Tac. *Ann.* 15.45, 16.23 (where see Furneaux on the date); Plut., *praec. ger. reip.* 815 D, perhaps refers to this event.

70. Hostility: W. Schmid, *Der Atticismus* 1 (Stuttgart, 1887) 38 n. 13. Re-

spect: Rostovtzeff, *SEHRE* 118. Assimilation: H. Fuchs, *Der geistige Wider-stand gegen Rom* (Berlin, 1938) 18, 50. For a contrary view, J. Palm, *Rom, Römertum und Imperium* (Lund, 1959) 17–20, 23–24, J. Touloumakos, *Zum Geschichtsbewusstsein der Griechen* (Göttingen, 1971) 54.

71. J. Jüthner, *Hellenen und Barbaren* (Leipzig, 1923) 79; Jones, *Plutarch* 124–125.

72. Jones, *Plutarch* 118 (decline: add *de def. orac.* 413 F–414 A), 68 (Rome's fortune), 122 (culture), 123 (gladiators).

73. Jones, *Plutarch* 123. On Roman litters, Mayor on Juv. 1.64; cf. Darem-berg-Saglio 3.1004.

74. Cf. Pliny, *Ep.* 8.24; Jones, *Plutarch* 127, 129.

75. For ancient estimates of this speech, J. E. Sandys' edition, pp. xxxiv–xxxvi.

Chapter 5. Alexandria

1. See now E. Wilmes, "Beiträge zur Alexandrinerrede (or. 32) des Dion Chrysostomos," diss. Bonn 1970; C. U. Crimi, *SicGymn* 26 (1973) 356–362.

2. For this body, Jos. *BJ* 2.490; P. Jouguet, *BSAA* 37 (1948) 90–92.

3. See the Appendix.

4. Cf. Jones, *Plutarch* 15. In the *Trojan*, also probably an early work, Dio refers to a visit to Onuphis, *Or.* 11.37.

5. Second city: Jos. *BJ* 4.456. Population: D.S. 17.52.6 gives 300,000, but this includes the territory, cf. Duncan-Jones, *ERE* 276.

6. See particularly Rostovtzeff, *SEHRE²* 415–420.

7. Str. 17.791–795, 798.

8. Str. 17.798.

9. Pliny, *Paneg.* 31.2; Tac. *Ann.* 2.59; for distributions at Alexandria, Jos. *contra Apionem* 63–64.

10. For good sketches of Roman Alexandria, Mommsen, *Römische Ges-chichte* 5³ (Berlin, 1886) 581–592 = *The Provinces of the Roman Empire* (Lon-don, 1909) 2.262–273; Friedländer, *Sittengeschichte* 1.431–440.

11. Friedländer (above, n. 10) 39 n. 6.

12. For this sense of ἀπάτη, Robert, *Hellenica* 11/12 (1960) 7–15, esp. 8.

13. For these at Alexandria, Cic. *pro Rab. Post.* 35; H. A. Musurillo, *The Acts of the Pagan Martyrs* (Oxford, 1954) 247–248; on their general popularity in the Greek East, Robert, *Hermes* 65 (1930) 118–119 (*OMS* 1.666–667).

14. For these, Robert, *REG* 42 (1929) 433–438 (*OMS* 1.221–226).

15. Robert, *REG* 42 (1929) 435–436 (*OMS* 1.223–224).

16. Mommsen (above, n. 10) 538–584 = 264–265; Friedländer (above, n. 10) 437.

17. Tac. *Hist.* 4.83–84; P. M. Fraser, *Ptolemaic Alexandria* (Oxford, 1972) 1.267–268.

18. A. Bouché-Leclerq, *Histoire de la divination dans l'antiquité* 3 (Paris, 1880) 383; A. Henrichs, *ZPE* 3 (1968) 67–68, Wilmes (above, n. 1) 14–15.

19. Bouché-Leclerq (above, n. 18) 387.

20. Bouché-Leclerq (above, n. 18), 384–386; Roeder, *RE* 1A (1920) 2406–2407; Kees, *RE* 15 (1931) 685–688.

21. Str. 17.793–794; Müller-Graupa, *RE* 16 (1933) 801–821; Fraser (above, n. 17) 1.305–319.

22. In this section, wrongly numbered 9 in Arnim's edition, Dio is usually thought to distinguish those (οἱ μέν) who do not go outdoors from those (οἱ δ') who stay in their lecture halls. The δέ, however, merely marks an opposition to the words immediately preceding, ἀπεγνωκότες ἴσως τὸ βελτίους ποιεῖν τοὺς πολλούς, cf. 9 ad fin., δέον ἐκκόπτειν τὴν ἀγερωχίαν οἱ δ' ἔτι αὔξουσιν: the true opposition to οἱ μέν is in τῶν δὲ Κυνικῶν at the beginning of 9.

23. Apparently unknown (not in *RE*).

24. Viz. Ptolemy XV, better known as Caesarion: H. Volkmann, *RE* 23 (1959) 1760–1761.

25. For Augustus' dispensation, Str. 17.797–798, Tac. *Hist.* 1.11, *Ann.* 2.59; on the Alexandrian council, D.C. 51.17.7, HA *Sept. Sev.* 17.2, Musurillo (above, n. 13) 84–88, V. A. Tcherikover and A. Fuks, *Corpus Papyrorum Judaicarum* 2 (Cambridge, Mass., 1960) nos. 150, 153.

26. Str. 17.819.

27. Tac. *Ann.* 2.59; D. G. Weingärtner, *Die Ägyptenreise des Germanicus* (Bonn, 1969).

28. For Vespasian, see below: note also Avidius Cassius, Vaballathus, and Domitius Domitianus. Cf. Mommsen (above, n. 10) 569–572 = 249–251.

29. Philo, *in Flacc.*, esp. 25–101.

30. Musurillo (above, n. 13); Tcherikover and Fuks (above, n. 25) no. 156.

31. Essentially, Musurillo (above, n. 13); Tcherikover and Fuks (above, n. 25) nos. 154–159; a new example in *POxy.* 42.3021.

32. Jos. *BJ* 2.487–498.

33. U. Wilcken, *APF* 5 (1909) 182–184. Note also Nero's Alexandrian teacher Chaeremon (*PIR²* C 706), and generally O. Montevecchi, *PP* 160 (1975) 48–58.

34. First intended visit: Tac. *Ann.* 15.36, Suet. *Nero* 19.1. Second: D.C. 63.18.1, J. Vogt, *Die alexandrinische Münzen* (Stuttgart, 1924) 1.32–33.

35. Suet. *Nero* 20.3.

36. D.C. 63.27.2, cf. Suet. *Nero* 40.2; also ibid. 45.1, special dust for wrestlers imported from Alexandria.

37. Suet. *Vesp.* 7.2; generally, Henrichs (above, n. 18) 51–80.

38. Suet. *Vesp.* 7; Tac. *Hist.* 4.81–82; D.C. 66.8.1; Musurillo (above, n. 13) no. V B; perhaps also *Sammelb.* 9528.

39. πόθος; the same word is used of Caracalla's visit to Alexandria, D.C. 77.22.1, Hdn. 4.8.6, but it is a usual motive of visitors, cf. Henrichs (above, n. 18) 56.

40. D.C. 66.8.2–5. For these anapaestic shouts cf. Philo, *in Flacc.* 139.

41. Suet. *Vesp.* 19.2, with Braithwaite's commentary. For similar taunts cf. E. Fraenkel, *Horace* (Oxford, 1957) 6–7.

42. D.C. 66.8.6; Suet. *Tit.* 5.3; *POxy.* 34.2725.

43. Jos. *BJ* 7.409–420; Euseb. *Chron.* ad Ol. 213, 3 (Armenian version, p. 216 Karst; Jerome's, p. 188 Helm²).

44. C. P. Jones, *Historia* 22 (1973) 305–307.

45. κόσμος: applied to a city this signifies both "adornment" (buildings and the like) and "order" (freedom from disruption).

46. Apparently Antiochus IV Epiphanes: N. Lewis, *CPh* 44 (1949) 32–33.

47. Despite his denial (81): thus Jones (above, n. 44) 304 n. 19, G. Highet, *GRBS* 15 (1974) 253; for the contrary view, J. F. Kindstrand, *Homer in der Zweiten Sophistik* (Uppsala, 1973) 19 n. 12.

48. See esp. Menander Rhet., ed. Spengel 3.346–347; L. Robert, *BCH* 101 (1977) 129–132.

49. Cf. *Or.* 39.1; Robert, *RPh* 41³ (1967) 59.

50. *Or.* 35.13–14; Menander (above, n. 48) 347–351; Robert, *JS* 1961, 155.

51. *Or.* 33.2, 35.13, Menander (above, n. 48) 349; Robert, *Laodicée* 280.

52. Menander (above, n. 48) 351–352.

53. *Or.* 35.14–15; *Or.* 39.1.

54. On Alexandria's territory, Jones, *CERP*² 304–305. The official name of the city was "Alexandria by Egypt" (*ad Aegyptum*). Cf. *Or.* 35.13.

55. *Or.* 33.17, 20.

56. For this sense of ᾄδω, cf. 10; W. C. Wright, ed., Philostratus, *VS* (Loeb) p. 575 s.v. ᾠδή.

57. *Or.* 33.1–16, esp. 14; *Or.* 34.1–6; *Or.* 35.1–12.

58. *Or.* 12.1–16, esp. 1, 12, 16; *Or.* 13.1–15, esp. 10.

59. Daremberg-Saglio, 3.1440–1442; Abert, *RE* 1 A (1920) 1762–1763.

60. Daremberg-Saglio, 1.1215–1216; Abert, *RE* 11 (1921) 533–534; Friedländer, *Sittengeschichte* 2.177–188.

61. Bowersock, *Augustus* 10.

62. Friedländer (above, n. 60) 187–188.

63. Suet. *Nero* 20.1, *Vesp.* 19.1, D.C. 63.8.4. The Alexandrian citharode Terpnus (*IGUR* 1034) is too humble to be the same man.

64. *Or.* 19.2. Contrast Strabo's story of a citharode at Iasos, 14.658.

65. Cf. Plut. *de frat. amore* 487 F (two Achaeans who quarreled over citharodes), Arr. *Epict.* 3.4.1 (a disturbance in Epirus over a *comoedus*). Claqueurs: Suet. *Nero* 20.3.

66. For these words applied to mortals, Nock, *Essays* 720–727, esp. 723 n. 18.

67. A. Cameron, *Porphyrius the Charioteer* (Oxford, 1973) 232–239.

68. R. MacMullen, *Enemies of the Roman Order* (Cambridge, Mass., 1966) 168–171.

69. Daremberg-Saglio 3.193–210; K. Schneider, *RE* 8 (1913) 1735–1745.

70. Daremberg-Saglio 1.1187–1201; Friedländer, *Sittengeschichte* 2.21–50; J. Regner, *RE* Suppl. 7 (1940) 1626–1664.

71. For the proverbial "bread and circuses," Mayor on Juv. 10.80–81, Friedländer (above, n. 70) 2.

72. Outbreaks: MacMullen (above, n. 68) 170–171; Cameron (above, n. 67) 232–252. Nero's exhibitions: Friedländer (above, n. 70) 29, 37.

73. That is, if it is the so-called "Lageion," as argued by A. Maricq, *RA* 37 (1951) 26–46, esp. 43, cf. Fraser (above, n. 17) 2.95–96, 99–101.

74. Above, n. 71.

75. J. H. Humphrey, *BASO* 213 (1974) 31–45; A. Cameron, *Circus Factions* (Oxford, 1976) 208–213.

76. Olck, *RE* 3 (1897) 457–461.

77. E. K. Borthwick, *CR* 22 (1972) 1–3, plausibly emends τὰ ὄντα to τὰ ὀθόνια.

78. Philostr. *VA* 5.26; cf. Chapter 4 at n. 53. With Apollonius' reference to the Trojan horse, cf. Dio, *Or.* 32.88.

79. Thus *Leg. Allegor.* 3.223; *de Agricult.* 74–76; *in Flacc.* 26; and generally the index to the Cohn-Wendland edition s.v. ἡνίοχος.

80. Tert. *de Spect.* 25.5; cf. T. D. Barnes, *Tertullian* (Oxford, 1971) 96 n. 1.

81. John Chrys., *Huit catéchèses baptismales inédites*, ed. A. Wenger (Paris, 1957), I 43; *PG* 48.1045, 53.54–55, 54.660–662, 58.644–646.

82. On Vespasian and the Cynics, Chapter 2 at n. 67. The Diogenes who abused Vespasian (D.C. 66.15.5) may be the Diogenes of Musurillo (above, n. 13) no. V, and an Alexandrian: C. H. Roberts on *POxy.* 20.2264. For possible Cynic influence on the *Acta Alexandrinorum*, Musurillo, 267–273, Roberts, 130 n. 4. Later, note the Cynic Agathobulus of Alexandria, Lucian *Peregr.* 17.

83. Cf. P. Riewald, *Diss. philol. Halenses* 20 (1912) 273–277, 287–296.

Chapter 6. Exile and Return

1. *Or.* 40.12, 50.8; so also Epictetus in Arrian, C. G. Starr, *CP* 44 (1949) 20–29.

2. *PIR²* F 355; thus already Emperius in Dio, ed. Arnim, 2.334, and Groag in *PIR²* F 355. The other cousin murdered by Domitian, Flavius Clemens (*PIR²* F 240), died only in 95, whereas Dio's exile was long (*Or.* 40.2, 12).

3. Suet. *Dom.* 10.4. On the date, *PIR²* F 355. Friends of Titus: D.C. 67.2–3.

4. A. Berger, *Encyclopedic Dictionary of Roman Law* (Philadelphia, 1953) s.v. relegatio.

5. *Or.* 1.50, 19.1–2.

6. *Or.* 40.2, 45.10–11.

7. *Or.* 13.12, 19.2, 45.1.

8. *Or.* 40.2, cf. 13.11.

9. Thus M. Pohlenz, *Die Stoa* 1⁴ (Göttingen, 1972) 365: "ein althellenischer Trieb, fremde Menschen und Völker kennenzulernen." Cf. Plut. *de def. orac.* 410 A-D, E. Fraenkel, *Horace* (Oxford, 1957) 270–271.

10. He claims never to have asked for money (*Or.* 3.15), but may have received gifts.

11. Above, Chapter 2 at n. 32.

12. *PIR²* F 123; Bowersock, *Sophists* 36.

13. Odysseus: *Or.* 1.50, 13.4, 33.14–15, 45.11. Socrates: *Or.* 33.9, 43.8–12. Similarly, Epaminondas, *Or.* 43.4–5; Aristotle, *Or.* 47.9–11.

14. *Or.* 13.14–28. There seems no reason to ascribe this speech, in part or in whole, to Antisthenes, as Arnim, 256–260.

15. *Or.* 4, 6, 8–10.

16. Xen. *Anab.* 3.1.5–7; Pl. *Apol.* 21 A-B.

17. Hom. *Od.* 11.121–134.

18. D. L. 6.20–21.

19. A. D. Nock, *Conversion* (Oxford, 1933), Ch. XI; O. Gigon, *MH* 3 (1946) 1–21.

20. Cf. Chapter 2 at n. 57.

21. Cf. Philostr. *VA* 4.25, for a student wearing the τρίβων.

22. *Or.* 32.8–11; *Or.* 34.3.

23. Before exile: *Or.* 11.6, 14, 31.122, 32.8–11, 22, 39, 97–98. After exile: *Or.* 33.9–10, 34.52, etc.

24. Philostr. *VS* 1.7, p. 488, quoted in full in Chapter 2.

25. Contrast Emperius, Dio ed. Arnim 2.335, "falsissima, ut pleraque quae de Dione tradidit Philostratus," with Arnim, *Dio* 246–247.

26. *VS* 1.8.2, p. 489. Cf. Bowersock, *Sophists* 36.

27. *Or.* 36.1.

28. On the date of Domitian's measure, Sherwin-White, *Pliny* 763–765. Apollonius: Philostr. *VA* 7–8, esp. 8.7.11.

29. *Or.* 3.13, 13.12–13, 45.1.

30. *Or.* 1.40, 7.8–9, 13.11, 40.2, 45.1.

31. *Or.* 12.18; *Or.* 35.20.

32. D. L. 7.168; Philostr. *VA* 5.19.

33. Synes. 314 line 25, 316 lines 1–2; on the text of 314 line 25, K. Latte, C&M 17 (1956) 95 = *Kleine Schriften* (Munich, 1968) 609. With Synesius' phrase ὅλοις τοῖς ἱστίοις cf. Philostratus' description of another "conversion," *VS* 1.25.5, p. 536, πλήρεσιν ἱστίοις. For a skeptical view of Dio's conversion see now J. L. Moles, *JHS* 98 (1978).

34. Thus P. Desideri, *AAT* 107 (1973) 576–577, 590–591; cf. G. R. Stanton, *AJPh* 94 (1973) 354.

35. This was apparently first propounded by E. Weber, *Leipz. Stud. zur kl. Philol.* 10 (1887) 218–223: more recently, R. Höistad, *Cynic Hero and Cynic King* (Uppsala, 1948). Contrast Nock (above, n. 19) 174: "Dio did not suddenly feel the attraction of a philosophic teacher or school."

36. *Or.* 34.2–3.

37. Thus especially Arnim, *Dio* 245, 464.

38. *Or.* 32.22; *Or.* 34.2–3.

39. Epictetus, 3.22 passim. Cf. A. Bonhöffer, *Epictet und die Stoa* (Stuttgart, 1890) v.

40. Arnim, *Dio* 260. On these see now M. Szarmach, *Eos* 65 (1977) 77–90.

41. Cf. Arr. *Epict.* 1.24.6–10, etc.; M. Ant. 8.3; Jul. *Or.* 6.

42. D.C. 68.29.1, Jul. *Caes.* 333 A, 335 D, HA *Hadr.* 4.9; cf. C. P. Jones, *Chiron* 5 (1975) 406.

43. See further Chapter 13 at nn. 52–53.

44. Cf. Synes. 316 line 10; perhaps also ΣLucian p. 221 Rabe.

45. Tac. *Hist.* 1.2, Suet. *Nero* 57.2. Thus Arnim, *Dio* 293–296.

46. Cf. Syme, *Tacitus* 518. On the phenomenon of "false" rulers, Millar, *Cassius Dio* App. V.

47. On the "golden sheep" mentioned by Dio, see Eur. *El.* 698–746, with Denniston's commentary ad loc.

48. This was first suggested by Arnim, app. crit. to *Or.* 66.6; cf. Momigliano, *Quarto Contributo* 261.

49. *Or.* 3.13, 13.12–13, 45.1.

50. *Or.* 7.2. On the location of the Hollows, W. Kendrick Pritchett, *Studies in Ancient Greek Topography* 2 (Berkeley and Los Angeles, 1969) 19–23; for a different view, H. J. Mason and M. B. Wallace, *Hesperia* 41 (1972) 136–140.

51. Cf. *Or.* 7.83 and Chapter 7 at n. 34.

52. *Or.* 1.52–56. On the site of Heraea, Paus. 8.26.1–3 with Frazer ad loc., Bölte, *RE* 8 (1912) 407–411.

53. Xen. *Mem.* 2.1.21–34.

54. See Chapter 13 at nn. 23–24.

55. *Or.* 19.1–2.

56. Dio himself uses the old name, "Borysthenes."

57. *Trist.* 1.2.85, 2.195, etc. So also Propertius on Olbia, 2.7.18.

58. *VS* 1.7.2, p. 488. Accepted by Arnim, *Dio* 301–305, and many others.

59. Thus Arnim, *Dio* 302; in his edition of two years previously he had not questioned the phrase.

60. *Or.* 13.16–20; see this chapter at n. 71.

61. Pliny, *Ep.* 1.5.10, 9.13.5, D.C. 68.1.2. Dio, *Or.* 36.25, may imply that he had not yet heard of his recall when in Olbia.

62. Chapter 13 at nn. 56–58.

63. *Or.* 40.5.

64. *Or.* 40.16, 41.1.

65. *Or.* 44.12. This letter should be different from that of *Or.* 40.5.

66. *Or.* 45.3–4 (embassy), 44.11 (favors), 40.33 (assize-district).

67. Thus Arnim, *Dio* 325.

68. See below, Ch. 13. For Trajan's *saeculum*, Tac. *Agr.* 3.1, Pliny, *Ep.* 2.1.6, 10.1.2, 2.2–3, 97.2.

69. *Or.* 40.18.

70. *Or.* 12.21, 25 (games), 16 (exile).

71. *Or.* 12.16–20. εὐθὺ τοῦ Ἴστρου in 16 cannot mean "straight *from* the Danube," as usually understood: see LSJ s.v. εὐθύς B I a.

72. *ILS* 5035.

73. *Or.* 44.1, 6, cf. 41.2 (honors), 40.17 (decree).

74. Chapter 13 at nn. 59–62.

75. *Or.* 44.1, 6.

76. For this date, see the Chronology.

77. *Or.* 40.13–15.

78. *Or.* 40.16–18, 41.7–9.

79. Below, Chapter 11.

80. *Or.* 44.11.

81. Below, Chapter 11.

82. According to the title, this was recited in Prusa.

83. *Or.* 12.15, 33.15, 34.2–3, 35.2–4, 11–12; earlier, *Or.* 32.22. For all this as the philosopher's uniform, Apul. *Met.* 11.8.

84. *Or.* 4.28, 12.4, 33.4–5, 35.10.

85. *Or.* 3.12–35.

86. Arr. *Epict.* 3.23.17, 19; Epictetus seems to have approved of Euphrates more than of Dio, 3.15.8. Cf. Apollonius of Tyana on Dio, *Ep.* 9, Philostr. *VA* 5.40.

87. Arr. *Epict.* 3.23.19; Philostr. *VS* 1.8.2, p. 490, 1.25.8, p. 539. Cf. also Charidemus of Messene, Dio, *Or.* 30.1.

88. D.C. 68.17.3, cf. J. and L. Robert, *La Carie* (Paris, 1954) 223.

89. Philostr. *VS* 1.8.2, p. 490, cf. D.C. 69.3.6; Fronto, p. 133 van den Hout; Luc. *Peregr.* 18. Note also the bust of Dio at Pergamum, *AA* 81 (1966) 473.

90. Arethas, Dio ed. Arnim 2.328; Phot. *Bibl.* 165 A, Suda Δ 1240 (Dio, ed. Arnim, 2.320, 328).

91. Thus in the essay of Theodorus Metochita (13th–14th century), cited in Dio, ed. Arnim, 2.329–332; on the author, K. Krumbacher, *Geschichte der byzantinische Litteratur*[2] (Munich, 1897) 550–554.

Chapter 7. Ideal Communities

1. Thus Arnim, *Dio* 457–458; P. A. Brunt, *PCPS* 19 (1973) 9.

2. Note the praise of Synesius, p. 317 lines 21–24, and of Burckhardt, "Dio Chrysostomus" 108: "eine der schönsten Idyllen der alten Literatur, unstreitig das für uns wertvollste Stück der ganzen grossen Sammlung." This section of the *Euboean* is the only passage from Dio in Wilamowitz, *Griechisches Lesebuch* 1 (Berlin, 1902) 19–32.

3. Chapter 6 at n. 50.

4. Thus G. Highet, *GRBS* 14 (1973) 35 n. 1.

5. S. Georgoudi, *REG* 87 (1974) 155–185, esp. 169–170 on Dio.

6. Thus, most recently, Highet (above, n. 4) 36 n. 2.

7. For an interesting discussion of the influence of this passage on Spengler, H. Petriconi, *A & A* 7 (1958) 58–60.

8. For these in Euboea, Philostr. *VA* 1.24; cf. J. A. O. Larsen, *ESAR* 4.485.

9. Apul. *Met.* 3.2–10, esp. 3.

10. Cf. *Or.* 34.1.

11. Pliny, *Ep.* 10.54.1. Cf. Liebenam, *Städteverwaltung* 312–328; Jones, *GC* 246; J. Zablocka, *Eos* 54 (1964) 166–180.

12. For the Hellenistic period, see the index of *OGIS* s.v. ἀτελεία: for the Roman, Jones, *GC* 189–190.

13. Wagner in Roscher, *Lexikon* 3 (1897) 25–27.

14. Euboea: Dio, *Or.* 7.8, 55, St. Byz. s.v. Καφηρεύς: perhaps also Apul. *Met.* 2.14, though this may refer to Thessaly. Epirus: Apul. *Met.* 7.7. Seriphos: L. Robert in *Études déliennes* (Paris, 1973) 470–471.

15. Ulp., *Dig.* 47.9.10.

16. ἐπιεικής, πρᾴως: for these two qualities in Greek political life, Robert, *Hellenica* 13 (1965) 223.

17. Generally, Liebenam, *Städteverwaltung* 315–317; Rostovtzeff, *Studien zur Geschichte des römischen Kolonates* (Leipzig and Berlin, 1910) 266.

18. C. Vatin, *BCH* 86 (1962) 57–63 (*Bull.* 1965.239); *Syll.*[3] 884, cf. Larsen

(above, n. 8) 477, J. Tréheux, *BCH* 77 (1953) 157–162, esp. 158 n. 4 on the date.

19. References in Duncan-Jones, *ERE* 292 n. 3.

20. *CIL* 8.25902, 25943.

21. P. Mazon, *CRAI* 1943, 85–86; against, J. Carcopino, ibid. 86–87.

22. Pages 57–63 Hense.

23. Cf. Philostr. *VS* 2.1.3–4, p. 549, and often in inscriptions: A. Wilhelm, *Beiträge zur griechischen Inschriftenkunde* (Vienna, 1909) 189–190; J. and L. Robert, *La Carie* (Paris, 1954) 323.

24. Robert, *Ét. anat.* Ch. IV; cf. *Bull.* 1973.451.

25. *Or.* 34.21.

26. Bibliography in Robert (above, n. 16) 207 n. 5; further, P. Herrmann, *AAWW* 111 (1974) 444.

27. *Or.* 56.10.

28. Chapter 4 at n. 25.

29. S. Reinach, *Traité d'épigraphie grecque* (Paris, 1885) 369; W. Larfeld, *Handbuch der griechischen Epigraphik* 2 (Leipzig, 1902) 763–767; Herrmann (above, n. 26) 444.

30. *Ep.* 4.13.5.

31. As does J. Day, *Studies in Roman economic and social history in honor of Allan Chester Johnson* (Princeton, 1951) 213; on this essay, L. Robert, *Hellenica* 11/12 (1960) 68 n. 3.

32. Plut. *de def. orac.* 413 F-414 A; cf. Larsen (above, n. 8) 481–482, Rostovtzeff, *SEHRE*² 253–254.

33. P. Collart, *CRAI* 1943, 87; Highet (above, n. 4) 35–40.

34. D. Reuter, "Untersuchungen zum Euboikos des Dion von Prusa," diss. Leipzig, 1932, esp. 51.

35. *Or.* 12.55–83.

36. Soli: *Or.* 34.14. Celaenae: title of *Or.* 35 (which may not be Dio's own).

37. St. Byz. s.v. Βορυσθένης: *Bull.* 1958.477, p. 327; E. Belin de Ballu, *Olbia: Cité antique du littoral nord de la mer noire* (Leiden, 1972) 20–22.

38. *IOSPE* 1² 40 line 2 (*CIG* 2.2059).

39. On these, Hdt. 4.53.3; Belin (above, n. 37) 33; A. Wasowicz, *Olbia pontique et son territoire* (Paris, 1975) 27.

40. *IOSPE* 1² 32, 34 (*Syll.*³ 495, 730).

41. Str. 7.303–304, *IGBulg* 1² 13 (*Syll.*³ 762); cf. Belin (above, n. 37) 136–138.

42. συνῴκησαν: for this sense, *Bull.* 1958.251.

43. *IOSPE* 1² 42 line 6, cf. Robert (above, n. 16) 213; Belin (above, n. 37) 145–152; Wasowicz (above, n. 39) 119–127.

44. E. H. Minns, *Scythians and Greeks* (Cambridge, 1913) 468–469.

45. Minns (above, n. 44) 467; *Bull.* 1970.44.

46. Belin (above, n. 37) 77–82, 139–140, 164–165; Wasowicz (above, n. 39) 33.

47. Thus Belin (above, n. 37) 164 n. 1; for the dedication, K. S. Gorbunova, *AR 1971–1972* (1972) 49.

48. *HA* Pius 9.9.

49. Belin (above, n. 37) 162; Wasowicz (above, n. 39) 121; *Inscriptiones Olbiae* 45 line 17 (*SEG* 3.584).

50. Thus Boeckh, *CIG* 2, p. 115; for the name at Olbia, indexes of *IOSPE* 1² and *IOlb*.

51. Rostovtzeff, *Iranians and Greeks in South Russia* (Oxford, 1922) 11. On this passage, J. Bidez and F. Cumont, *Les Mages hellénisés* (Paris, 1938) 1.91–98; M. Pohlenz, *Die Stoa* 2 (Göttingen, 1955) 45–47.

52. Rostovtzeff, *SEHRE²* 659.

53. *IOSPE* 1² 42 line 12. Compare a self-taught poet of Cremna in Pisidia, *Bull.* 1973.475 no.1.

54. Rostovtzeff, *ABSA* 22 (1918) 1–22; id., *SEHRE²* 154. Note esp. *IOSPE* 1² 40 (*CIG* 2.2059), with Robert, *OMS* 4.352–353.

55. *IOSPE* 1² 181, 79 (*CIG* 2.2087, 2060).

56. Nero: *ILS* 986. Trajan: Belin (above, n. 37) 167–172. However, Trajan's role depends upon the reading *Tyrae* in "Hunt's Pridianum," which is not accepted by the latest editor, Robert O. Fink, *Roman Military Records on Papyrus* (Case Western Reserve, 1971) no. 63 col. ii line 21.

57. Synes. p. 317 lines 24–26.

58. Honigmann, *RE* 3 A (1927) 787. On the vexed question of the location of the Essenes and their connection with Qumran, R. de Vaux, *Archaeology and the Dead Sea Scrolls* (Oxford, 1973), esp. 126–138.

59. Pliny, *NH* 5.73.

Chapter 8. Apamea

1. That the present collection is not Dio's own is shown by the inclusion of two spurious works, *Or.* 37 and *Or.* 64, both by Favorinus (A. Barigazzi, *Favorino di Arelate: Opere* [Florence, 1966] 245–247).

2. Thus Arnim, *Dio* 447.

3. Str. 12.577. The classic account is by G. Hirschfeld, *ABAW* 1875, 1–26; important material also in W. M. Ramsay, *Cities and Bishoprics of Phrygia* (Oxford, 1895–1897) 396–483; more recent bibliography in W. Ruge, *RE* 20 (1941) 815, Magie, *RRAM* 983–984.

4. Thus J. Burckhardt, "Dio Chrysostomus" 106–107: "Celänä [wird] ironisch gepriesen als der glückseligste und wohllebendenste Ort der Welt, etwa mit Ausnahme Indiens"; so also W. Schmid, *Der Atticismus* 1 (Stuttgart, 1887) 74. This aspect of the speech has often been ignored. With 17–22 on India, Lucian, *Vera Hist.* 2.6–16, has often been compared.

5. Thus Arnim: the manuscripts read "Orbas" or "Norbas": cf. Ruge, *RE* 18 (1939) 876.

6. Hirschfeld (above, n. 3) 17; Robert, *Noms indigènes* 355.

7. Str. 12.577–578; Hirschfeld (above, n. 3) 17–23; Ramsay (above, n. 3) 396–412, 451–457.

8. Ramsay (above, n. 3) Pl. I; F. Imhoof-Blumer, *SNR* 23 (1923) 316 no. 356.

9. On the communications of Apamea, Hirschfeld (above, n. 3) 6–10; B. Levick, *Roman Colonies in Southern Asia Minor* (Oxford, 1967) 10–15.

10. For this sense of προκαθῆσθαι, LSJ cite Hdt. 7.172.2.

11. For the general system of tribute collection in this period, W. Schwahn, *RE* 7 A (1939) 62–70.

12. Str. 13.361. Generally, Ramsay (above, n. 3) 447–450; on the border with Apollonia to the east, Robert, *Noms indigènes* 357–359.

13. Swoboda, *RE* Suppl. 4 (1924) 969–970; Jones, *GC* 271–274; for the financial status of those living on the territory, *Or.* 7.28–31.

14. Cf. Nörr, *Imperium und Polis* 50–52.

15. ὑποζύγια may mean "donkeys" (LSJ s.v.), which would be even less flattering.

16. παρ' ἔτος: see below.

17. On the "dioceses" and the system of assizes generally, Ch. Habicht, *JRS* 65 (1975) 64–91, G. P. Burton, ibid. 92–106; for Apamea as an assize-city, Habicht 80–87.

18. L. Robert, *RPh* 8³ (1934) 276–278 = *OMS* 1175–1177.

19. *Or.* 40.33, 44.11.

20. Modest., *Dig.* 27.1.6.2. On these, see Chapter 9 at n. 31.

21. Habicht (above, n. 17) 71.

22. Jurors: Robert (above, n. 18) 279 = 1178 n. 0. For governors misled by their assessors, Philostr. *VA* 5.36.

23. Thus Ramsay (above, n. 3) 428 n. 5, 462, followed on this point by Mommsen, *Gesammelte Schriften* 5 (Berlin, 1908) 523 n. 2. The texts are as follows: *JOAI* 47 (1964–65) Beibl. 29–30, line 21, explained in *Bull.* 1968.462 (Ephesus, a *prytanis*); *Didyma* 279 b 12, cf. Robert, *Gnomon* 31 (1959) 666 = *OMS* 1631 (Miletus, a *stephanephoros*); *IGRR* 4.1638 (Philadelphia, a *tamias*); ibid. 788–790 (Apamea, a gymnasiarch and *agoranomos*).

24. References in n. 23.

25. Thus rightly Ramsay (above, n. 3) 428 n. 5; for the other view, e.g. Burton (above, n. 17) 98. For this meaning of παρά, cf. LSJ s.v. C I 9: an epigraphical example perhaps in *Phoenix* 27 (1973) 320.

26. Sherwin-White, *Pliny* 531–532.

27. Robert, *RPh* 41³ (1967) 47.

28. *IGRR* 4.791, explained by Robert, *CRAI* 1968.582. On the distribution of neocorates in Asia, K. Hanell, *RE* 16 (1935) 2425–2426; on the sharing of expenses by the cities of the province, Robert, *Hellenica* 7 (1949) 208–212.

29. Thus Robert (above, n. 27) 48 n. 4.

30. On this board, Deininger, *Provinziallandtage* 38–40; M. Rossner, *StudClas* 16 (1974) 107–108.

31. Thus Bowersock, *Augustus* 117; Deininger, *Provinziallandtage* 43–50; Rossner (above, n. 30) 102–107.

32. *BMC* Phrygia 101, *ILS* 8820 = *IGRR* 4.780. The *archiereis* of *BMC* Phrygia 102 and *IGRR* 4.791 (on which see Robert, *CRAI* 1968.582) are high priests of the city cult, not the provincial.

33. Robert, *BCH* 54 (1930) 265–266 = *OMS* 969–970, with additions in *CRAI* 1967.284 n. 1; *Bull.* 1969.541; *BCH* 101 (1977) 90 n. 3.

34. Arr. *Epict.* 1.19.26–29, cf. Bowersock in *Culte des Souverains* 182–184.

35. *Or.* 13.20, 34; *Or.* 79.1, 13. See Chapter 14 at n. 26.

36. Cf. Tac. *Ann.* 12.63, with Furneaux's n.

Chapter 9. Tarsus

1. Two others, *Or.* 79 and 80, were spoken "in Cilicia," according to the manuscript titles; but nothing in the text confirms this, and *Or.* 79 at least seems to have been delivered at Rome, Chapter 14 at n. 23.

2. Cf. Arnim, *Dio* 438–447, 460–463, and the Chronology on *Or.* 33 and 34.

3. An excellent account in W. Ruge, *RE* 4 A (1932) 2413–2439; cf. also W. M. Ramsay, *Cities of St. Paul* (London, 1907) part II, C. B. Welles, *MUB* 38 (1962) 43–75, and now L. Robert, *BCH* 101 (1977) 88–132.

4. Ruge (above, n. 3) 2435–2436, Robert (above, n. 3) 94, 130.

5. Ruge (above, n. 3) 2432.

6. Ruge, *RE* 11 (1921) 388; id. (above, n. 3) 2435.

7. Plut. *Ant.* 26, cf. Ruge (above, n. 3) 2422, Robert (above, n. 3) 130–132. For the Cydnus on coins of Tarsus, F. Imhoof-Blumer, *SNR* 23 (1923) 355–357.

8. Ruge (above, n. 3) 2438–2439.

9. Ruge (above, n. 3) 2417–2418.

10. F. Imhoof-Blumer, *JHS* 18 (1898) 174–178, Ruge (above, n. 3) 2415, Robert (above, n. 3) 98–116. On the legend of Perseus in other cities of Cilicia, and also at Iconium in Lycaonia, Robert, *JS* 1973, 199–200; id. (above, n. 3) 116–119.

11. Höfer in Roscher, *Lexikon* 3.323–324; Ruge (above, n. 3) 2415; Robert, *Noms indigènes* 500; id. (above, n. 3) 96.

12. Str. 14.676, cf. Robert (above, n. 3) 107.

13. Imhoof-Blumer (above, n. 10) 171–174; Robert, *CRAI* 1961, 177 (*OMS* 1464); id. (above, n. 3) 97–98, 107–109.

14. For coins of Athena at Tarsus, *BMC* Lycaonia, Isauria, Cilicia 191–192; for Athena in the legend of Perseus, Robert (above, n. 3) 127.

15. Robert (above, n. 3) 113–114.

16. App. *BC* 4.64, D.C. 47.31.

17. Cf. Ruge (above, n. 3) 2422, 2426–2427.

18. Cf. the similar grant to Termessus Major, *ILS* 38 col. II lines 31 ff. Thus S. J. De Laet, *Portorium* (Bruges, 1949) 280–281.

19. For "laws" meaning "autonomy" in inscriptions, *IG* 12, 1, 2, *Syll.*[3] 793 n. 5 (R. Bernhardt, *Imperium und Eleutheria* [Hamburg, 1971] 208 n. 569, 216 n. 597). Antony: App. B. C. 5.7; cf. Bernhardt, *Imperium* 172, 190.

20. [Lucian], *Macrob.* 21. Cf. *PIR*[2] A 1288.

21. Str. 14.674–675. Cf. Bowersock, *Augustus* 39, 48. On Boethus, Robert (above, n. 3) 106.

22. Str. 14.673.

23. Philostr. *VA* 1.7, 6.30–34, 43. On Philostratus' source Maximus of Aegaeae (*VA* 1.3), Bowersock, introduction to the Penguin translation (Harmondsworth, 1970) 11; Robert (above, n. 10) 185.

24. Welles (above, n. 3) 68.

25. K. Mras, *WS* 64 (1949, publ. 1950) 76 n. 18; F. Millar, *JRS* 58 (1968) 127.

26. C. Bonner, *HTR* 36 (1942) 1–8.

27. *Or.* 8.13; Arr. *Epict.* 2.20.10.

28. Pl. *Gorg.* 455 B, 514 D-E, with Dodd's nn.; Robert, *RPh* 13³ (1939) 166 (*OMS* 1319); L. Cohn-Haft, *The Public Physicians of Ancient Greece* (Northampton, Mass., 1956) 56–57.

29. Bowersock, *Sophists* 69, esp. n. 3.

30. Conceivably this comparison inspired Philostratus' account of Dio in the Roman camp, Chapter 2 at n. 16.

31. Nicomedia: see Chapter 10 at n. 13. Ephesus the "first metropolis": e.g. *BMusInscr* 541; for the importance of both under Augustus, D.C. 51.20.6.

32. For such rivalries, note especially the inscription of Nervan date from Beroea, J. M. R. Cormack, *JRS* 30 (1940) 50–52; with τὸ τῆς μητροπόλεως ἀξίωμα there, cf. Dio, *Or.* 33.46.

33. Cf. Aphrodisias' claim to have been free "from the beginning," Robert, *AC* 35 (1966) 411.

34. "Even better" perhaps refers to a legend which made the Athenian Erichthonius one of the founders: Robert (above, n. 3) 114. On Aegaeae's Argive descent and this decree, Robert, ibid. 119–129.

35. On this phenomenon generally, Magie, *RRAM* 637–638; D. Musti, *ASNP* 32 (1963) 225–239; Robert (above, n. 10) 202–203. On the Panhellenion, J. H. Oliver, *Hesperia* Suppl. 13 (1970), ch. IV.

36. Athenodorus: note his father's name Sandon (Cic. *ad fam.* 3.7.5, Str. 14.674), clearly derived from the Asiatic god Sandan worshiped at Tarsus, cf. Ruge (above, n. 3) 2415, 2424, Robert, *Noms indigènes* 99, 500. Paul: *Acts* 21.39, cf. Ruge (above, n. 3) 2420, 2424.

37. Philostr. *VA* 1.7.

38. *Or.* 31.116. On Arados' legends, J.-P. Rey-Coquais, *Arados et sa Pérée* (Paris, 1974) 250–251, cf. 118.

39. L. Robert, *Hellenica* 5 (1948) 66–69; for the other view, e.g. Ruge (above, n. 3) 2424.

40. For this term, H. J. Mason, *Greek Terms for Roman Institutions* (Toronto, 1974) 157–158.

41. Deininger, *Provinziallandtage* 167–168.

42. Briefly, Magie, *RRAM* 599; Chapter 10. On Tarsus' feuds, Ruge (above, n. 3) 2428; Robert (above, n. 3) 127–128.

43. See now Robert (above, n. 10) 161–211, and n. 34 above.

44. Chapter 4 at n. 37.

45. Ruge, *RE* 14 (1928) 916–917; on the site, Robert, *CRAI* 1951.256–259; *AS* 24 (1974) 28–29.

46. Text in *SEG* 12.511; the other disputant is "Antioch by the Pyramos," usually called Magarsos, which seems temporarily to have absorbed Mallos, Robert (above, n. 45) 258.

47. Ruge (above, n. 3) 2438; cf. Jones, *CERP*² 206.

48. On this sentence, *Chronology* on *Or.* 34.

49. Ruge, *RE* 3 A (1927) 935–938.

50. D.C. 47.31.2.

51. Ruge (above, n. 3) 2426, 2428.

52. G. Downey, *A History of Antioch* (Princeton, 1961) 241.

53. Jones, *Plutarch* 118.

54. Reading Μαλλόν, with Casaubon. Valesius' ἄλλους is tempting.

55. See now Ch. Habicht, *JRS* 65 (1975) 75 no. 19, 83 no. 9; Chapter 12 at n. 32.

56. Jones, *Plutarch* 118.

57. Cf. Downey (above, n. 52) 239–242.

58. Philostr. *VS* 1.8.3, p. 490; cf. Bowersock, *Sophists* 90.

59. 23 K., cf. *Syll.*[3] 849.

60. Cf. Aristides 23.59–65.

61. Chapter 10 at nn. 23–24.

62. Cf. Pliny, *Ep.* 8.24.6, on the "contempt" of free cities for a Roman official.

63. Pliny, *Ep.* 8.24.9, on the temptations of a *longinqua provincia*.

64. It is tempting to suppose that the "two in succession" are the Capito and Tutor of Juv. 8.93; cf. H. Castritius, *Historia* 20 (1971) 80–83. For other "brutal" governors of Cilicia, Plut. *de def. orac.* 434 D, Philostr. *VA* 1.12.

65. Pliny, *Ep.* 4.9.16–19 (leniency), 4.9.14, 5.20.4 (prejudice), 4.9.20 (Bithynia). Cf. P. A. Brunt, *Historia* 10 (1961) 217, 220.

66. Cf. *Or.* 38.33–40, and Chapter 10 at nn. 35–37.

67. On the league generally, Magie, *RRAM* 65–66, Deininger, *Provinziallandtage* 10–12; for its activity in Dio's day, Philostr. *VA* 4.5–6. Brunt (above, n. 65) 220, and Kienast, *Historia* 20 (1971) 76, take Dio to mean the *koinon* of Asia.

68. For governors compared to Minos or Rhadamanthus, Robert, *Hellenica* 4 (1948) 21–22; id. (above, n. 3) 99 n. 49.

69. Jones, *GC* 47, 311 n. 62.

70. For this phrase (ἀναγκαῖοι καιροί) in inscriptions, cf. Robert, *Ét anat.*, Index s.v. καιροί.

71. Plut. *praec. ger. reip.* 805 B, E.

72. Chapter 10 at n. 50.

73. For the social and political aspects of the *gerousia*, E. A. Turner, *APF* 12 (1937) 179–186, Magie, *RRAM* 855–860, *Bull.* 1959.65; for the religious, J. H. Oliver, *The Sacred Gerousia*, *Hesperia* Suppl. 6 (1941), cf. *Bull.* 1944.25, 1959.65, 1969.193.

74. Str. 14.674–675. That would give added point to the gibe against him, ἔργα νέων, βουλαὶ δὲ μέσων, πορδαὶ δὲ γερόντων.

75. Sherk, *RDGE* no. 63. Note also how the people let the *gerousia* burn at Nicomedia, Pliny, *Ep.* 10.33.2.

76. For the Youths generally, C. A. Forbes, *NEOI: A Study of Greek Associations* (Middletown, Conn., 1933); at Tarsus, Str. 14.673, and cf. n. 74 above. For a letter of the Pergamene Youths to Hadrian, *Syll.*[3] 831.

77. On the guilds generally, Fr. Poland, *Geschichte des griechischen Vereinswesens* (Leipzig, 1909) 106–129, esp. 117, Stöckle, *RE* Suppl. 4 (1924) 155–

211, esp. 163–164, Broughton, *ESAR* 4.841–846, Rostovtzeff, *SEHRE*[2] 178–179. Ruge (above, n. 3) 2432, and Broughton, *ESAR* 4.844, suppose that "Linenworkers" was merely a generic term for the lower classes at Tarsus; similarly, L. Cracco Ruggini in *Assimilation et résistance à la culture gréco-romaine* (Bucharest and Paris, 1976) 463–491. But the growing evidence for guilds at Tarsus (Broughton, *AJA* 42 [1938] 55–57, Robert, *Hellenica* 7 [1949] 201–205, id. [above, n. 3] 91–96) and the parallel of organized linenworkers in other cities (e.g. Anazarbus, *IGRR* 3.896) make this unlikely.

78. *Acts* 19.24–40.

79. For a different view, Jones, *GC* 174.

80. Duncan-Jones, *ERE* 10.

81. κηδεμόνα ὄντως: the same phrase in *Or.* 32.26. For κηδεμών in such a context, E. Peterson, *RhM* 78 (1929) 221–222, Nock, *Essays* 728–730, Mason (above, n. 40) 152. For ὄντως, Robert, *Hellenica* 11/12 (1960) 551–552.

82. Arr. *Epict.* 1.19.29, cf. F. Millar, *JRS* 55 (1965) 147. For gold and purple mentioned together in inscriptions, *Bull.* 1953.193 no. 22, 1964.590.

83. Gymnasiarch: Robert, *Documents de l'Asie Mineure méridionale* (Paris, 1966) 83. *Demiourgos:* Ruge (above, n. 3) 2427, and generally Robert, *Noms indigènes* 478–479. For the expenses of eponymous magistrates, Jones, *GC* 234–235.

84. Plut. *praec. ger. reip.* 819 E–820 F.

85. For this term, Jones, *GC* 162.

86. For bravery (*andreia*) as a civic virtue, Robert (above, n. 33) 429–431.

87. The expressions are Mommsen's, quoted in Chapter 3, n. 43. Arnim, *Dio* 460, calls it "eines der reifen Meisterwerke Dios."

Chapter 10. Concord

1. Chapter 9 at n. 39. Note also Dio, *Or.* 38.11, 13–15, 39.4, 8; Plut. *praec. ger. reip.* 824 B-D; Aristid. 23.29, 48, 51, 53; Philostr. *VA* 4.8; earlier, *TAM* 3, 1, no. 7 (*Bull.* 1942.160); L. Robert, *StudClas* 16 (1974) 68 n. 42.

2. J. de Romilly, *Mélanges Pierre Chantraine* (Paris, 1972) 199–209.

3. Robert (above, n. 1) 64–68.

4. Robert, *Villes*[2] 366.

5. M. Jessop Price, *NC* 11[7] (1971) 131 no. 19.

6. Robert, *OMS* 4.91. Cf. C. J. Cadoux, *Ancient Smyrna* (Oxford, 1938) 275: "the single word ὁμόνοια ('concord') indicates no more than an exchange of diplomatic civilities, probably sometimes reflecting the cessation of some dispute."

7. On these, J.-P. Callu, *La politique monétaire des empereurs romains de 238 à 311* (Paris, 1969) 29–33, referring to "un vaste réseau d'alliances": against, Robert (above, n. 1) 68 n. 41.

8. For cities celebrating their alliance with Rome, Robert, *JS* 1975.203.

9. D. Kienast, *JNG* 14 (1964) 51–64.

10. Jones, *GC* 172; W. Gawantka, *Isopolitie* (Munich, 1975) 198–199.

11. W. Ruge, *RE* 17 (1936) 471.

12. On the harbor of Nicomedia, Ruge (above, n. 11) 481–482; Robert, *Hellenica* 11/12 (1960) 35, 228 n. 2. On its land communications, Ruge (above, n. 11) 487.

13. Robert, *HSCP* 81 (1977) 3–4.

14. Ruge (above, n. 11) 230, 472–473; Robert (above, n. 13) 22–30.

15. In the east, besides the examples cited above, Chapter 9 at nn. 42–61, note Athens and Megara (Philostr. *VS* 1.24, p. 529); in the west, Pompeii and Nuceria (Tac. *Ann.* 14.17), Vienna and Lugdunum (Tac. *Hist.* 1.65), Oea and Leptis (ibid. 4.50).

16. Dio, *Or.* 38.38 (Greece); J. M. R. Cormack, *JRS* 30 (1940) 50–52 (Macedonia); Dio, *Or.* 34.48, Hdn. 3.3.3, 3.6.9, Liban. 18.187 (Syria).

17. Note the feud of Athens and Sparta over προπομπεία, Dio, *Or.* 38.38; Robert, *OMS* 4.93–94, shows that the occasion was the Eleutheria held at Plataea.

18. *Or.* 34.49–52, 38.24–26, 38; Aristid. 23.42–52, 24.25–26.

19. Pliny, *Ep.* 10.114–115. Cf. Ruge (above, n. 11) 482.

20. Ruge (above, n. 11) 240–241.

21. The quaestor who settled the financial affairs of a *civitas amplissima* shortly before 100 (Pliny, *Pan.* 70.1) is usually thought to be Sex. Quinctilius Maximus, quaestor of Bithynia (*ILS* 1018).

22. Plut. *de Is. et Osir.* 380 B–C, Juv. 15.33–83.

23. Aristid. *Or.* 23; with 23.60 cf. Dio, *Or.* 38.23–24; with 23.74, Dio, *Or.* 38.20. On πρωτεῖα generally, Robert, *Laodicée* 287, Habicht, *Inschriften des Asklepieions* 78; for the later history of the dispute in Asia, Habicht 72–74.

24. Cf. *Or.* 38.50, Aristid. 23.28, 72, 80.

25. Cf. Broughton in *ESAR* 4.709.

26. Rostovtzeff, *Studien zur Geschichte des römischen Kolonates* (Leipzig and Berlin, 1910) 260 n. 3.

27. H. Dessau, *Geschichte der römischen Kaiserzeit* 2.2 (Berlin, 1930) 599 n. 1.

28. Bowersock, *Augustus* 116 n. 7.

29. P. A. Brunt in A. H. M. Jones, *The Roman Economy* (Oxford, 1974) 182. It is possible that Dio uses the word "tithes" simply to avoid the repetition of the word "tribute," and does not imply a fixed quota.

30. Robert (above, n. 13) 20, 24–25, referring to A. M. Schneider, *Die Stadtmauer von Iznik (Nicaea)* (Berlin, 1938) 45 no. 11, 46, nos. 14, 15.

31. Cf. *Or.* 33.46, 34.43–48.

32. As S. J. de Laet, *Portorium* (Bruges, 1949) 356. For customs dues in Asia, Broughton (above, n. 25) 799–800, Rostovtzeff, *SEHRE²* 609–610. J. and L. Robert, *Bull.* 1976.160, suggest that the "certain people" who already "do favors" of the kind that Dio proposes are the associations of importers (*naucleroi*) known to have been influential in Nicomedia.

33. Robert, *RPh* 41³ (1967) 48.

34. Aristid. 23. 32–34.

35. Chapter 11 at n. 62. Dio may be referring here to the proconsul Julius Bassus, who is thanked in inscriptions of Nicaea for an unstated benefaction, Schneider (above, n. 30) 46 nos. 14, 15.

36. *Syll.*[3] 849, cf. Robert (above, n. 23) 286 n. 4.

37. *MAMA* 6.6, with the discussion of Robert (above, n. 23) 287–288.

38. Kienast (above, n. 9) 59–61.

39. Cf. *Or.* 41.10, 47.17.

40. Ruge (above, n. 11) 471; Robert, *RPh* 13[3] (1939) 168–170 (*OMS* 1321–1323). On the site of Astakos, S. Şahin, "Neufunde von antiken Inschriften in Nikomedeia (Izmit)," Diss. Münster, 1973, 66–70; *Bull.* 1974.574.

41. Dio, *Or.* 39.1; cf. Robert (above, n. 40) 169 (1322).

42. Ruge (above, n. 11) 228–229.

43. Ruge (above, n. 11) 229 (Nicaea in Locris), 228, 239 (Dionysus), 240 (Heracles).

44. Coins: Ruge (above, n. 11) 239–240. Inscriptions: Schneider (above, n. 30) 45 nos. 11 and 12, with the comments of Robert (above, n. 13) 9–18.

45. Ruge (above, n. 11) 243; Schneider (above, n. 30).

46. Millar, *Cassius Dio* 11.

47. Men. Rh. p. 350 Spengel; Robert (above, n. 33) 59.

48. Robert, *JS* 1961.105–106; id. (above, n. 8) 202–203.

49. For this as a claim of cities, Robert (above, n. 8) 204.

50. Chapter 9 at n. 72.

51. Ruge (above, n. 11) 236–237; only coins of Gordian mention the council and assembly, but earlier ones showing "Concord of the Nicaeans" perhaps mean the same. For similar coins in Nicomedia, Ruge (above, n. 11) 481.

52. Plut. *praec. ger. reip.* 823 F–825 F; note, however, 808 C. On class struggle generally in the eastern cities, Broughton (above, n. 25) 810–812; Magie, *RRAM* 600; Rostovtzeff, *SEHRE*[2] 126, 148, 179.

53. Philostr. *VA* 6.38.

54. Ruge (above n. 11) 239–240 (Zeus, Athena, Aphrodite, Homonoia, Nemesis).

55. Hirschfeld, *RE* 1 (1894) 2664 no. 5; Ruge, *RE* 16 (1933) 1104–1105; Magie, *RRAM* 1268 n. 34; Bowersock, *Augustus* 63, 66. The notion that Apamea was a "double community," consisting of both a Greek *polis* and a Roman colony, is not likely; see F. Millar, *JRS* 58 (1968) 222. Privileges: Pliny, *Ep.* 10.47.1. Trade: Robert (above, n. 1) 68.

56. Cf. Jones, *Plutarch* 111.

57. Chapter 2 at n. 60.

58. Liebenam, *RE* 5 (1905) 1805.

59. *Or.* 34.45; Robert, *Laodicée* 287–288.

60. Robert, *Gladiateurs* 175 (θέα), 34–36 (theaters), 35 (stadia), 270–275 (imperial cult).

61. Tac. *Ann.* 14.17; cf. R. MacMullen, *Enemies of the Roman Order* (Cambridge, Mass., 1966) 169, and pl. III there.

62. Plut. *praec. ger. reip.* 822 C.

63. Robert (above, n. 1) 67–68.

64. Thus P. Herrmann, *OAth* 10 (1971) 37 lines 3–4.

65. Chapter 6 at n. 75.

66. R. Münsterberg, *NZ* 8² (1915) 119, Artem. p. 235 Pack.

67. Cf. Plut. *praec. ger. reip.* 814 C; Jones, *Plutarch* 113, 115.

68. Chapter 2 at n. 60.

69. Cf. Plut. *praec. ger. reip.* 808 C, 824 D.

70. Robert, *Gladiateurs* 253.

Chapter 11. Local Politics

1. Pliny, *Ep.* 10.32.1, 34.1.

2. Chapter 1 at nn. 21–27.

3. *Or.* 50.2.

4. Chapter 12 at n. 20.

5. Qualification: Liebenam, *Städteverwaltung* 33, 234; Sherwin-White on Pliny, *Ep.* 10.110.2. Bankruptcy: Dio, *Or.* 46.3, 66.2, Pliny, ibid.

6. Pliny, *Ep.* 10.79–80; on the disputed reading in 79.2, Sherwin-White ad loc. On the censors, Chapter 1 at n. 24.

7. *Or.* 48.13.

8. Pliny, *Ep.* 10.79.3.

9. *Or.* 49.15, 50.10.

10. *Or.* 44.3–5, 8, 46.3.

11. *Or.* 48.9–10.

12. *Or.* 50.1, 3.

13. Lib. 11.133–138. Cf. Robert, *Hellenica* 11/12 (1960) 571 n. 1.

14. Chapter 7 at n. 25, Chapter 9 at n. 76.

15. Robert, *BCH* 52 (1928) 411 (*OMS* 882).

16. *Or.* 34.23.

17. Liebenam, *Städteverwaltung* 250, Jones, *GC* 174.

18. *Or.* 48.17; cf. Liebenam, 247–248.

19. Chapter 12 at n. 75.

20. *Or.* 56.10; cf. Chapter 7 at n. 27.

21. Chapter 10 at n. 56.

22. Jones, *Plutarch* 111.

23. *Or.* 34.1.

24. *Praec. ger. reip.* 813 A-C.

25. *Or.* 7.62. Cf. *OGIS* 595, lines 35 ff. (council of Tyre, second century), *Syll.*³ 898 lines 13 ff. (third century).

26. The *psephos* of *Or.* 45.9 seems to refer to the assembly, that of *Or.* 49.15 to the council.

27. *Or.* 48.17, cf. *Or.* 51.6.

28. *Or.* 49.15.

29. *ILS* 6089, sect. 60; cf. Liebenam, *Städteverwaltung* 300.

30. Pliny, *Ep.* 3.20, 4.25. This is the sense presumably intended by Arnim's ἐδεήθη.

31. *Or.* 45.7–10.

32. So Arnim, *Dio* 386. However, there seems no evidence for Arnim's view that Diodorus was Dio's son, as observed by C. Vielmetti, *SIFC* 18 (1941) 108 n. 1.

33. Robert, *Documents de l'Asie Mineure méridionale* (Paris, 1966) 83.

34. The phrase *megiste arche* is used of the archonship in Bithynian inscriptions: *CIG* 2.3749 (Nicaea), *IGRR* 3.69 with n. 5 (Prusias ad Hypium): in Pontus, *IGRR* 3.90 (Amastris). Arnim, ibid. (above, n. 32), thinks that Dio refers to a permanent *praefectura morum*; against, I. Lévy, *REG* 12 (1899) 274 n. 4.

35. Similarly, he reproaches the Tarsians for taking advice from a speaker "even if he is a mere gymnasiarch" (*Or.* 34.31).

36. *Or.* 46.8; *Or.* 43.6.

37. *Or.* 45.10.

38. *Or.* 46.14.

39. Chapter 12 at n. 70. Cf. Jones, *Plutarch* 121; G. P. Burton, *JRS* 65 (1975) 104.

40. Ulp. *Dig.* 1.16.7.1; Dio, *Or.* 40.9.

41. Modest., *Dig.* 50.10.3.1; Dio, *Or.* 45.15.

42. Chapter 12 at n. 70.

43. Chapter 12 at n. 81. Cf. Burton (above, n. 39) 104–105.

44. J. H. Oliver, *Hesperia* 23 (1954) 163–167 (*Bull.* 1955.28).

45. *Praec. ger. reip.* 815 A; cf. Jones, *Plutarch* 121.

46. *Or.* 45.8, 10; *Or.* 47.19.

47. For "tyranny," cf. *Or.* 41.3, 47.18, 23–24 (in other contexts, *Or.* 38.35, 43.11), Philostr. *VS* 2.1.2, p. 547, 2.1.11, p. 559; popularity, Pliny, *Ep.* 6.31.3; oppression of *minores*, Tac. *Ann.* 15.20.

48. *Or.* 45.8, 10.

49. *IGRR* 4.914 lines 9–10; presumably not a strike, as suggested by Rostovtzeff, *SEHRE*[2] 621 n. 45. Cf. Augustus, *RG* 1.1 (Greek translation); *SEG* 9.8 line 7; Plut. *praec. ger. reip.* 813 A.

50. Pliny, *Ep.* 10.34.1.

51. Chapter 9 at n. 72; Chapter 10 at n. 50.

52. Chapter 11 at n. 58; Chapter 11 at n. 66.

53. *Or.* 43.7.

54. *Or.* 50.3–4.

55. Cf. Jones, *Plutarch* 112.

56. *ILS* 6089, sect. 58; cf. Liebenam, *Städteverwaltung* 33.

57. For torture employed by governors, P. D. Garnsey, *Social Status and Legal Privilege in the Roman Empire* (Oxford, 1970) 141–147; for exile, id. 111–122.

58. δῆμος can of course refer generally to the citizenry of a city, not necessarily to the assembly as opposed to the council: so also δημόται, 12.

59. Bassus: *PIR*[2] I/J 205; W. Eck, *Senatoren von Vespasian bis Hadrian* (Munich, 1970) 156. Rufus: *PIR*[1] V 177; Eck, 164. P. A. Brunt, *Historia* 10 (1961) 214 n. 77, thinks that Dio's proconsul need not be either of these.

60. Thus H. Dessau, *Hermes* 34 (1899) 86; Arnim, *Dio* 374–381, had favored Bassus.

61. For the possibility that Bassus is the governor unfavorably referred to in the *Nicomedian*, Chapter 10, n. 35. Sherwin-White, *Pliny* 352, argues that the charges against Rufus were aggravated by that of cruelty (*saevitia*): that would fit Dio's description well.

62. Pliny, *Ep.* 6.7.1.

63. Pliny, *Ep.* 7.10; Sherwin-White on *Ep.* 7.10.3.

64. Tac. *Ann.* 15.20–22.

65. *CIL* 3.3162 III lines 14–16; H.-G. Pflaum, *Le marbre de Thorigny* (Paris, 1948).

66. Pliny, *Ep.* 10.58–60. For the date of the proconsul who had allegedly condemned him, Velius, or perhaps Vettius, Eck (above, n. 59) 128 n. 77.

67. Pliny, *Ep.* 10.81–82; see Chapter 12 at nn. 85–87.

68. Jones, *Plutarch* 117: Robert, *Annuaire du Collège de France 1973* 485–486.

69. Bowersock, *Sophists* 93–100; Oliver, *Hesperia* Suppl. 13 (1970).

Chapter 12. Benefactions

1. Pliny, *Ep.* 6.31.3; for the inscriptions, *PIR²* C 788; R. Syme, *JRS* 58 (1968) 139.

2. Cf. M. P. Charlesworth, *PBSR* 15 (1939) 2–6; among private persons, note *IGRR* 4.1302 lines 14–17; P. Herrmann, *OAth* 10 (1971) 37 line 3; Apul. *Met.* 3.11.

3. Tac. *Ann.* 4.38; for other examples of the formula, A. Henrichs, *ZPE* 4 (1969) 150.

4. Not statues, as the context makes clear: for the distinction, *Or.* 51.9, Apul. *Met.* 3.11, Dittenberger on *OGIS* 537 n. 7, 571 n. 4, *Bull.* 1976.344.

5. Gold *eikones* (see previous n.) are said to be customary for "those who have most greatly benefited the people" in Augustan Cyme, *IGRR* 4.1302 lines 8–9; several "gold" statues were awarded to a benefactor of Miletus under Caligula, *Didyma* 107 (*OGIS* 472). For "gold" meaning "gilded," J. and L. Robert, *La Carie* (Paris, 1954) 110; cf. *Bull.* 1976.581.

6. For this as the meaning of *agalma*, Chapter 4 at n. 26.

7. Note that an Augustan benefactor of Cyme refuses a temple: *IGRR* 4.1302 line 16. Cf. Habicht in *Culte des Souverains* 79.

8. *SEG* 18.143, on which Robert, *REA* 62 (1960) 324–342 (*OMS* 840–858).

9. Robert, *AC* 37 (1968) 414–416; a new example in Herrmann (above, n. 2) 37 lines 3–4, 19. In Italy, Duncan-Jones, *ERE* 129.

10. They are granted to Diodorus Pasparos of Pergamum ca. 70 B.C. (*IGRR* 4.292 lines 48 ff.; on the text, Robert, *Ét. anat.* 48–50), but not to the Augustan benefactors L. Vaccius Labeo of Cyme (*IGRR* 4.1302) or Barcaeus of Cyrene (Robert, *RPh* 13³ [1939] 158–163 [*OMS* 1311–1316]).

11. On this, see most recently Robert (above, n. 8) 327–328 (843–844); id.

(above, n. 9) 420–421; id. *CRAI* 1969.42–44; Bowersock, *Augustus* 5–13; id., *Sophists* 43–50; Millar, *Emperor* 494–495.

12. Cf. Strabo's tribute to Prusa's good government, 12.564.

13. On this as a civic virtue, Robert, *Hellenica* 13 (1965) 222.

14. Presumably different from the letter which Dio brought back on his return from exile, *Or.* 40.5, but identical with that of *Or.* 47.13. For letters of emperors to prominent Greeks, W. Williams, *JRS* 64 (1974) 94 n. 63; Millar, *Emperor* 469–472.

15. Cf. above, n. 11; D. Kienast, *RE* Suppl. 13 (1973) 587–590; Millar, *Emperor* 385.

16. *Or.* 40.13–15; in 14, ⟨ἂν⟩ αὐτῷ must clearly be read (Dindorf). On this incident, Millar, *Emperor* 414–415.

17. Philostr. *VS* 1.21.6, p. 520, cf. Bowersock, *Sophists* 44. For an unsuccessful petition of Smyrna to Trajan in 101 or 102, Millar, *Emperor* 438–439.

18. H. Herter, *RE* 16 (1935) 2352–2355; C. J. Cadoux, *Ancient Smyrna* (Oxford, 1938) 220–223.

19. *Or.* 45.4; C. P. Jones, *Chiron* 5 (1975) 403–406.

20. *Or.* 45.7, cf. *Or.* 40.14, 44.11, 48.11. Law of Pompey: Pliny, *Ep.* 10.112.1. These were evidently extra councillors: for the average size of councils in eastern cities, Liebenam, *Städteverwaltung* 229 n. 5.

21. Pliny, *Ep.* 10.112.1, cf. 39.5.

22. *Bull.* 1956.159. Cf. Millar, *Emperor* 427.

23. Robert, *BCH* 60 (1936) 196–197 (*OMS* 903–904), with earlier bibliography in 196 (903) n. 1; id., *Laodicée* 264; P. D. Garnsey, *Historia* 20 (1971) 309–325; Duncan-Jones, *ERE* 82–88, 147–153.

24. *Or.* 40.10, 33.

25. *Or.* 45.6. διοίκησις clearly refers to the assizes, cf. *Or.* 45.10, 48.11: see now G. P. Burton, *JRS* 65 (1975) 95. On the different meanings of ἡγεμών, Chapter 3 at n. 23.

26. Pliny, *Ep.* 10.58.1, with Sherwin-White's commentary.

27. *Or.* 40.10.

28. *Or.* 40.10, cf. 33. On this practice, Chapter 8 at n. 22.

29. *Or.* 48.11.

30. Chapter 8 at n. 18.

31. *Or.* 35.17, 40.33. Cf. Burton (above, n. 25) 100.

32. Robert, *Hellenica* 7 (1949) 228–232.

33. Cf. Broughton, *ESAR* 4.709.

34. *Or.* 40.33.

35. W. H. Waddington, E. Babelon, S. Reinach, *Recueil général des monnaies grecques de l'Asie Mineure* 1 pt. 4 (Paris, 1912) 577–578.

36. Robert, *Hellenica* 11/12 (1960) ch. IV, esp. 59.

37. Waddington et al. (above, n. 35) 577 no. 7.

38. Lucian, *Alex.* 58; see Robert (above, n. 36) 62.

39. R. Bernhardt, "Imperium und Eleutheria," Diss. Hamburg, 1971, 229–240; Millar, *Emperor* 431.

40. *Or.* 44.5, 11–12.

41. Cf. Pliny, *Ep.* 10.103–104; note his attitude toward the colony of Apamea, ibid. 47–48.

42. *Or.* 45.13–14.

43. As D. Nörr, *Imperium und Polis* (Munich, 1966) 50 n. 50.

44. As Rostovtzeff, *SEHRE²* 257. In his note (654 n. 4) Rostovtzeff supposes that the "phylarchs of concord" at Prusias ad Hypium (*IGRR* 3.65) were "carrying out a συνοικισμός in Dio's sense," but the expression is obscure, cf. F. Gschnitzer, *RE* Suppl. 11 (1968) 1083.

45. Cf. Augustus' synoecism of Nicopolis in Epirus (Bowersock, *Augustus* 93–94).

46. *Or.* 38.47.

47. *Or.* 31.121, 32.4, 7.

48. For the same honor, Plut. *praec. ger. reip.* 820 D.

49. All three occur in a list of honors from the territory of Caunus, G. E. Bean, *JHS* 74 (1954) 87 no. 22 (*Bull.* 1956.274 b), cf. Robert, *AE* 1969, 22–23.

50. *Or.* 46.3.

51. *Or.* 31.110, cf. Chapter 4 at n. 39.

52. L. Couve in Daremberg-Saglio, 3.590 b.

53. Robert, *REG* 42 (1929) 433–438 (*OMS* 221–227), a dancer; id., *Hermes* 65 (1930) 106–113 (*OMS* 654–661), a pantomime.

54. Robert, *Hermes* 65 (1930) 114–116 (*OMS* 662–664), adducing this passage.

55. On Amoebeus, Crusius, *RE* 1 (1894) 1872–1873; on the two Poluses, F. Stoessl, *RE* 21 (1952) 1425–1426.

56. Duncan-Jones, *ERE* 245–246.

57. *Praec. ger. reip.* 802 D, cf. Jones, *Plutarch* 116. On the pyrrhic, Robert, *Hellenica* 1 (1940) 151–152.

58. Robert (above, n. 36) 570–573.

59. *Praec. ger. reip.* 811 C.

60. *Syll.³* 850. For official discouragement of games, cf. also Pliny, *Ep.* 4.22, Duncan-Jones, *ERE* 137.

61. *Or.* 40.5, cf. above, n. 14.

62. Pliny, *Ep.* 10.8.1 (Duncan-Jones, *ERE* 27); *Syll.³* 850; Millar, *Emperor* 421–422.

63. Philostr. *VS* 1.25.2, p. 531, 2.1.3, p. 548; *IGRR* 4.1431 lines 33–42. Cf. Bowersock, *Sophists* 44–46; Millar, *Emperor* 420–421.

64. *Or.* 40.13–15.

65. *Or.* 45.4, cf. Chapter 12 at n. 19; J. and L. Robert, *La Carie* (Paris, 1954) 223–225, cf. Chapter 13 at n. 14.

66. *Or.* 40.8–9, cf. Pliny, *Ep.* 10.70.1.

67. *Or.* 40.11, 47.13. On the still unidentified site of Caesarea, Robert, *Villes²* 190 n. 1, 474 s.v. Menthon; also *OMS* 4.134.

68. Macer, *Dig.* 50.10.3. pref.

69. *Or.* 40.5, 45.15. Cf. the προτροπή given by a governor of Arabia to the

building of a temple, G. W. Bowersock, *Le monde grec: Hommages à Claire Préaux* (Brussels, 1975) 515. For Roman supervision of building, *Dig.* 50.10; Jones, *GC* 136; Robert (above, n. 57) 47–48.

70. *Or.* 48.2. For the interference of governors in a city's internal affairs, cf. previous n.; also Magie, *RRAM* 1391 n. 61, 1504 n. 29; Nörr (above, n. 43) 35–39; Burton (above, n. 25) 104–105.

71. *Or.* 40.3. Thus, correctly, G. Sautel, *RIDA* 3³ (1956) 429. For epigraphical examples of such promises, Robert, *Ét. anat.* 378–382; id. (above, n. 57) 50–51.

72. Ulpian, *Dig.* 50.12.1.2–5.

73. For such negotiations over promises, Robert (above, n. 57) 50–51.

74. Dio's funds: *Or.* 47.12. Curator: Pliny, *Ep.* 10.81.1, cf. Sautel (above, n. 71) 428–429. Subscribers: *Or.* 40.6, 48.11. Public moneys: *Or.* 48.9. On subscriptions, Pliny, *Ep.* 10.39.1, 40.1; Robert, *BCH* 57 (1933) 505–517 (*OMS* 473–485), 59 (1935) 421–424 (*OMS* 178–181).

75. *Or.* 40.6, cf. *Or.* 45.16.

76. *Or.* 40.7; for the marble of Bithynia, Robert (above, n. 36) 35, *JS* 1962, 43. Plutarch: *praec. ger. reip.* 811 B-C.

77. *Or.* 40.8–9, cf. *Or.* 47.11.

78. *Or.* 47.16–17. Macrinus is unknown (A. Stein, *RE* 14 [1928] 168 no. 1, is aberrant); Prusias is evidently Prusias I, not the disgraced Prusias II. Pliny, *Ep.* 10.49–50, refers to the same construction. For the "inscribing" of benefactors, Apul. *Met.* 3.11, Liebenam, *Städteverwaltung* 34.

79. *Or.* 40.12, 47.18; *Syll.*³ 852 lines 33–35.

80. Apart from the frequent references in Pliny, *Ep.* 10, note *Syll.*³ 833.

81. *Praec. ger. reip.* 814 E-F, cf. Jones, *Plutarch* 118.

82. Robert (above, n. 32) 80–81.

83. John Chrysost., Migne, *PG* 54.659, cited by Robert (above, n. 36) 571 n. 3.

84. For "satraps" of highly placed Romans, *Or.* 7.66, 50.6, Jones, Plutarch 114 n. 27. For such accusations of individuals before the emperor, Millar, *Emperor* 443.

85. Pliny, *Ep.* 10.17 B, cf. Dio, *Or.* 48.9–10.

86. Pliny, *Ep.* 10.81–82. Cf. Sautel (above, n. 71) 428–429. For the length of time sometimes taken to complete buildings, Duncan-Jones, *ERE* 87–88.

87. On the burial of prominent citizens inside a city, sometimes in buildings given by themselves, Habicht, *Inschriften des Asklepieions* 25.

88. Philostr. *VS* 1.25.3–4, pp. 44–46. Cf. Bowersock, *Sophists* ch. IV; Millar, *Emperor* 91–93.

Chapter 13. Trajan

1. J. R. Asmus, *Julian und Dio Chrysostomus*, Tauberbischofsheim, 1895, 1–31.

2. J. Scharold, *Dio Chrysostomus und Themistius*, Burghausen, 1912, 9–40.

3. J. R. Asmus, *ByzZ* 9 (1900) 85–151.

4. Cf. Arethas in Dio, ed. Arnim 2.325.

5. For dialogues read to an emperor, cf. Suet. *Aug.* 89.3. Similarly, it is uncertain whether Christian apologies were really read or heard by the emperors to whom they were addressed; cf. P. de Labriolle, *La réaction païenne* (Paris, 1942) 75.

6. J. Palm, *Rom, Römertum und Imperium in der griechischen Literatur der Kaiserzeit* (Lund, 1959) 26–29.

7. Rostovtzeff, *SEHRE*² 120. A position similar to Rostovtzeff's is taken by Momigliano, *Quarto Contributo* 263.

8. Syme, *Tacitus* 41.

9. Philostr., *VS* 1.7, p. 488; quoted in full, Chapter 2 at n. 15.

10. D.C. 68.7.4.

11. Cf. Pliny, *Ep.* 6.31.12.

12. Cf. Pliny, *Ep.* 10.41.5, D.C. 68.17.1.

13. Suet. *Caes.* 44.3, with Butler and Cary ad loc.

14. Crito: Chapter 12 at n. 65. Plutarch: Jones, *Plutarch* 31–32; for another view, R. Flacelière, *CRAI* 1971, 168–185.

15. Xen. *Mem.* 2.1.21–34.

16. Pliny, *Pan.* 15.5, 19.3; cf. Syme, *Tacitus* 38.

17. Pliny, *Pan.* 2.3. The use of *dominus* or κύριος in private intercourse, as in Pliny's letters to Trajan, is another matter: cf. Sherwin-White, *Pliny* 557, L. Robert, *RPh* 48³ (1974) 242 n. 403.

18. Pliny, *Pan.* 18.1, cf. *Ep.* 8.14.7.

19. J. Beaujeu, *La religion romaine à l'apogée de l'empire* 1 (Paris, 1955) 72–73; *Bull.* 1964.188.

20. Nock, *HSCP* 41 (1930) 24 = *Essays* 221; Magie, *RRAM* 1451 n. 7.

21. 39–40; cf. 7, 11, 28, 30, 62, 82.

22. Pliny, *Pan.* 85, cf. Dio, *Or.* 1.82.

23. Heracles: Paul L. Strack, *Untersuchungen zur römischen Reichsprägung des zweiten Jahrhunderts* 1 (Stuttgart, 1931) 95–104; Beaujeu (above, n. 19) 80–87; G. W. Bowersock in *Le Culte des Souverains*, 192–194. II Traiana: Ritterling, *RE* 12 (1925) 1484–1485.

24. Strack (above, n. 23), ibid.

25. Cf. E. Fraenkel, *Horace* (Oxford, 1957) 451 n. 4.

26. Suet. *Caes.* 7.1.

27. Illustrated by A. R. Birley, *Marcus Aurelius* (London, 1966) facing p. 211.

28. Cf. Dio, *Or.* 45.1.

29. O. Weinreich, *Studien zur Martial*, Tübinger Beiträge zur Altertumswissenschaft 4 (Stuttgart, 1928) 125–132, discussing Martial 14.73.

30. Weinreich (above, n. 29) 130; note Philostr. *VA* 8.4.

31. Chapter 6 at n. 1.

32. Pliny, *Pan.* 14.5, cf. 82.7; 80.4–5, cf. Dio, *Or.* 1.84.

33. Attempts to show Dio influenced by Pliny (F. Trisoglio, *Il Pensiero Politico* 5 [1972] 3–43) or Pliny by Dio (J. Morr, *Die Lobrede des jüngeren Plinius und die erste Königsrede des Dio von Prusa*, progr. Troppau, 1915 [*non vidi*]) have not carried conviction.

34. Chapter 6 at n. 67.
35. Thus Arnim, *Dio* 325–327.
36. *PIR*² D 19.
37. Cf. Florus, praef. 8, cited by Syme, *Tacitus* 218 n. 7.
38. Arnim, *Dio* 407, proposes a date shortly before the second Dacian war.
39. Homer: O. Murray, *JRS* 55 (1965) 161–182. Achilles: e.g. Cic. *ad fam.* 5.12.7 (Alexander at Sigeum), Arr. *Anab.* 7.14.4 (his mourning for Hephaestion).
40. The parallel is made explicit in *Or.* 47.9.
41. Arnim, *Dio* 405, argues precisely for 18 September 103 or 104.
42. Cf. Nock, *JRS* 37 (1947) 114 = *Essays* 672.
43. Pliny, *Pan.* 81, cf. D.C. 68.7.3; P. A. Stadter, *GRBS* 17 (1976) 157–167, plausibly connects Arrian's *Cynegeticus* with this imperial hobby. For Spanish hunting generally, G. Lafaye, Daremberg-Saglio 5 (1912) 696 n. 5; note the epigram of Arrian from Cordoba, *Bull.* 1973.539.
44. Cf. the endings of *Or.* 32, 35, 48. The next piece in the collection, the *Libyan Tale* (*Or.* 5), seems to be a kind of appendix to *Or.* 4; cf. Arnim, *Dio* 412–414.
45. R. Höistad, *Cynic Hero and Cynic King* (Uppsala, 1948) 220, argues for Domitian's reign.
46. Momigliano, *Quarto Contributo* 265; id., *RSI* 61 (1949) 126–127 = *Quinto Contributo* 1005–1007.
47. Glory: above, n. 12. Alexander: D.C. 68.17.1, 30.1.
48. A tiny detail in the description of the Miserly Spirit seems to hint at Domitian, "those mistresses we know of" (96), cf. Plut. *Popl.* 15.5, Suet. *Dom.* 22.
49. Momigliano, *Quarto Contributo* 262.
50. Cf. Pliny, *Ep.* 6.31.
51. *Or.* 1.49, 3.28–29.
52. Chapter 6 at n. 43.
53. *Or.* 6.54–59; with *Or.* 6.59 cf. *Or.* 1.82.
54. Suda, Δ 1240, where the manuscripts have ἐγκώμιον Ἡρακλέους καὶ Πλάτωνος: the emendation of καί to κατά, and the elucidation of the work, are due to C. Gallavotti, *RFIC* 59 (1931) 504–508.
55. Suda, Δ 1240. Cf. J. R. Hamilton, *Plutarch, Alexander: A Commentary* (Oxford, 1969) lx–lxii.
56. *FGrHist* 707; cf. Dio, ed. Arnim, 2 pages iv–ix.
57. F 5 = Dio, ed. Arnim, 2 page ix.
58. Jacoby dates it tentatively between 96 and 100.
59. The sole fragment runs "inde Berzobim, deinde Aizi processimus" (Priscian, 6.13, *GLK* page 205).
60. Pliny, *Ep.* 8.4.
61. *FGrHist* 200. Cf. Chapter 12 at n. 65, Chapter 13 at n. 14.
62. E. L. Bowie does not mention Dio's *Getica* when surveying the historiography of the period, *P&P* 46 (1970) 10–28 = *Studies in Ancient Society*, ed. M. I. Finley (London and Boston, 1974) 174–195.

Chapter 14. Rome

1. Contrast Aristides' praises, *Or.* 26.6–13, with the denunciation of Juv. 3, for example. Modern parallels come readily to mind.

2. Thus Pliny, *Ep.* 10.40.3.

3. App. praef. 39. It may be that the philosopher Lucius who talks of Alexander as "my king," Philostr. *VS* 2.1.9, p. 557, was also Alexandrian.

4. Chapter 5 at n. 31.

5. H. A. Musurillo, *The Acts of the Pagan Martyrs* (Oxford, 1954) nos. 8, 11.

6. Luc. *Peregr.* 18, 33 (Rome), 17 (Agathobulus, presumably in Alexandria).

7. Cf. Bowersock, *Augustus* 105–108; like Alexandria, Athens had fervently supported Mark Antony.

8. *Or.* 36.17.

9. *Or.* 35.10; cf. Epictetus on the priest of Augustus at Nicopolis, Arr. *Epict.* 1.19.26–29. On this, Bowersock in *Le Culte des souverains* 182–183.

10. Jones, *Plutarch* 116.

11. Arr. *Epict.* 1.19.26–29 (priesthood); 1.10, 1.25.26–27, 4.1.55, 4.7.21–24 (office).

12. 1.26.10–12.

13. 3.7.21.

14. *Or.* 31.62, 32.35.

15. *Or.* 39.1 (Nicaea), 11.137–138 (Ilion), 41.9–10 (Apamea).

16. Cf. Dio, *Or.* 32.71–72, Plut. *praec. ger. reip.* 814 A, 825 C; cf. Jones, *Plutarch* 117–118.

17. Chapter 4 at nn. 70–73.

18. Cf. Vespasian's famous justification for revoking the freedom of Achaea, that "the Greeks had forgotten how to be free," Paus. 7.17.4.

19. Chapter 6 at nn. 45–46.

20. *Or.* 45.1.

21. Contrast Paus. 7.17.3, Philostr. *VA* 5.41; cf. Jones, *Plutarch* 80.

22. Chapter 8 at n. 35.

23. Cf. Jones, *Plutarch* 124–125.

24. Chapter 6 at n. 75.

25. ὑπό τινος Σωκράτους: but the speech apparently is Dio's own, cf. Chapter 6 at n. 14. The phrase shows that Dio's remark to Trajan, Σωκράτης . . . ὃν καὶ σὺ γιγνώσκεις (*Or.* 3.1), does not satirize the emperor.

26. Cf. the attack on Roman morals in Lucian's *Nigrinus*, also set in Athens.

27. Above, Chapter VII.

28. ἐν ἄστει καὶ κατὰ πόλιν: there seems no ground to suppose that this specifically denotes Rome, with P. A. Brunt, *PCPS* 199 (1973) 9 n. 2.

29. "Quo cuncta undique atrocia aut pudenda confluunt celebranturque," Tac. *Ann.* 15.44.3.

30. As Arnim, *Dio* 457–458.

31. 136, cf. 118, 124, 140.

32. Elsewhere Dio uses δουλεύειν and its cognates of political subjection: *Or.* 31.125, 34.51.

33. Chapter 7 at n. 22.

34. Cf. D.C. 68.5.5; for Domitian's concubines, Chapter 13, n. 48.

35. Pliny, *Ep.* 4.1, 4.19, etc.

36. Pliny, *Pan.* 46, *Ep.* 7.24.

37. Pliny, *Ep.* 1.6.

38. F. Millar, *JRS* 59 (1969) 12–29, esp. 27–28. Cf. Gordian III's appeal to the memory of the Persian wars at the beginning of his own eastern expedition, L. Robert, *CRAI* 1970, 13–17.

Index

This index covers the text, Chronology, and notes (the notes only when they discuss special points). Cross-references have been kept to a minimum, so that a reader interested in Syria, for example, should consult "Antioch," "Apamea," and so on, as well as "Syria." Works of literature are indexed under their authors' names. Greek words are transliterated into Roman characters. Names of modern persons are not included.